THE COMPLETE
ENCYCLOPEDIA OF
CONTAINER PLANTS

THE COMPLETE
ENCYCLOPEDIA OF
CONTAINER PLANTS

Detailed descriptions of hundreds of species

NICO VERMEULEN

REBO
PUBLISHERS

Explanation of the symbols after each item in the A to Z:

☼   The plant requires a light position in winter.

☀   The plant may be placed in a dark position in
    winter, but a light one is also possible.

°C(°F) Minimum winter temperature.

❋   The plant is fully hardy and may be left out of doors
    in winter (dug in if appropriate).

(1)   Annual, or perennial best treated as an annual.

© 1998 Rebo International b.v., Lisse, The Netherlands

Text: Nico Vermeulen
Photography: Nico Vermeulen
Production: TextCase, The Netherlands
Translation: Mary Charles for First Edition Translations Ltd, Great Britain
Typesetting: Hof&Land Typografie, The Netherlands
Cover design: Minkowsky Graphics, The Netherlands

ISBN 90 366 1584 4

Contents

Preface

In the world of gardening, plants in pots and other containers have rapidly become all the rage. They give plant lovers an opportunity to enjoy a splendid display of exotic flowers on a balcony or a patio. Such interest also makes it worthwhile for growers to include less familiar items in their range of plants.

Many new species of plants have come on to the market in recent years but, unfortunately, you are unlikely to find most of them in books currently available. It was therefore a real challenge to track them down and photograph them at various nurseries, and to discuss their management with the growers. Without the help of these specialized nurserymen, it would have been impossible to publish a book describing so many pot or container plants.

Although this publication may rightly be called an encyclopedia of container plants, other groups of plants have not been forgotten. Traditional conservatory plants should be taken indoors in winter as they are frost-tender. Most plant lovers have limited winter storage facilities, or else none at all. The book was therefore extended to include numerous annuals and hardy plants suitable for growing in pots. At the end of each description you will see at a glance whether the plant should be taken indoors in winter, and whether it is an annual or a fully hardy plant.

The index contains the botanical as well as the common English name of the plant. Following the introduction on plant care, the various plants are described under their botanical names in alphabetical order.

This encyclopedia uses the new nomenclature which is gradually being adopted. The Royal Horticultural Society's new standard scientific work *Dictionary of Gardening* provided the criteria in most instances, and deviation occurred only if the new name was not found at any nursery, or if more up-to-date studies such as the revised edition of *Passion Flowers* (1996), by Vanderplank, were available.*
The Naamlijst van houtige gewassen (1995) (List of names of woody plants) and *Naamlijst van vaste planten* (1996) (List of names of perennials) published by the Dutch Research Station for tree nurseries (Proefstation voor de boomkwekerijen) were also consulted. As the usual synonyms are also included, you will always be able to find the plant for which you are searching. There is a vast selection of plants for pots, baskets, balcony troughs and tubs, and a suitable plant can be found for virtually any position. This encyclopedia will help you to find the right one.

N. Vermeulen

Preceding page: *Phygelius x rectus* 'Trewidden Pink'

* The Dutch edition "Passiebloemen" is available only from the "Nationale Collectie Passieflora's" (National Collection of Passion Flowers); see the list of growers.

Introduction

Attempts at growing southern plants in northern countries were made as early as the Middle Ages. Plants from Mediterranean regions were brought across the Alps to northern Europe and tried out there. Most of these endeavours were doomed to failure until glass and greater prosperity created fresh opportunities. Glass could be used to protect plants from the cold while giving them sufficient light. Prosperity was indispensable for the creation of special areas where Mediterranean plants could survive the winter. Originally such areas were not greenhouses, but buildings with one wall consisting mainly of windows. This is where the first container plants - frequently orange trees - were housed, and the structures themselves were therefore called orangeries. Later on, all plants that had to be taken indoors for the winter became known as "orangery" plants. They were usually large plants which were grown in containers, hence their present name container plants. It is, however, also possible to grow winter-hardy plants in containers, so that there are more container plants than "orangery" plants.

As time went on, plants from countries outside Europe began to appear.

The development of worldwide shipping led to the arrival of innumerable new species, which were then tried out in orangeries. They were often referred to as "Cape" plants, after the Cape of Good Hope.

Opportunities nowadays are immense. Plants from all over the world are brought to different countries, so their potential for flourishing outside their native habitat can be assessed. Nothing is too extraordinary for growers to turn into a saleable product. Plants are grafted on to stronger rootstocks, propagated by means of tissue culture, and treated with growth retardants to keep them compact. Hybridization and selection occur on a large scale, thus creating a constant flow of new cultivars, each one just slightly better adapted to a more northerly climate than the last.

Preceding page: a pot made of Cretan earthenware

Sundry pots

Pots and containers

Pots, tubs, and troughs are more than just packaging for a root ball. They can enhance the beauty of a plant or detract from it. Plant, position, and pot should be in harmony with one another. If a profusely flowering plant is placed in a richly ornamented and glazed pot, the design of the decoration will compete with the flowers, whereas a handsome foliage plant would show up well in such a container.

The position, too, plays an important part. A black concrete container with a *Brugmansia* in it looks splendid against the plain, severe background of, say, wooden fencing; a nostalgic environment would be quite out of keeping with the plant. Such surroundings call for a garlanded cast-iron urn and profusely flowering plants. Richly decorated earthenware or baskets full of flowers also look well in a setting of that kind.

Clearly, not every handsome urn will show up to its best advantage on your patio. Pots, tubs, and urns should blend with their environment. The visual effect of a pot may even be so striking that filling it with plants would seem superfluous. It could then become a decorative feature for a garden or a patio, and be placed there because of its own beauty. This

may be enhanced if you arrange plants round it, or let the pot merge with the greenery. Perhaps it may even look as if it had been left there in some distant past. If it is too obvious that the pot has been put somewhere deliberately, the effect will be lost.

Pots and containers with plants growing in them should satisfy not only an aesthetic ideal, but must also the plants' requirements. If they are out of doors, it must be possible for excess water to drain away easily through holes in the bottom of the container. Many pots do not have any, which means that you must drill some yourself. This may seriously damage glazed pots, or even break them, and you should therefore consider the risks when buying certain types of container.

One advantage of earthenware pots is that roots can also absorb oxygen through the sides. This may be particularly important to plants that grow naturally in light, stony, or sandy soil. Clay pots also have some major drawbacks. As a lot of moisture evaporates through their sides, you will need to water far more often. If the water runs out through the bottom of the pot after frequent watering, nutrients will also be washed away. During the evaporation process, salts are left behind on the sides of the pot. Roots will go in search of this nutrient and therefore grow towards the

Glazed pot from Sicily

A lead container

sides of the pot, where there is also more oxygen, and form a felt-like layer of rootlets. If you repot the plants, these rootlets will be lost, whereas there will be fewer roots in the centre of the root ball. This problem does not arise if pots with solid sides are used.

Pots with solid sides immediately suggest plastic pots and concrete containers. Despite the fact that oxygen cannot penetrate the sides of the container, most plants do better in them than in earthenware pots. To ensure satisfactory growth you should not water excessively (as the soil will remain moist for a longer period). You should also make sure that the soil stays airy enough to let oxygen penetrate. Special container plant compost is often coarse-fibred and varied. You can further improve its quality by mixing in coarse sand or other minerals.

Not only plastic pots, but also wooden tubs, glazed troughs, and metal urns and containers have sides that are impenetrable to oxygen. If you wish to combine clay pots with the advantages of plastic, you can line the earthenware with plastic. Containers made of such metals as lead, which are now reproduced from antique models, should always be lined with plastic to prevent the moist soil from combining with the metal.

Instead of smooth plastic, you can also use thin bubble wrap, the kind in which fragile items are packed. Bubble wrap insulates and prevents the roots from being scorched if the plant is placed in full sun, particularly if the pot is dark on the outside. The use of bubble wrap is strongly recommended for plants that are to remain out of doors in winter.

Frost-resistant earthenware

Fully hardy plants can remain out of doors during frosty spells, even though they are less tolerant of frost when grown in pots or containers than they are in open ground. If, however, hardy plants are to remain out of doors, their pots should also be frost-resistant. Most earthenware, the cheaper kind in particular, should not be left out of doors in winter. Because of the relatively low temperatures at which the clay is baked, the earthenware is porous. This absorbs any water, and if frost follows on a wet spell, the pores are still full of it. The water expands as it freezes, which fractures the earthenware. The damage does not become visible until the thaw sets in and large strips of earthenware break off the pot.

Fortunately, there are also pots which can remain out of doors in winter. These are known as "Cretan" pots, which are fired at very high temperatures. (The kilns are heated with the oleaginous seeds of olives.) There are also other kinds of frost-resistant earthenware, and such information is often indicated on the pots. If in doubt, ask the supplier for a warranty.

It may seem strange, but frost-resistant pots may also freeze. The moist soil in the pot expands as it freezes, and then causes vertical cracks in the pot. This occurs most frequently if the pots are narrower at the top, and the freezing soil cannot expand upwards. For winter use, you should therefore only select pots which taper towards the bottom. If frozen, the soil can then always expand upwards unrestrictedly.

A pot made of Cretan earthenware

Moving tubs and heavy pots

Conservatory plants overwinter indoors. Large specimens are often cultivated in wooden tubs, while others are kept in big pots, or containers made of plasticized cement. Up to a certain weight, it is still possible for them to be lifted by one person without any mechanical aids. Bend your knees, embrace the pot, and straighten your legs: in that way you will protect your back. If you are moving house, it may well be possible for you to cut back the plant beforehand and make carrying it through doorways and up or down stairs considerably easier.

If you can no longer lift the container on your own, you will need some help. Wooden tubs need handles to enable them to be lifted with their contents. Handles screwed into the wood are not strong enough for the purpose, and should be welded to bands fitted round the tubs, preferably with links to other bands lower down or, even better, passing right underneath the bottom of the tub. In this way, a tub can be lifted by two people.

Again, you should always lift from the knees, and keep your back straight.

If the tub is too heavy even for two people, you will need some kind of a truck or trolley, or an old-fashioned flat cart on two wheels of the type used for transporting "orangery" plants in the old days. That kind of cart tilts down to the ground at the back, after which the tub is pushed on to it until it is in the centre. The cart is then returned to a horizontal position and towed away.

A more time-consuming method is to transport the tub on rollers. Use a lever to raise one side of the container and push a plank underneath it. Then place round tree trunks under the plank so that it can roll over them. The trunks released at the back in the course of the rolling process are then repositioned in front of the plank. You do of course need a straight, flat surface. In ancient times, the heavy blocks of stone for the Pyramids were transported in this way, so why shouldn't you be able to do the same with your conservatory plant?

Lemon trees are taken out of doors in Tuscany

1 Planting up pots and hanging baskets

To grow a plant successfully in a container or hanging basket, you need to ensure optimum growing conditions at the time of planting. If you follow the guidelines in this chapter, your plants will thrive in their container or hanging basket.

The soil

If the plant is to grow well, its roots will need moisture, nutrients, and oxygen. For species such as bog plants, the emphasis is on moisture rather than oxygen, but a light soil mixture is essential for most species if they are to achieve adequate growth.

Special container plant compost is generally available, and proves very satisfactory. The peat component is coarse-fibred, and sand and clay are often added. Small lumps of clay retain moisture and are highly nutritive. You can of course make your own mixture. Find out what is required for each species and add more peat for plants that like acid soil, and extra clay for those that prefer clay. Coarse

sand may be either lime-rich (often recognizable by its chalky white colour) or deficient in lime (yellow). You can aerate the potting compost with sand containing the appropriate amount of lime. It is also possible to use other mineral substances such as gravel for the same purpose. Sand and gravel are of course heavy and can be replaced by pearlite if the container is to stand on a balcony.

Guidelines for planting

1. Good drainage is of paramount importance for nearly all container plants. It must be possible for moisture to drain away satisfactorily through the bottom of the pot. Drilling a lot of fairly large holes in the bottom should prove effective. A single hole may be enough, but only if it is not clogged. You should therefore put one or more pieces of broken clay pots (crocks) over the hole, with the convex side uppermost.
2. You can further improve the drainage by putting some gravel or chippings on top of

Drill large holes in the bottom of the pot

Put one or several crocks over the hole

13

Put a layer of gravel or stone chippings on top of the crocks

Cut a piece of anti-root material to size and put it on top

the crocks. If the container is to stand on a balcony or flat roof, you also need to consider its total weight, and in that case it may be better to substitute the kind of plastic chips often used in packaging to protect such items as electric appliances.

3. A layer of horticultural fleece or similar material should be placed on top of the gravel or chips. Although this will let moisture through, it will prevent the soil from

clogging up the spaces between the chips. First check whether the material really does let water pass through it; if not, make a few holes. Cut out the material to fit the pot and place it on top of the gravel.

4. Partly fill the pot with special potting compost for container plants or with your own mixture. Make a small hollow in the surface by pushing the soil up against the sides.

Partly fill the pot with soil

Make a hollow in the soil

Put the plant upright in the pot and fill the area round the root ball with soil

5 Stand the root ball, which should be pre-soaked in a bucket of water until it is thoroughly wet, in the hollow. Make sure the plant is upright and that the crown is not too far from the centre of the pot.
6 Fill the space round the root ball with soil, and press it down slightly so that the plant is firmly in position.
7 Finally, fill the pot with soil up to about 2.5cm (1in) below the rim. Remember that the level of the soil will continue to drop slightly after you have watered the plant. Make sure that the level of the soil is ultimately at least 2.5cm (1in) below the rim of the pot, so that the water can sink into the soil and not cascade over the edge.

Bulbs in pots

Pots and containers do not need to be left empty all winter. You can plant bulbs in them in autumn; they will flower the following spring. When the bulbs are over, the pot or container will be available again for summer-flowering annuals.

When planting bulbs, do not use excessively tapering pots. To prevent the bulbs from freezing, you should not plant them too near the edge of the container. Follow the general instructions for filling pots and containers, and make sure that these have good drainage if they are to remain out of doors.

Large bulbs need to be planted deeper than small ones, and it is therefore possible to combine large and small bulbs in a single container. You might choose some tulips that flower in April, and plant a layer of *Iris reticulata* above them for flowering in February. Or else combine *Scilla* and *Puschkinia* for a blue carpet in March. You can also create a lovely effect with a combination of tall and short plants in toning colours - early narcissi and scillas, for instance - which will flower simultaneously.

Remember that bulbs that are fully hardy in open ground may freeze in pots. The pots themselves should also be frost-resistant. If there is a severe frost, put the pots of bulbs in a cool place such as a shed, where there may even be a few degrees of frost. On no account should you take the pots into the house, where it is always too hot for bulbs to develop healthily. The pots may be kept in the dark until the tips of the bulbs project above the soil. At that stage they will need light.

If you do not have a cool place where the bulbs can overwinter, you should stand the pots as close to the house as possible. Wrap the pot in insulating material such as straw or bubble wrap in the event of severe frost.

Another good method is to dig the bulbs into the garden, pots and all. In that way, they will be protected against frost while still absorbing enough moisture (if the pots are porous).

Bulbs also need moisture while they are still underground, so you must not forget to water pots that are kept in a shed, or under the eaves, or up against the house. After the bulbs have flowered, you should take them out of their pots and plant them somewhere in the garden so that the foliage can die down.

The pots can then be filled with annuals or other plants.

Hanging baskets

Hanging baskets have become immensely popular. At one time, they were used almost exclusively to adorn English houses and pubs, but now they are to be seen suspended from outbuildings or houses, enhancing patios all over Europe. This is an excellent development, as many plants appear to thrive in hanging baskets, mainly because their roots can absorb more oxygen in that way than they would in traditional containers.

Yet there are also some drawbacks. Hanging baskets require daily watering during the summer months. The moisture in the baskets evaporates on all sides, which makes plentiful watering a necessity. The second drawback applies only to traditional moss-lined baskets. This kind of lining consists of sphagnum moss from peat moors. If you are aware that living peat moors are becoming increasingly rare and that some species of animals and plants dependent on them will become extinct if the moors disappear, you will appreciate the problem.

Fortunately, there is an alternative: a circular insert of coconut fibre with incisions which enable you to form it into a rounded shape. After lining the basket, you cut off the strip of fibre projecting above the top of the basket. All the following instructions on how to plant a moss-lined basket also apply to those lined with coconut fibre, except that you may need to cut holes in the material, through which the root balls can be inserted.

Planting up hanging baskets

Hanging baskets consist of a metal framework which may be galvanized or coated with plastic. They are often sold with enough sphagnum moss for their first season. Step-by-step instructions on how to fill the baskets are given below.

1. Line the sides of the basket with a thick layer of sphagnum moss. The thickness of the layer must be the same throughout, and there should not be any holes in it.

Line the basket with sphagnum moss

Fill the basket with container plant compost

2. Place a saucer in the bottom of the lined basket, or make a small bowl from a piece of plastic. This will serve as a reservoir to enable the water to be reabsorbed in the soil instead of running straight through.

Make a hole in the moss lining in the side and insert the root ball of a plant

Insert several more plants in the side

Plant up the top of the basket with several more plants

3. Fill the saucer or plastic bowl with container plant compost, preferably containing some clay; this will help to retain the water and nutrients.

4. Make a hole in the moss lining the side of the basket and push the root ball of a plant through it. If the ball is too big and the plant is small, you can also slide the plant into a cardboard cylinder (taken from a roll of lavatory paper) and then push it through the moss from the inside.

Fill the basket with soil

5. Make further holes in the side of the basket (see point 4). There is usually room for three to five plants round the side of an average basket.

6. After inserting the plants in the side, put some more soil in the basket, but not too much, as there are more root balls to be added.

7. Fit a few plants into the top of the basket and press the soil down firmly all round them. Add more soil if required.

8. Water the basket thoroughly, or plunge it into a bowl of water (not too cold).

9. Fix the basket to the chain as described in the directions.

10. Find a suitable place for the basket and hang it in the sun or semi-shade, depending on the requirements of the plants you have chosen.

Press the soil down firmly round the plants

Hanging baskets in autumn

Annuals become unsightly in autumn and at a given moment you will decide to empty the basket. It often happens that only the metal basket is preserved and the moss is thrown away. That is unnecessary, as the moss can quite well be used for a second season, but only if you leave the basket out of doors to prevent the moss from drying out and turning brittle. Put the basket in a shady place, for instance under a shrub. Damp sphagnum moss retains its resilience and can therefore be used during the following season.

Planting bulbs in hanging baskets

Bulbs that can thrive in pots will also do well in hanging baskets, so why not fill the baskets with bulbs in autumn? Try inserting crocuses into the soil through the sides. They will sprout in spring, curl upwards and flower magnificently. Tulips, narcissi and other harbingers of spring may be fitted into the top.

Suitable plants for hanging baskets

Trailing plants or species which grow horizontally are especially suitable for hanging baskets. They will clamber over the rims and hang down flowering profusely or trailing graceful foliage. The following species are particularly suitable for hanging baskets:

Bacopa, see *Sutera*
Begonia semperflorens group
Begonia sutherlandii
Bidens ferulifolia
Brachycome iberidifolia
Browallia species

Catharanthus roseus
Chaenorrhinum organifolium
Convolvulus cneorum
Convolvulus sabatius
Cymbalaria species
Erigeron karvinskianus
Felicia amelloides
Hedera helix
Helichrysum petiolare
Impatiens walleriana
Laurentia axillaris
Lobelia erinus
Lobelia 'Richardii'
Lobularia maritima
Lysimachia congestiflora
Nemophila species
Nierembergia hippomanica
Pelargonium x *peltatum*
Petunia (trailing species)
Plectostachys serphyllifolia
Plectranthus forsteri
Portulaca grandiflora
Sanvitalia procumbens
Scaevola aemula
Silene coeli-rosa
Sphaeralcea species
Sutera cordata
Thymus species
Verbena (trailing species)
Viola cornuta

Courtyard of "De Rhulenhof" nursery and show garden, Ottersum, the Netherlands

2 Managing container plants

Watering

Each entry in the alphabetical section will tell you at which time of the year your plant will need a lot of water or very little. The actual amount will depend largely on circumstances:

- The more leaves the plant has, the more water will evaporate and the more you will need to water it.
- The same plant will absorb more water in a warm position than in a cooler one. Pay special attention to this when evergreen plants are kept indoors for the winter. You will also need to give them extra water in hot weather.
- If a plant is in a windy spot, more water will evaporate than in a sheltered position.

Container plants occasionally receive a deluge of rain water in summer, and will then require less watering. This depends largely on the condition of the leaves: whether the rain water runs down the stems into the pot, or whether the leaves act as an umbrella. In subtropical regions, the leaves are often turned outwards to prevent water reaching the centre of the plant. The water drips down beyond it and is caught by the roots. If, however, the plant is in a pot, the water might fall outside the pot so that the roots dry out.

Obviously, you should not forget pots standing under the eaves or a lean-to roof. Pots placed close to walls (especially when sheltered from the prevailing wind) also need extra water, even in rainy weather. Nevertheless, the most important rule for watering container plants is this: they are more likely to die of excessive watering than from lack of water. The consequences of drought soon become apparent, but if the roots rot away in soggy container-compost, you will not notice the first symptoms until it is too late. It is therefore better to be a little careful with water than over-generous.

Feeding

In open ground, the plant's roots go in search of essential minerals. Pot plants need to find their minerals in a relatively small space, which must therefore contain sufficient nutrients. Good potting compost will always include them. If the acidity of the soil corresponds to the plant's needs, the roots will be able to extract the minerals from the soil.

The minerals, however, are consumed in the course of the season and are also washed away by watering. Plants that have remained in the same soil for several years are most likely to suffer from a lack of nutrients in the long term. The solution in such cases is to add fertilizers.

In spring, you can use a nitrogenous fertilizer such as well-rotted cow manure or one containing dried blood to stimulate leaf formation. Cow manure is also very suitable for plants that have not been repotted. Carefully remove the top layer of soil and replace it with fresh compost enriched with some well-rotted cow manure. Later in the season, it is better to add a fertilizer with a relatively low nitrogen (N) content. Phosphorus (P) and potassium (K) will respectively ensure that the plant flowers profusely and hardens off better in autumn.

If you prefer to keep the feeding simple, you can use fertilizer granules enclosed in a semi-porous capsule which enables the nutrients to

Iron pot with *Petunia surfinea*, *Convolvulus sabaticus*, *Helichrysum petiolare*, and *Brachycome iberidifolia*

be released from the granules gradually (more rapidly in warm and moist conditions than in dry or cool weather). You need only mix the granules in with the top layer of compost once, in spring, to ensure that the plants are provided with enough nutrients for an entire season.

Pests and diseases

Some plant lovers become quite panicky if they find small creatures or inexplicable spots on their plants. This is quite unnecessary. In nature, plants are nibbled at by all kinds of creatures without suffering unduly - provided they are growing in the right place. The lax, etiolated growth of plants in dark positions appears to be very popular with insects, which feast on the shoots in large numbers. The plant will lose its vigour, and mildew and viruses will finish it off.

This is a completely natural process, and it would therefore be better to regard pests and diseases as nature's aids.

With a little understanding of natural processes, pests and disease suddenly cease to be something nasty. You will learn from them. If a plant is diseased or infested with insects, there is something wrong with its manage-ment. Healthy plants are also visited by small creatures, but never in vast quantities. A healthy plant is quite capable of overcoming disease.

If you want to enjoy beautiful plants, you must look after them properly. A lot of attention is devoted to that subject in this encyclopedia. What is the best position in summer; should it be sunny or shady? What should be done with the container plant in winter? How much water and food do the plants need in summer or winter? What are the ideal temperatures? These hints and your own "green-finger instinct" will help you to keep your plants in the best of health. You will also find that the occasional small creature on the plant will not immediately lead to an infestation that will destroy it.

Everywhere I went in the course of my visits to countless specialized nurseries, I saw small creatures through the enlarging eye of my camera's macrolens. Some growers using chemical pesticides will regard this as an insult. Other modern growers, however, know that there are small creatures wandering about on their plants - their control methods could not do without them. These insects produce larvae that will go in pursuit of the "pests" in the greenhouse, but the latter will never be totally eliminated. The predators will

Petunias in a pot

have died or departed long before they have found the last of their prey.

You should abandon the idea that plants should be entirely pest-free. The strict requirements insisted on by markets in this respect are completely outdated. They lead to an unacceptable use of toxic substances, and cause damage to our environment. Careful management will make it unnecessary to resort to chemical pest and disease control. If any of your plants are suddenly infested, check the relevant entries in this encyclopedia to see what is wrong with their position or management. If the atmosphere in a heated living-room is too dry and your plants are covered in red spider mite or thrips, move the plant to a cooler position, preferably out of doors if the plant can stand it. Are the tips of your plants infested with aphids? Stop giving them nitrogenous fertilizers in any case, and move them to a cooler and lighter position. In warm, dark places, they produce the kind of lax shoots and weak buds that aphids love. If you adapt and alter the way you are managing your plants, the infestation will disappear of its own accord. You can accelerate the process by washing the aphids off the plant with a jet of water. This also works well for thrips.

Prevent infestation by scale insects by growing the plants in a well-ventilated atmosphere and ensuring that the potting compost is not too moist. When scale insects have established themselves, they are difficult to get rid of, either by chemical or biological means. Repot the plant in light soil and put it out in the fresh air. If the plants are slightly affected, you can scratch away the scales and lightly touch up the spots with a paintbrush dipped in methylated spirits (mineral spirit). Too dry an atmosphere, a warm, dark winter position, and excessively moist soil are your plants' worst enemies. Pay special attention to those aspects when looking after plants.

Overwintering

This encyclopedia includes descriptions of annuals, fully hardy plants, and conservatory plants. Only the final group requires constant care during the winter. Fully hardy specimens can be plunged into a hole in the garden in their pots, or moved to an unheated greenhouse; annuals survive as seed; but conservatory plants must be taken indoors.

When you should do so, and where the plants should be kept varies depending on the species. Special attention is devoted to their ideal winter position in this encyclopedia. The conditions in which the species grows in the wild are often described as well, since it provides important information about overwintering.

Tropical plants cannot tolerate temperatures below 10-12°C (50-53°F) for any length of time. That is the reason why they are not often grown as container plants. Some of them may be kept in a living-room during the winter, but most species cannot tolerate the dry heat of centrally heated houses. They do best in greenhouses and conservatories. Before buying that kind of plant, work out how much it will cost you to keep a greenhouse or a conservatory at a temperature of at least 12°C (53°F). There is a ten to one chance that you will decide to abandon the idea of purchasing the plant.

The most rewarding container plants come from subtropical or Mediterranean regions: countries around the Mediterranean; the Atlantic islands (Madeira, the Canary Islands, and the Azores); the south of the United States; dry regions in Central America; the cool regions of the Andes and the southern tip of South America; the Pacific islands; Australia; New Zealand; and South Africa. The climate in those regions often includes warm periods interspersed with cool and/or rainy spells followed by drought. Plants develop the same rhythm and only grow in

Pots on a flight of steps in La Palma

the favourable months. Growth is halted for the rest of the year, and some plants even shed their leaves. Several species retain the rhythm of the region they originally came from, and grow and flower in northern winters. There are also numerous container plants which have adapted to change and therefore flower in northern summers and rest in winter.

The way in which they rest during the winter varies according to the species. Some die down to the soil; others shed some of their leaves when they do not have enough light, and some are entirely evergreen. This kind of information is also included in the alphabetical section of this encyclopedia. This introduction merely includes some general rules for winter management, so that it will be easier for you to relate the detailed information given elsewhere in this book to the general background.

The ideal temperature for most genuine container plants varies between 5 and 10°C (41-50°F). The plants are then in a frost-free environment cold enough to prevent new growth. The temperature at which a plant begins to grow depends partly on the species, but for many plants the starting signal occurs at about 12°C (53°F). That temperature should therefore not be reached in winter, as

winter growth is bad for plants. Northern winters are too dark to enable southern plants to continue to grow healthily. The plant produces lax, pale green shoots which exhaust it and and make it susceptible to infestation by pests. The thin shoots must be removed in spring, as constrictions will otherwise develop in the stems.

The lighter the plant's position, the less damaging a high temperature will be. If the plant grows, it will obviously need watering. In that case, the following rule applies: the more you water in winter, the more likely the development of mildew will be.

Because the soil remains moist for a long time and water evaporates from the surface of the leaves, the humidity will increase, particularly when the temperature drops sharply at night. Cold air cannot contain much moisture. This relatively high humidity prevents evaporation and, because plants are not growing at this time, very little moisture evaporates. All in all, there are many good reasons why evergreen plants do not need much water in cold periods.

The great disadvantage of a humid atmosphere is that fungi can multiply rapidly. You would therefore be wise to check the plants regularly and carefully remove any fallen leaves (prime sources of fungoid growth). Also remove any

A pot of grape hyacinth bulbs waiting for spring

withered leaves that are still on the plants. All container plants like an airy winter atmosphere which will ensure that they are less susceptible to pests and fungi. Throw open doors and windows as often as possible, which means until the minimum temperature for the most heat-loving plant has been reached. Do not worry if your plants are too cold for a short period. Even heat-loving species can briefly tolerate lower temperatures without suffering as a result.

Plants which tolerate greater cold should be left out of doors for as long as possible. This will harden them off and give them an optimum amount of fresh air. Make sure, however, that the potting compost does not become excessively moist, as that will make them increasingly frost-tender. It is therefore advisable to shelter the pots from rain and give them very little water, if any.

Some species, including camellias, laurels, olives, pomegranates, yuccas, corokias, and the strong *Trachelospermum* may be moved out of doors again in early spring. A few degrees of frost will not harm them. Keep to the rule: if it is not too cold for a plant out of doors, then put it out of doors. If the temperature drops, bring it indoors again. This may be a laborious process, but if the plant's winter quarters are at ground level, it need not be a problem. You can put the plants on some kind of trolley like those used in hospitals, or on a simple tea trolley. It will then be a simple matter to wheel them indoors again in the evening.

Winter storage for conservatory plants

Lovers of pot and container plants without enough room to accommodate them in a suitable place in winter, can confine themselves to annuals or fully hardy species. Many plants of that description are included in this encyclopedia. If, however, you are absolutely devoted to genuine conservatory plants, which definitely need to be indoors in winter, there is another option: try to find somewhere else to house the plants for the winter season. Some nurseries may make greenhouse space available for enthusiasts' plants, but this is not a standard service. If you find a local nursery willing to look after your plants over the winter months, a charge will probably be made for the service. Your plants will however be provided with a light, frost-free position and enough care to enable them to survive the winter. Generally speaking, the 'overwintering' season extends from October to May.

A corner of the "Overhagen Nursery", Velp, the Netherlands

A

a

Abelia floribunda

The Mexican shrub *Abelia floribunda* will
grow out of doors all the year round in regions
with a very mild climate. In most places in
Europe, however, the plant will need to be
taken indoors in winter. If there are more than
a few degrees of frost, you should take the
plant indoors and let it overwinter in a light
place; keep it cool and fairly dry.
The supple stems develop in spring, and the
plant produces flowers on new wood in early
summer. The freely borne racemes of flowers
appear in beautiful shades of deep pink to
cherry red.

☼ 0°C (32°F)

Abelia floribunda

Abutilon x hybridum

This collective name includes innumerable
hybrids of abutilon species, with flowers
varying from white to shades of yellow,
orange, or red. If you keep these plants
growing well throughout the summer by giving
them plenty of water in hot weather, they will
eventually grow up to about 2m (6ft) tall.
It is quite all right to stand them in a sunny

Preceding page: *Anisodontea capensis*

position out of doors. Sunshine is harmful
only if they are not given enough water, in
which case the leaves will curl up and drop
off. Indoors, all abutilons need to be sheltered
from the hottest sunshine. The plant prefers a
cool and light position in winter. Although
some hybrids can tolerate a few degrees of
frost out of doors (which will make the plant
shed its leaves), they will survive the winter
best at temperatures between 10 and 16°C (50-
61°F). Most leaves will remain on the plants,
and the soil should therefore be just moist
enough to compensate for transpiration
through the leaves. At higher winter temperatures, the plants will need more water as they
will then continue to grow and flower.
Prune in autumn and again in early spring if
required. After pruning, each stem should be
left with enough viable tips. Pruned plants will
sprout more vigorously in spring. Abutilons
are subject to infestation by red spider mite,
whitefly, greenfly, scale insects, and cottony
maple scale. An airy but draught-free position
will help to prevent this kind of infestation.

☼ 5°C (41°F)

Abutilon x hybridum

Abutilon x hybridum 'Albus'

This freely branching shrub produces velvety
dark green leaves. The white to creamy white
flowers also create a downy impression.

25

Abutilon x *hybridum* 'Albus'

Because of its slow growth, this cultivated plant will retain its beauty over a long period.

☼ 5°C (41°F)

Abutilon x *hybridum* 'Donna'

The flowers are orange yellow at first but fade to salmon pink as they age. Unlike most abutilons, the veining in this hybrid is not deeper in colour, but translucent white. It belongs to the Darwinii group.

☼ 5°C (41°F)

Abutilon x *hybridum* 'Donna'

Abutilon x *hybridum* 'Eric Lilac'

Pinkish-red pendent flowers with deep red veining are suspended elegantly between the leaves. The leaves are large and velvety green like those of one of the plant's ancestors, *Abutilon darwinii*. A large group of hybrids is called the Darwinii group after this species.

☼ 5°C (41°F)

Abutilon x *hybridum* 'Eric Lilac'

Abutilon x *hybridum* 'Eric Rose'

This cultivar from the Darwinii group makes an altogether lighter impression than 'Eric Lilac'. It has pale pink flowers with delicate deep-pink to red veining.

☼ 5°C (41°F)

Abutilon x *hybridum* 'Eric Rose'

Abutilon x *hybridum* 'Kentish Belle'

This is a free-flowering, very rewarding abutilon belonging to the Megapotamicum group, with pendent flowers suspended in pairs from the leaf axils. The elegant leaves appear on rather lax-growing vertical stems, which arch under the weight of the flowers. The petals are orange yellow with orange veining. The strikingly large calyx is a wonderful shade of deep red.

☼ 5°C (41°F)

Abutilon x *hybridum* 'Kentish Belle'

Abutilon x *hybridum* 'Laura'

A fairly new cultivar from the Darwinii group, with orange- yellow flowers shading to blush pink at the edges.

☼ 5°C (41°F)

Abutilon x *hybridum* 'Laura'

Abutilon x *hybridum* 'Pink Niedorp'

Pink petals open out into a wide bell with deep pink veining; the plant belongs to the Darwinii group.

☼ 5°C (41°F)

Abutilon x *hybridum* 'Pink Niedorp'

Abutilon x *hybridum* 'Red Princess'

Another cultivar belonging to the Darwinii group. It has shiny, deep red flowers.

☼ 5°C (41°F)

Abutilon x *hybridum* 'Red Princess'

Abutilon x *hybridum* 'Souvenir de Bonn'

Because of its vigorous growth, 'Souvenir de Bonn (synonym: 'Andenken an Bonn') is used as a rootstock on which lax- growing abutilons are cultivated. It is hard to keep the shrub itself looking its best, as the shoots rapidly become straggly, and therefore need frequent pruning.

In spite of this, 'Souvenir de Bonn' is often for sale because the leaves of this cultivar have interesting markings. The margins of the large leaves are creamy white to greenish yellow, a characteristic which persists in plants grown from seed. The flowers are salmon pink with deep pink veining.

☼ 5°C (41°F)

Abutilon x *hybridum* 'Souvenir de Bonn'

Abutilon megapotamicum

The red and yellow flowers which occasionally have purple stamens gave the plant its nickname Belgian flag (which is red, yellow and black).

The bulbous flowers dangle like lanterns between the velvety foliage. The pointed leaves grow on long pliable stems which are easy to train and may produce a profusion of flowers.

Abutilon megapotamicum originally came from Brazil, but will nevertheless tolerate temperatures as low as -10°C (14°F) when planted in open ground. Container plants should however be taken indoors before the temperature drops to below 5°C (41°F), as they would otherwise lose their leaves.

For management, see *Abutilon* x *hybridum*.

☼ 5°C (41°F)

Abutilon megapotamicum

Abutilon pictum

The first thing to strike one about the yellowish orange flowers of this species, often sold under the name *Abutilon striatum*, is their dark, thickened veins. In summer, this sturdy shrub will grow out of doors in a large pot with humus-rich soil. Provide a light and dry position for it in winter, with a minimum temperature of 10°C (50°F).

It is likely that you will buy a cultivar. 'Thompsonii' is especially popular because of its yellow-mottled leaves, the result of what is called the mosaic virus. Unfortunately, this attractive-looking disease is not passed on when you grow the plant from seed. Grow cuttings of this handsome cultivar in soil at about 20°C (68°F), or in tepid water.

☼ 10°C (50°F)

Abutilon pictum 'Thompsonii'

Abutilon striatum

See: *Abutilon pictum*

Abutilon sonneratianum

About 150 species of abutilon grow in many of the tropical and subtropical regions of America, Africa, Asia, and Australia.

Abutilon sonneratianum, from southern Africa, is a typical example of the original species, with their relatively small, predominantly yellow or orange flowers. A huge range of cultivars, sold as *Abutilon* x *hybridum*, has been developed from them.

They flower freely over a long period: from about April to October in tubs out of doors; all the year round in heated winter gardens, conservatories, and greenhouses.

☼ 5°C (41°F)

Abutilon sonneratianum

Acacia

Acacias grow in the dry regions of Australia, Africa, and America. The Australian species in particular are favourite plants for subtropical greenhouses, conservatories, and winter gardens, but they are also suitable for growing in containers. In nature, acacias grow in seemingly arid places, but the long roots nearly always appear to find water deep down in the earth, or else their widely branching root system manages to extract it from the surface, where the moisture condenses as the temperature drops at night. This explains why acacias do better in ground soil in a greenhouse than when they are enclosed in a container. If you grow the plant in a container, do not forget that the plants are adapted to arid conditions, and keep the soil moderately moist during the growing season. Moisture should obviously not be allowed to stagnate. Good drainage and an airy soil mixture are essential for keeping the plant healthy. The soil should also be fairly acid. Deficiency disease is likely to occur in limy soil, when the leaves will lose their deep colour and turn yellowish green.

The soil should not dry out even in winter, because the leaves, which remain on the plants, always lose a small amount of moisture by evaporation. Put acacias in a light position where the temperature is not too high. They will flower better if they overwinter in a cool place at a maximum temperature of 10°C (50°F). Most species will tolereate a few degrees of frost, and all of them like fresh air. For this reason, genuine enthusiasts always keep the plants out of doors for as long as possible, and also take them out again during periods when there is no frost.

Most species flower in late winter or early spring, and it is remarkable to note that the plants that have remained out of doors in their containers flower best of all. The small globular flowers, usually yellow or creamy white, grow in compact clusters. As cut flowers, they are sold as mimosa, but they are not related to the genuine *Mimosa*. The false acacia, *(Robinia pseudoacacia)*, is also called acacia sometimes, but is not related to it.

Only a few dozen of the 1,000 species of genuine acacias are cultivated. The others are too thorny, or grow poorly or too fast, in which case they become bare lower down. All acacias, in fact, are subject to this problem, and pruning is therefore unavoidable. Cut the shrubs or trees back into shape after they have flowered. You can propagate acacias by cuttings, but that is not an easy task and should really be left to a professional grower or a thoroughly experienced amateur. Although sowing is not very easy either, it is the best method of propagation for the average plant lover. The seeds are very hard and should be presoaked in water until they have visibly swelled. This may take from 12 hours to as long as 8 days. Some enthusiasts accelerate the process by plunging the seeds into boiling water for 20 minutes, or by bringing water to the boil, putting the seeds into it, and leaving them in the cooling water until they have doubled in size (after 2-3 days). You can subsequently sow them at a temperature of just over 20°C (68°F). The results will vary considerably. It will usually be 1-3 weeks before the seeds begin to germinate, but sometimes the process takes a whole year. A description of three of the most commonly cultivated species is given below.

☼ 15°C (59°F)

Acacia cultriformis

KNIFE-LEAF WATTLE

What appear to be the leaves of *Acacia cultriformis*, turn out to be thickened leaf stalks known as phyllodes. In the case of this species from New South Wales in Australia, they are blueish green and end in a sharp point. In areas where severe frosts are unknown, the prickly shrubs are sometimes grown as impenetrable hedges. In north-west Europe, *Acacia cultriformis* blooms in late winter and early spring, producing small heads of fluffy yellow flowers. The branches have a natural tendency to arch, which may be encouraged by targeted pruning, so that you can keep the plant relatively compact.
For further management, see *Acacia*.

☼ -5°C (23°F)

Acacia cultriformis

Acacia dealbata

MIMOSA, SILVER WATTLE

Acacia dealbata is also referred to as mimosa, but this is not correct. As early as the nineteenth century, its flowering stems were cut in the south of France and in Italy and sold further north as cut flowers (labelled mimosa).

The Australian species grows naturally into a tree with beautiful pinnate foliage. By means of its surface root system, the tree absorbs the moisture it requires from a wide area. A large container and constant moisture are therefore essential. Since this often turns out to be an insuperable problem, false mimosa is usually found growing in glasshouses and winter gardens. Not much heating is required as a rule, since the species will survive temperatures as low as -10°C (14°F) in open ground. For further management, see *Acacia*.

☼ -5°C (23°F)

Acacia dealbata

Acacia floribunda

See: *Acacia retinoides*

Acacia retinoides

In countries where frosts are rare, *Acacia retinoides* is often cultivated because of its long flowering season; it is subsequently left to naturalize. The Australian plant grows into a bushy tree about 5m (16ft) tall in those subtropical regions. Unlike most other acacias, *A. retinoides* will tolerate lime in the soil, which explains why this species in particular can become naturalized to such an extent. The fact that it is hardly frost-tender also plays a part. Even in south-west England, the shrub will survive out of doors against a south- or west-facing wall. You should therefore leave it out of doors in its container for as long as possible.

New racemes of fragrant yellow flowers will appear between 18cm (7in) phyllodes (flattened leaf stalks) throughout the year. The shrub grows rapidly and may pruned be as much as you like.

For further management, see *Acacia*.

☼ -5°C (23°F)

Acacia retinoides

Acacia semperflorens

See: *Acacia retinoides*

Acca sellowiana

See: *Feijoa sellowiana*

Acer palmatum

JAPANESE MAPLE

Japanese maples are fully hardy in a garden. The leaves turn wonderful shades of red and orange before they fall. The trees themselves remain small and are naturally graceful. Specially grafted trees in pots resemble overgrown bonsais.

Grow Japanese maples in frost-resistant pots

Acer palmatum (Palmatum group and Dissectum group)

or containers with large drainage holes. Use a clayey, but neutral to slightly acid soil, which should be kept moderately moist throughout the summer.

Shelter Japanese maples from strong winds and fierce sun, but give them plenty of light. If the temperature falls below -5°C (23°F), you should protect the pot and its contents by wrapping it in insulating material and standing it against a wall of the house. In the event of severe frost, it would be advisable to take the plant indoors temporarily, and keep it in a cool position, in the dark if need be.

There are many cultivars of Japanese maple on the market, often with five to seven pointed lobes to their leaves. Those of the cultivar 'Ornatum', better known as *Dissectum atropurpureum*, are so deeply divided that they look like ribbons. The autumn colours are magnificent.

Acer palmatum 'Ornatum'

Acidanthera bicolor

See: *Gladiolus callianthus*

Acnistus

When visiting specialized container plant nurseries, enthusiasts will come across three plants which closely resemble one another: *Acnistus, Dunalia*, and *Iochroma*. These vigorous shrubs bear clusters of tubular flowers at the tips of branches. The colours always vary from blue to orange red, sometimes with a little white mixed in. The plant sold as *Acnistus arborescens* is a good example of this.
The whitish tubular flowers have wide lavender-pink flanges. The oblong felt-like leaves grow on green stems which become woody as they age.
Acnistus australis has a similar bushy growth, but bears lilac-blue tubular flowers with flared mouths.
The close relationship between *Acnistus* and *Iochroma* is apparent from the ease with which the two genera can be crossed. *Acnistus australis* can be crossed with *Iochroma cyaneum*. The result is a shrub bearing narrower, carmine to wine-red flowers in larger clusters than those of *Acnistus*.

Acnistus species can be managed in the same way as *Iochroma* species. In summer, the shrubs prefer a warm and sunny spot which, because of their fragile branches, should not be too windy. In this kind of "tropical" position, the plant will need to be watered freely and fed regularly to maintain its growth. It should be taken indoors quite early on, at

Acnistus australis

least before night temperatures fall below 5°C (41°F). A light and airy winter position at temperatures between 10 and 15°C (50-59°F) is best.
The plant will then retain its foliage and should be given enough water to make up for transpiration. In emergencies, you may let the plant overwinter in a dark position at lower temperatures, but in that case it will shed its leaves, and will also be slow to start growing again in spring.
The plants will remain manageable if you prune them hard in spring and autumn. In summer, you can take greenwood cuttings which will root easily under glass at a soil temperature of about 20°C (68°F).

☼ 5°C (41°F)

Acnistus arborescens

Acnistus australis x *Iochroma cyaneum*

Aeonium arboreum

The large rosettes of *Aeonium* will eventually grow on branching stems about 60cm (24in) tall. The green leaves appear only at the tips of the stems. Dark-leafed cultivars such as 'Atropurpureum' (dark red), or 'Schwarzkopf' (deep aubergine) are most frequently on sale, though the variegated 'Variegatum' (creamy white and green) is also very popular.

Put this - originally Moroccan - plant in a roomy pot in summer, and stand it out of doors in a sunny position. Any soil mixture will do, though the plant has a preference for mineral soil with clay and sand. It likes moderate watering in summer, and should therefore be protected against excessive rainfall.

In winter, *Aeonium arborescens* will need very little water, if any. Put it in a light position in a cool but frost-free place.

☼ 0°C (32°F)

Aeonium ciliatum

Aeonium arboreum 'Zwartkop'

Aeonium ciliatum

Each of the greyish-green leaves of the rosettes of *Aeonium ciliatum* is adorned with a pinkish red margin. The rosettes sometimes appear at the tips of thin stems which will eventually become prostrate, so that older specimens can be cultivated as hanging plants. They should be managed in the same way as *Aeonium decorum*.

☼ 5°C (41°F)

Aeonium decorum

Aeonium decorum comes from the island of Gomera in the Canaries, and forms small, thick-leafed rosettes. The bottom leaves always fall, so that the rosettes eventually have longish stems. On Gomera, these grow to about 50cm (20in). The rosettes flower in late summer and then die.

Cultivate the plant in a mineral soil mixture (clay, sand, and gravel) with some humus. In summer, water the plant as soon as the soil has dried out. The plant needs a cool (minimum temperature 5°C/41°F) and dry, but sunny position.

☼ 5°C (41°F)

Aeonium decorum

Aeonium tabuliforme

This species comes from Tenerife. Its small, softly fringed leaves overlap in spirals to form flat rosettes. As the leaves are thin, the plant also needs watering in winter. In summer, at a minimum temperature of 15°C (59°F), it should be given average amounts of water, a little less in winter. In autumn, when the plants will tolerate considerably lower temperatures out of doors, the rosettes produce multi-headed, pale yellow flowers approximately 25cm (10in) tall, with an equal spread. The flowering rosettes will subsequently die, so you will need to collect the seed.

☼ 5°C (41°F)

Aeonium tabuliforme

Agapanthus

AFRICAN LILY

Because they produce large umbels of magnificent flowers in late summer and are also easy to manage, African lilies are among the most rewarding of container plants. Idle folk can enjoy them even more, as infrequent repotting stimulates their growth - the plants can be left until their roots break a plastic pot or crack a stone container.

This South African plant needs a lot of water and food, and prefers a warm and sunny position in summer. Some African lilies retain their leaves in winter, whereas species growing in areas where rainfall alternates with

Agapanthus africanus

long periods of drought have foliage which dies down. Cultivated species shed their leaves in winter if you put them in a cold dark place. The leaves will sprout again in late winter, but the large rounded umbels of blue or white flowers will not appear until July or August.

After the plant has flowered, you should gradually give it less water and stop feeding it. When grown in pots, the plants will even tolerate a few degrees of frost and should be left out of doors for as long as possible. Some cultivars, including those of the Headbourne Hybrids group and others that are easily available, can be left out of doors in open ground under a winter covering, provided the soil is fairly dry. If they are left to overwinter in too warm an area (above 10°C/50°F), fewer, if any, new flower buds will form.

The approximately ten species of African lilies, which all grow naturally in South Africa, are very easy to hybridize. This has advantages (many lovely new hybrids have been created) as well as disadvantages. Throughout the centuries in which they have been cultivated, countless hybrids have been created naturally; they, in turn, have been hybridized either deliberately or unintentionally. It has consequently become impossible to provide cultivated plants with correct names. The following species and forms are therefore described merely as being typical of various groups.

☼ of ● 5°C (41°F)

Agapanthus africanus

The leaves and flower stems of this magnificent evergreen species are shorter than those of the well-known *Agapanthus praecox*. The leaves of *Agapanthus africanus* are about 30cm (12in) long and usually remain upright. The flower stem, which is about 50cm (20in) tall, bears up to 30 violet blue flowers. This plant definitely needs to be kept frost-free.

☼ 5°C (41°F)

Agapanthus africanus 'Albidus'

This is an evergreen cultivar which, unlike the species, can tolerate a few degrees of frost. According to recent research, it should really be called *Agapanthus* 'Umbellatus Albus'. The flowers are transparent with purple stains at the tips of petals.

☼ 0°C (32°F)

Agapanthus africanus 'Albidus'

Agapanthus africanus 'Albus Nanus'

This plant forms dense clumps of evergreen leaves, slightly shorter than those of the species. Pure white flowers are borne on stems which are about 40cm (16in) tall.

☼ 5°C (41°F)

Agapanthus 'Lilliput'

The ancestry of this hybrid is unknown, but the shape of its flowers is related to that of *Agapanthus campanulatus*. Like *A. campanulatus*, *Agapanthus* 'Lilliput' is comparatively hardy. Its leaves are narrow and pointed, which makes them look almost grass-like. They are about 10cm (4in) long and wither in autumn. The violet blue flowers grow to about 40cm (16in) in height.

☼ 0°C (32°F)

Agapanthus africanus 'Albus Nanus'

Agapanthus praecox orientalis

The more compact subspecies *orientalis* of the evergreen *Agapanthus praecox*, which produces flower stems up to 1m (3ft) tall, is more likely to be available for sale than the ordinary species. The rounded umbels of up to

Agapanthus 'Lilliput'

100 flowers are borne on stems more than 60cm (24in) tall. The flowers are a shade of watery blue, with darker stripes.

○ of ● 5°C (41°F)

Agapanthus praecox orientalis

Agapanthus umbellatus

See: *Agapanthus africanus* or *Agapanthus praecox*

Agave

CENTURY PLANT

The sturdy rosettes of agave species grow naturally in tropical America. The leaves and huge flowers are so decorative that they were also planted in other hot countries and became naturalized there. As soon as the rosette has grown to its full extent, which rarely happens in more northerly regions, a very tall flower stem shoots up from the centre. The rosette dies after it has flowered, but young plants usually develop at the base

Agave species

Agave americana

of the plant. As container plants, agaves are virtually indestructible. The only things that they cannot stand are soaking wet soil and frost. In summer, they may be put out of doors in full sun; in winter they prefer a light, cool position. They need hardly any water during the winter.

○ 0°C (32°F)

Agave americana

The leaves of this most famous of all agaves can grow to almost 2m (6ft) in their natural habitat. In pots and containers, however, they will remain considerably smaller. The species will tolerate a few degrees of frost, but the variegated forms usually available in countries like the Netherlands or Great Britain, are more vulnerable:
Agave americana 'Marginata' has broad yellow margins to its leaves;
Agave americana 'Medio-picta' has a wide, creamy white band down the centre of its

Agava americana 'Medio-picta'

leaves; *Agave americana* 'Striata' has yellowish or yellowish-white striped leaves; *Agave americana* 'Variegata' has creamy white edges to its leaves.

☼ 0°C (32°F)

Agave attenuata

You will not prick yourself on this Mexican agave, which grows in many gardens in the Canary Islands and Madeira.
The greyish-green leaves, which can grow up to 50cm (20in) long, are spineless. As the lower leaves fall, the rosette gradually begins to acquire a short stem. Its spectacular flower stem, approximately 3m (10ft) tall, can only be seen in southern countries.

☼ 5°C (41°F)

Agave attenuata

Agave bovicornuta

Like *Agave americana*, *Agave bovicornuta* comes from Mexico but is about half its size. Its leaves are waxy, light green, and have narrow, prickly, reddish-yellow edges and a red spine at their tips.

☼ 0°C (32°F)

Agave ferox

The impressive, spiny leaves of *Agave ferox* grow to 30cm (12in) wide and about 2m (6ft) long.
They arch gracefully, and give the plant a vase-like appearance.

☼ 0°C (32°F)

Agave ferox

Agave filifera

THREAD AGAVE

Agave filifera looks as if it is permanently in mourning. Leaf margins break away, leaving white fibres which curl over and eventually fall. The rosette does not grow beyond 50cm

Agave bovicornuta

(20in) in diameter, which makes the plant suitable for a comparatively small pot.

☼ 0°C (32°F)

Agave filifera

Agave parryi

Agave parryi's rosette, blueish grey with a lovely bloom, only grows to about 50cm (20in) in diameter over a period of many years. The edges of the thick leaves have chocolate-brown spines.

Put this plant, which hails from the scorching south-west of the United States and the adjoining region of Mexico, in full sun to preserve its bloom.

☼ 0°C (32°F)

Agave parryi

Agave titanota

The short, greyish-green leaves of this plant have striking chestnut-brown edges with curved spines facing in all directions. The plant is highly decorative and therefore also suitable for a comparatively small pot or bowl.

☼ 0°C (32°F)

Agave titanota

Ageratum houstonianum

FLOSS FLOWER

Some of the floss flower's cultivars are short enough to grow in a shallow bowl. There are numerous cultivars on the market, all of them bearing button-shaped flowers in shades of blue, mauve, pink, or white.

They are grown mainly as annual bedding plants, and may be sown indoors in early spring. After they have been pricked out and hardened off, you can put them out of doors

Ageratum houstonianum

in a sunny or partially shaded position. Keep the soil uniformly moist, but not excessively wet.

(1)

Ageratum mexicanum

See: *Ageratum houstonianum*

Albizia julibrissin

SILK TREE

The leaflets forming the doubly pinnate leaves of *Albizia julibrissin* close up in the evening. The tree's common name, silk tree, refers to its flowers, which appear in late summer. They consist of a tuft of soft, silky, shiny stamens, each of them about 3cm (1 1/4in) long. Although the silk tree (especially the cultivar 'Rosea') is almost winter-hardy in countries like Great Britain, the containerized plant, which may grow several metres tall (6ft or more) over the years, should still be taken indoors in winter if it is frosty. Water and light are scarcely required in that event, as the small tree sheds its leaves anyway.

In summer, you should keep the well-drained sandy soil evenly moist, but not excessively wet, and feed the plant sparingly, as rapid growth leads to vulnerable plants.

● -5°C (23°F)

Albizia julibrissin

Alchemilla mollis

LADY'S MANTLE

Alchemillas are fully hardy deciduous garden plants, which also do very well in pots. They are scarcely demanding but do have some preferences, including humus-rich soil which should remain cool and moist if possible. This means that it is better to stand the pot in partial shade. Even if you cannot meet these requirements, *Alchemilla mollis* will survive. If they are too dry, the leaves will droop, but they will soon revive after you have watered them.

The plant can spend the winter out of doors in its pot, but it would be wise to insulate it in the event of severe frost.

❄

Alchemilla mollis

Allamanda cathartica

GOLDEN TRUMPET

In tropical greenhouses, this Brazilian climber will cover the walls up to a great height. In a pot or container, the plant can be kept bushy by pruning in spring. Anyone who can find a warm position for the plant in summer (over 20°C/68°F) will be able to admire its large yellow flowers. This *Allamanda* also prefers light, humus-rich, highly nutritive soil, and plenty of water during the growing season. Let the plant overwinter in a light position with high humidity in moderately moist potting compost at a minimum temperature of 12°C (53°F).

○ 12°C (53°F)

Allamanda neriifolia

See: *Allamanda schottii*

Allamanda schottii

This plant is sometimes called the golden trumpet bush because of its shrubby growth. If the plant's position is warm enough, racemes of golden yellow flowers with orange- brown-striped throats will appear in summer. In favourable conditions, the flowers are follow-ed by large prickly fruits containing seeds that you can use for propagation. *Allamanda schottii*, which requires the same kind of care as *Allamanda cathartica*, is only sold in small quantities at present, but it is a promis-ing novelty for anyone who can provide it with enough warmth and moisture.

☼ 12°C (53°F)

Allamanda schottii

Allium albopilosum

See: *Allium christophii*

Allium christophii

The Dutch common name Persian star refers to the light purple flowers, which have a metallic glint. They sparkle in their dozens in large spherical umbels (20cm/8in in diameter) without actually dominating the scene. Be-cause of their subdued colour, the flowers are not otherwise spectacular. After they have flowered, the small stars will dry and remain on the plant for a long time. Alliums can over-winter in the garden, but may also be grown in large pots. Plant the bulbs in autumn (or winter), at a depth of about 10cm (4in) and the same distance apart, in nutritive, moisture -retentive, but well-drained soil. Keep the potting compost moist, even in winter. You should only bring the pots indoors in the event of severe frost, as the bulbs need to overwinter in a cool spot. Their foliage begins to die down during the flowering period in June-July, but you can conceal this by having some low-growing plants round the base. Remove the bulbs from the soil as soon as all the leaves have died down, and keep them in a relatively warm place during the summer. You may also leave the bulbs in a pot for the summer, but in that case you should put the pot in a warm dry spot.

❄

Allium christophii

Aloe barbadensis

See: *Aloe vera*

Aloe barbadensis

Aloe striatula

Aloes are popular garden plants in places where frosts are unknown. Tall stems with dense rows of tubular flowers rise above thick succulent rosettes. The flowers are red, orange or yellow (often with green), or any shade in between; those of *Aloe striatula* vary from yellow to orange. The species will tolerate a few degrees of frost in open ground, but pots should be taken indoors before the first night frost. Indoors, the plant should be placed in a light, cool spot, preferably between 5 and 10°C (41-50°F). You should only water the plant if the leaves begin to shrivel.
Plants with well-developed root systems may be placed in full sun in summer.
Give them plenty of water, but let the potting compost dry out completely afterwards. The soil should be light, well drained, and preferably contain minerals (therefore a lot of sand, stones and clay).

☼ 5°C (41°F)

Aloe vera

Aloe vera contains oils that are very popular in the cosmetic industry, and you will often

Aloe striatula

find pictures of the plant on the packaging of face creams and shampoos. The species originally came from the Cape Verde Islands, but it has become naturalized in many other places. You will therefore find it in the Canary Islands, in countries bordering the Mediterranean, and in South and Central America. The succulent leaves grow in a compact rosette; stems with lemon-yellow flowers emerge from them in summer. They should be managed in the same way as *Aloe striatula*.

☼ 5°C (41°F)

Alpinia purpurata

RED GINGER

Alpinia purpurata owes its common name to the red flowers which adorn it. The spikes of red bracts may ultimately grow to almost 50cm (20in) tall, and appear at the tips of large-leafed shoots measuring about 2m (6ft) in height. The shoots themselves emerge from ginger-like rhizomes. A few tentative attempts have been made to introduce this Malaysian ornamental ginger as a container plant. It tolerates low temperatures, but will only flower in warm and, above all, moist tropical conditions.
Warm summers are therefore essential for inducing the plant to flower in a container. It should be given a sheltered position, shaded from fierce sunlight - a closed greenhouse is still better - so that the leaves do not dry out. In summer, *Alpinia purpurata* needs a lot of water and food. Plant it in a large container with very humus-rich soil and keep the soil permanently moist. You should also frequently give it plant food. After the plant has finished flowering, you should gradually

reduce the amount of water and stop adding fertilizer. In normal circumstances, it will retain its foliage in winter, which means that it should be placed in a light position which is preferably not too cool. This plant should really appeal to advanced enthusiasts. The rhizomes are easy to divide, so that propagation is not a problem, and you can use the young plants to try out this "new" introduction's tolerance. *Alpinia purpurata*'s flowers also develop what are known as "adventitious buds," complete young plants which easily take root in moist soil at room temperature. Other species which are available for sale sporadically include:

Alpinia calcarata, Indian ginger, which grows about 1m (3ft) tall and produces whitish-yellow flowers with purplish-red veins;

the spice *Alpinia galanga*, 'laos', which will only produce its yellow and greenish-white flowers indoors in an atmosphere with high humidity;

Alpinia zerumbet, which needs less moisture and heat to bear its pinkish white and yellow flowers with pink throats.

○ 13°C (55°F)

Alpinia purpurata

Alyogyne huegelii

This relative of the hibiscus grows naturally in Australia, but *Alyogyne huegelii* has also been flowering in the conservatories and on the patios of European homes for some time now. The bushy plant grows up to about 1.5m (5ft) tall, and bears outstandingly beautiful deep pink flowers in among its soft, deeply lobed leaves. While the plant is in full growth, you should water it freely and occasionally feed it.

Alyogyne huegelii

Move it indoors in late summer, as soon as night temperatures fall to below 10°C (50°F). That is also the minimum temperature at which the plant can survive the winter comfortably. Give it just enough water to keep its leaves, but definitely not more.

In winter, the roots are highly susceptible to rot. At temperatures over 15°C (59°F), *Alyogyne* will need more water. The plant will continue to grow and should then be cut back hard in spring.

○ 10°C (50°F)

Alyogyne huegelii 'Trumpet Serenade'

Alyssum maritimum

See: *Lobularia maritima*

Amaryllis belladonna

BELLADONNA LILY

The official name of the amaryllis sold by florists is *Hippeastrum*, which closely resembles *Amaryllis belladonna*. This South African bulb grows wild in the Azores and the Channel Islands, where frosts are rare. The genuine *Amaryllis* is sold only by specialized firms. Plant the bulb in a large pot in spring, with the apex just showing above the surface. You should give the plant average amounts of water and fertilizer while the plant still has its ribbon-like green leaves, which sometimes wither early in summer. The plant is then keeping to its natural cycle, but is definitely not dying. Do not water during that leafless period. Always find the warmest possible position for it on the patio or in a conservatory or greenhouse. In late summer, a sturdy flower stem may emerge from the leafless bulb, but usually this will not occur until a year later. Leaves will, in any event, appear again in autumn, so that the plant will require a light, frost-free position in winter and very little water. Do not repot an amaryllis more often than is strictly necessary.

○ 0°C (32°F)

Amaryllis belladonna

Ampelopsis

INDOOR VINE

Ampelopsis brevipedunculata var. *maximowiczii* 'Elegans' is something of a mouthful, and it is simpler to use the plant's most recent name: *Ampelopsis glandulosa* 'Elegans'. This variegated form is the only one that will grow satisfactorily in a living-room. The species itself is green-leafed and climbs exuberantly in all directions. In spite of its common name 'indoor vine', 'Elegans' will stay healthier if you treat it like a container plant. As soon night temperatures cease to fall below 5°C (41°F), you can put this plant out of doors in a pot, preferably in a sheltered position and shielded from the hottest midday sun. The leaves, which have green as well as greyish-green and cream spots (often with a pinkish bloom), therefore remain intact. The plant's decorative appeal is also greatest in the shade, as the leaves light up magnificently in a semi-dark position. Never allow an ampelopsis to dry up, and feed it regularly. You may, if you like, shorten excessively invasive shoots which wind their tendrils round other plants. A light position, high humidity, and a temperature from about 10 to 15°C (50-59°F) will enable the plant to keep its leaves. Overwintering in the dark is possible, but then you should definitely not give the plant too much water.

○ 10°C (50°F) or ● 5°C (41°F)

Ampelopsis glandulosa 'Elegans'

Anigozanthos

KANGAROO PAW

The eleven species of kangaroo paw all come from western Australia. They were regarded as a curiosity when they were discovered, and were removed from their natural habitat on such a massive scale that their survival was in doubt. Now they are often grown from tissue cultures. The name nearly always refers to cultivars of unknown origin, though the sturdy, yellow-flowered species *Anigozanthos flavidus* is often recognizable. The kangaroo paw will always remain a rare plant, as keeping it in a healthy condition is far from simple. Make sure the plant has a lot of light and warmth in summer - a sheltered position in full sun is best. In cool summers, it is preferable to keep the plant in a greenhouse or conservatory - or in a light position in a living-room. Keep the root ball permanently moist, or the flower buds will die off, but make sure that excess water can drain away satisfactorily. Most specimens die in winter because of lack of light. Put the plant in a very light, cool position (between 5 and 15°C/ 41-59°F) and give it just enough water to prevent the root ball drying out. Always use rain water or softened (boiled) water.

☼ 5°C (41°F)

Anigozanthos

Anisodontea capensis

This small shrub from South Africa will flower throughout the summer. If you keep the plant growing with plenty of water and fertilizer, new flowers will appear from late spring onwards. The shrub prefers a warm and sunny position in the garden, with some protection against fierce midday sunlight. It is best to move this *Anisodontea* indoors as soon as the first night frost occurs, though the plant can in fact stand a few degrees of frost. Usually, it will still be in flower at that time.
It is not advisable to let the plant continue to grow throughout the winter, so gradually reduce the amount of water you give it, and put it in a cool, light position. The plant may be cut back hard in spring, after which it will begin to grow again, followed by another long summer of abundant flowers.

☼ 0°C (32°F)

Anisodontea capensis

Antigonon leptopus

CORAL VINE

If this climber from Mexico is not given sufficient support, it will trail along the ground. This member of the polygonum family has become naturalized in many tropical countries but, further north, it is an extremely rare plant which is suitable for a greenhouse or a conservatory, and may flower with dense trusses of small white to pink flowers about a year after it has been sown. Put the coral vine in a sunny position and water it freely in summer. The temperature may fall to about 10°C (50°F) in winter. Keep the plant relatively dry during this period; you may also prune it severely while it is dormant.

☼ 10°C (50°F)

Antigonon leptopus

Apios americana

POTATO TREE

This climber with its butterfly-shaped flowers grows out of tubers which were a major source of food for North American Indians. The plant winds its way upwards for about 3m (10ft) in a single season, and flowers profusely. The flowers, however, have rather muted colours, and are not very spectacular.

It is a real enthusiast's plant and is increasingly available.

The leaves die down in winter, but the tubers are fully hardy.

Don't be tempted to grow the plant in open ground as it will become rampant. It is better to cultivate it in a large container in a sunny position out of doors. Water freely.

❄

Apios americana

Apios tuberosa

See: *Apios americana*

Aporocactus flagelliformis

RAT'S-TAIL CACTUS

The thin pendent stems of this cactus have golden spines and grow very long. If you look after it well, the plant will bear candy-pink flowers, about 10cm (4in) long, every spring.

The rat's-tail cactus needs a good period of dormancy during the winter. Water only if the "tails" begin to shrivel up, and hang the plant in a light, cool place where the temperature does not exceed 15°C (59°F). Resume watering gradually when small pinkish-red dots (the

buds!) appear in spring. Then hang the plant in a warm and very light position, but not in full midday sun.

After the final night frost, you may move the rat's-tail cactus out of doors again, not only because the plant looks so decorative suspended from a pergola or arbour, but mainly because it is particularly fond of fresh air. Indoors, the cactus is often fatally susceptible to attack by red spider mite.

☼ 2°C (36°F)

Aporocactus flagelliformis

Araujia sericifera

CRUEL PLANT

The sweet herbal scent of the cruel plant's flowers attracts moths, which insert their prosboces into the flowers in their search for nectar. An unpleasant surprise awaits them. The flower holds on to the proboscis and, no matter how much the moth struggles, its tongue will remain imprisoned and will not be released until early morning. A small package of pollen now adheres to the moth. The moth often makes the same mistake in a different flower the following evening, and the pollen is released as the moth struggles to free itself. The plant owes its bad reputation largely to moths which die during their imprisonment and remain suspended from the flowers. After pollination, a follicular fruit, over 10cm (4in) long, is formed.

Put the araujia in a large pot with nutritive,

moisture- retentive soil, and give it plenty of water and food while in full growth. This climber, which originally came from Argentina and Peru, likes warmth.

A greenhouse or conservatory would therefore be best for it, but a warm and sunny position out of doors is also suitable.

The evergreen *Araujia* should be kept relatively dry in winter. It needs a light position where the temperature does not fall below 10°C (50°F).

☼ 10°C (50°F)

Araujia sericifera

Ardisia crenata

CORALBERRY, SPICEBERRY

Ardisia is often sold as a houseplant, but it is far better to treat it as a container plant. As soon as the night temperatures cease to fall below 5°C (41°F) in spring, this small deep-green shrub may be taken out of doors. It bears small pink or white flowers in summer. They are pollinated out of doors, but not always indoors, and only the pollinated flowers develop into red berries, the plant's most decorative feature, in autumn. If the plant does produce berries, move it to the coolest possible position in a living-room so that you can enjoy it to the full.

In summer, the shrub prefers to be out of doors in partial shade and out of the wind. Keep the humus-rich potting soil constantly moist. In winter, it requires a cool position (5- 12°C/41-53°F) and only a little water.

The plant is easy to propagate from seed in spring.

☼ 5°C (41°F)

Argyranthemum 'Flamingo'

MARGUERITE

Arygranthemum 'Flamingo' is one of the lovely, newish marguerites in the Frutescens group. This rather low, open- structured shrub is adorned with an abundance of pink flowers with "scorched" centres. Management is the same as for *Argyranthemum frutescens*.

(1)

Argyranthemum 'Flamingo'

Argyranthemum frutescens

MARGUERITE

Innumerable cultivars of the wild marguerites from the Canary Islands are labelled *Argyranthemum frutescens* in garden centres.

Ardisia crenata

The foliage may be greyish or blueish green and deeply divided.

The flowers of the genuine marguerite are white with yellow centres, whereas those of the cultivars are often pink, white, yellowish, cream, or lilac. All too often, *Euryops* species with their golden yellow flowers are sold incorrectly named *Argyranthemum*.

Marguerites like sun and warmth, but also a lot of fresh air. They will flower magnificently even in partial shade, where transpiration will be reduced, and they will consequently need watering slightly less often.

Remember, however, that these thirsty container plants should never be left to dry out.

You should also feed them regularly to keep them flowering throughout the summer.

Move your marguerites indoors before the first night frost, so that you can briefly enjoy the flowers indoors. Although it is possible to take cuttings in autumn, most plant lovers find it simpler to buy a new, flowering specimen in spring.

(1)

Argyranthemum frutescens

Asarina erubescens

CLIMBING GLOXINIA

Pink flowers, each one up to 7cm (23/4in) long, are formed at the tips of *Asarina erubescens'* scandent stems throughout the summer. This Mexican climber will grow as tall as the supports provided for it (up to 3m/10ft in a single season).

In a large pot with bamboo stakes, the plant will remain a compact bush full of flowers. Stand the pot in a sunny or half-shady position, and give it plenty of water. Round fruits containing winged seeds are formed at the end of the season; you should sow them under glass in February if you wish to have plants the following season. It is also possible to cut back asarinas hard in autumn and let them overwinter in a frostfree, fairly dry and light place.

(1) or ☼ 0°C (32°F)

Asarina erubescens

Asclepias curassavica

SILK WEED, BLOOD FLOWER

Silk weed is excellent combined with other container plants, as its somewhat lanky appearance is too conspicuous on its own. Its flowers, which appear in May-June, are red and orange, yellowish orange, or sometimes whitish orange. Fresh umbels appear at the tips of shoots throughout the summer, and are followed by long fruits. When they burst open, the reason for the plant's name becomes obvious: each small seed has silky pappus attached to it.

Put the asclepias in well-drained soil in a sunny position in summer, and water freely. Adding fertilizer will benefit the flowers. The evergreen silk weed needs little water in winter, but it should be kept in a place where its ideal temperature, 10-15°C (50-59°F), prevails. If you sow seeds indoors in January-March, the seedlings will flower the same summer.

☼ 10°C (50°F)

Asclepias curassavica

Aspidistra elatior 'Milky Way'

Asclepias fruticosa

SILK WEED

The pale flowers of this species are less important than its decorative bladder-shaped fruits. In southern Africa, they are sprayed with silver paint and used as Christmas decorations.
See *Asclepias curassavica* for management and propagation.

☼ 10°C (50°F)

Aspidistra elatior

CAST-IRON PLANT

This aspidistra is as strong as its name suggests. Of Chinese origin, it will grow in very varied conditions, and eventually fill its pot with thick rhizomes from which long leaves subsequently emerge in spring. Do not stand the plant in full sun, and do not leave its rhizomes in water for too long, as not even the cast-iron plant can endure that.
Aspidistra elatior grows almost 1m (3ft) tall and does best on a shady, mossy patio, where Mediterranean plants are unlikely to survive. The dark green leaves suggest the atmosphere of Victorian country houses.
Besides the green-leafed species, there are also cultivars with yellow or white specks or

stripes on their leaves. 'Milky Way', the most familiar example, has small cream spots. 'Variegata Ashei' has small white stripes, and 'Variegata Exotica' a more irregular pattern of stripes.

☼ 0°C (32°F)

Aster amelloides

See: *Felicia amelloides*

Azalea mollis

See: *Rhododendron molle*

Asclepias fruticosa

B _____ *b*

Bacopa 'Snowflake'

See: *Sutera cordata* 'Snowflake'

Ballota pseudodictamnus

Everything about this low subshrub from the coasts of Greece is soft: its stems, its leaves, and even the white- velvety, saucer-shaped calyces enclosing the small whitish- purple flowers.

This is an excellent pot plant, which may be grown in sandy soil in full sun, and even then will need relatively little water. The white "velvet" will look its best if untouched by water.

The plant will tolerate temperatures as low as -15°C (5°F) in well-drained soil but, if grown as a pot plant, had better be moved indoors to a cool, light place in frosty weather. It may be propagated by cuttings.

☼ -5°C (23°F)

Ballota pseudodictamnus

Basella alba

Basella alba is a tropical vegetable. Its leaves and tender young stems are braised or cooked in a wok.

You can grow the climber yourself from seed. Sow indoors or in a greenhouse in early spring and let the seedlings grow on at room temperature.

The young shoots can be harvested after about three months; the plants will subsequently branch widely. In summer, the climber can be put out of doors in a large pot; the red cultivars 'Rubra' and 'Rosebud' are particularly suitable for growing as ornamental container plants. They are also called red basella because of their wine-red stems and leaf veins. Water freely and give the plants plenty of fertilizer to encourage satisfactory growth.

Crimson berries containing the seeds develop out of the small bladder-shaped flowers. The seed can be collected as soon as the berries shrivel up. Be careful with the juice, which may stain. It is used as a dye in Asia!

(1)

Basella alba 'Rosebud'

Begonia Cane-groep

BUSH BEGONIA

Out of all the many kinds of bush begonia, one group is particularly suitable for cultivating in containers. It consists of hybrids of the tall begonia species with clearly visible sections of bare stem resembling sugar cane. The nodes, from which the oblong leaves emerge, are enclosed by membranous scale leaves. The leaves have a characteristic shape, with an off-centre, pointed, and pendent tip, along which, in their natural environment, rain water can quickly drain off. The leaves are green to reddish green and often have silvery spots. White, pink, red, or orange flowers are suspended from the leaf axils in large panicles.

The ancestors of cane-stemmed begonias were

Begonia Cane-groep

mostly introduced from Brazil. Well-known houseplants such as *Begonia* 'Lucerna' (with large racemes of white to pale pink flowers) and *Begonia* 'Picta' (with striking silver-spotted leaves) were descended from *Begonia maculata*. Leaf margins are usually smooth, but when crossed with *Begonia aconitifolia*, they become sinuate and sometimes lobed, and the plant is referred to as 'Superba Cane'.

Because of the cane-stemmed begonias' sturdy growth, the group is very suitable for growing in containers. Tall plants may well need some support, especially if they have first been grown indoors. If you want to achieve a compact, bushy growth, you should cut back the plant to a few buds above the soil in spring. The new growth will consist of strong vertical stems which do not branch much, as

well as somewhat laxer, more horizontal ones. Depending on the required shape, you can cut back either the vertical stems or the more arching kind.

Depending on the cultivar, and on how it is supported or pruned, 'cane-stemmed' begonias will grow between 50cm and 3m (20in-10ft) tall. In spite of this, you should plant them in relatively small pots with well-drained soil, which can dry out thoroughly between watering sessions. A sheltered spot which catches morning or evening sunshine is the best position, as these begonias prefer a shady location during the hottest part of the day.

It is sensible to move the plants indoors in autumn. They will still be flowering, so that you will be able to enjoy them indoors as well. To prevent mildew, you should remove dead leaves and all dead flowers. Begonias left out of doors in the damp autumn air are susceptible to mildew. Remove any affected leaves (those with powdery white spots) and throw them away, or cut back the plant to a few buds above the soil. If you let this begonia overwinter in a living-room, you should water it regularly to preserve its leaves. If you put it in a cool place, the potting compost should remain fairly dry, in which case the leaves will normally be shed. After the plant's spring pruning, it will soon sprout again.

In summer, you can easily take tip cuttings, approximately 10cm (4in) long, and put them in water or moist sphagnum moss to grow roots.

Do not cover with plastic. The cuttings will have developed rootlets after about a month, and will then grow rapidly into flowering plants.

☼ 5°C (41°F)

Begonia coccinea

ANGELWING BEGONIA

This shrubby Brazilian species grows up to 1m (3ft) tall. Its stems are succulent and break off easily.

Even the shiny green leaves with deep-red edges are succulent; they are clearly wing-shaped, hence their common name. The pinkish-red male flowers grow to over 2cm (3/4in) in diameter; the red female flowers are slightly larger.

Begonia coccinea can be managed in the same was as the cane-stemmed begonias

☼ 5°C (41°F)

Begonia fuchsioides

FUCHSIA BEGONIA

At first sight, the stems, leaves, and flowers of this Venezuelan begonia closely resemble those of a fuchsia. The small toothed leaves, lax red stems, and panicles of small globular flowers are very similar. Because of its dense bushy shape, *Begonia fuchsioides* makes a delightful container plant. You should, however, move it indoors in good time in autumn, because it dislikes temperatures below 10°C (50°F). *Begonia fuchsioides* then turns into an ideal houseplant which may continue to flower throughout the winter. In summer, you should give the plant average quantities of water and a semi-shady position. Propagation is best carried out in summer by taking stem cuttings with several leaf buds.

○ 10°C (50°F)

Begonia fuchsioides

Begonia coccinea

Begonia minor

Begonia minor is one of the thousand or so natural begonia species growing in the warmer regions of America, Africa, and Asia. In 1777, *Begonia minor* (also known as *Begonia nitida*) became the first species to be brought to Europe. Even today, it is one of the few botanical species still cultivated. The plant originally came from Jamaica, but it is now grown as a garden plant throughout the tropics and subtropics.

Begonia minor does best in the shade, and prefers a cool shady position even when grown as a houseplant. Its stems, which grow towards the light up to a height of 2m (6ft), will eventually cover an entire north-facing window.

Begonia minor prefers to be out of doors in summer. It will then have light and fresh air, which will keep it more compact. Stand the plant in partial shade and shelter it from fierce midday sunlight. You can grow the plant in a relatively small pot. The potting compost should become packed with roots, which can then effectively absorb the moisture in the soil. Let the soil dry out between watering sessions, and put the plant in a drier position during lengthy periods of rain.

As soon as the temperature falls below 5°C (41°F) in autumn, you should move the plant to a cool position indoors, where it will continue to flower and provide you with further enjoyment.

○ 5°C (41°F)

Begonia minor

Begonia nitida

See: *Begonia minor*

Begonia Semperflorens group

These begonias are particularly well known as bedding plants because of their pink, red, and white flowers which can be used to fill separate colour sections. As they flower uninterruptedly right through the summer, they are prime favourites of gardeners who wish to use bedding plants for creating colourful patterns. People who like handsome flower troughs full of colour often choose Semperflorens begonias.

These plants were the result of crossing *Begonia semperflorens* with *Begonia schmidtiana*, both of which grow naturally in Brazil. Nowadays, other begonias are also used for similar hybridization, so that the origins of the Semperflorens hybrids can no longer be traced.

They are all plants with succulent leaves and stems which break easily, and some shelter from strong winds is therefore advisable. They may be moved out of doors after the final night frost, and will then continue to flower in full sun or partial shade until the first night frost. Water moderately, but make sure that the soil ball dries up thoroughly before they are next watered, as the risk of mildew will be considerable otherwise.

Manage the begonias like houseplants in autumn, preferably in not too warm a position. If they becomes unsightly, just discard them. In spring you simply buy new plants, which are easy to sow, or - in the case of sterile, fully double flowers - to propagate by cuttings.

(1)

Begonia Semperflorens group

Begonia sutherlandii

The orange flowers of this African tuberous begonia form a splendid contrast with its olive-green leaves. Nowadays, they are often sold specially for patio hanging-baskets. This is a good choice, since *Begonia sutherlandii* likes fresh air and is tolerant of low temperatures. You need not move the plant indoors until the first night frost is expected.

The begonia will continue to flower indoors for a while. If it overwinters in a warm, light position, the plant will keep its leaves and should be watered as soon as the soil has dried up. If you are only interested in having the plant flower out of doors in summer, you should put the *Begonia sutherlandii* in a cool, dry spot and cease to water it. The foliage will then die down, but the tuberous roots will stay alive. Put the plant in a frost-free spot, in the dark if need be, and give it just enough water to prevent it drying out too much. The radical tubers will sprout again in April-May, when you should gradually increase the amount of water that you give the plant. The small bulbils formed in the leaf axils can be used to propagate the plant. They mature in autumn and can then be potted up. If the resultant plants are well cared for, they will flower for a second season.

○ 15°C (59°F) or ● 0°C (32°F)

Begonia 'Tamaya'

This new cultivar is a begonia grafted on to the rootstock of a different species. Foliage

Begonia sutherlandii

and flowers of the grafted plant closely resemble those of *Begonia corallina-*, but, because they are suspended from a short stem, 'Tamaya' looks just like a bonsai. This effect is emphasized by the fact that the plant is usually on sale in a decorative china container. Like genuine miniature trees, you need to trim the plant to keep it in shape. This should be done after it has flowered, as the flowers, which are suspended from a remarkably long ovary, are much too pretty to cut off.

'Tamaya' will adorn the patio, and flower beautifully in summer. Make sure that excess water can always drain away and do not water until the soil feels dry. A light position, but not in fierce midday sunshine, is best for the plant. When night temperatures fall to below 7°C (45°F), 'Tamaya' should be taken indoors and treated as a houseplant.

☼ 7°C (45°F)

Begonia 'Tamaya'

Begonia Tuberhybrida-hybrids

TUBEROUS BEGONIA

Most of the thousand or so species of begonia are evergreen plants. In mild climates without frost and long spells of drought, they usually continue to grow throughout the summer and winter. Begonias from mountainous regions such as the Andes are the exception to the rule. In these mountains, *Begonia boliviensis*, *Begonia clarkei*, *Begonia davisii*, *Begonia pearcei*, *Begonia veitchii* and *Begonia froebelii* have alternating growing seasons and periods of dormancy. Stems and leaves die down when the plant is dormant; a thickened tuber in the soil stores reserve food.

The tuberous begonias grown out of doors in beds, pots, and troughs are hybrids of the species mentioned previously. Their flowers vary from single to fully double, and may be white, pink, red, orange, yellow, or multi-coloured.

To indicate the differences between their flowers, tuberous begonias have been divided into innumerable groups and given group names, including the following examples: the Camelliiflora group, with flowers resembling those of camellias; the Picotee group, with a coloured edge to each flower petal; the Multiflora group, with large numbers of small flowers; and the Pendula group, with pendent flowers making the group very suitable for hanging baskets. Tuberous begonias are ideal for those who have to contend with lack of space in winter. Stems and leaves die down in autumn. Remove any remains to prevent mildew, and leave the tubers in their pots of soil, which should be stored in a cool dark place. The ideal winter temperature is between 5 and 10°C (41-50°F). It is also possible to remove the tubers from their pots in autumn, and to store them in peat or sawdust. By keeping the peat or sawdust very slightly moist, you will prevent the tubers from drying out unduly and thus retarding growth.

In spring, you should return the tubers to pots of fresh, slightly moist, soil. Plant the tuber deep enough to enable you to add soil up to the top of the tuber. (Note: the convex side is

Begonia Tuberhybrida hybrid

the bottom of the tuber from which the roots will develop.) Besides roots and new shoots, small excrescences will develop at the sides of the tuber in this phase. They can be broken off and planted separately in pots, where they will grow into new plants. When the new shoots are well developed, you should add enough soil to the pots to cover the tuber completely.

If you cannot manage to let the tubers over-winter in a cool place, just throw them away at the end of the season and buy new ones. These days, tuberous begonias are also grown as annuals: they are then sown in early spring for summer flowering the same year.

Tuberous begonias will thrive in either partial shade or full sun. Give them average amounts of water and let the soil dry out before water-ing again. Missing out on watering from time to time is definitely not fatal; wind, however, is something that begonias really cannot endure, as the succulent stems break off easily. For the same reason, it is also best to avoid planting them along paths or in places where they may be damaged by children or domestic pets. Large-flowered and double cultivars are particularly subject to the danger of the stems breaking under the weight of the blooms.

You should therefore support them with small stakes, but be careful not to push supports into the tubers.

● 5°C (41°F)

Begonia Tuberhybrida hybrid

Bellis caerulescens

BLUE DAISY

Blue daisies grow wild in the North African Atlas Mountains. Frosts occur there regularly,

but never combined with damp conditions. That is the reason why this enchanting daisy will not become naturalized in northern lawns. It needs a dry and light position in winter, and can then tolerate some frost. Its root ball, however, needs some protection against more severe frost, simply because it is grown in a pot.

Apart from that, blue daisies are trouble-free plants which bloom profusely in summer. Their whitish flowers are slightly larger than those of the common daisy, and look as though they have just been dipped in poster paint for a moment. Sow these daisies in autumn. Cover the seed very lightly or not at all, as *Bellis* germinates in the light.

○ -5°C. (23°F)

Bellis caerulescens

Bellis rotundifolia caerulescens

See: *Bellis caerulescens*

Berberidopsis corallina

CORAL PLANT

In the forests of Chile, *Berberidopsis* will climb trees up to a height of 4m (13ft). In western European climates, it is an ideal plant for embellishing shady places. Cultivate this evergreen climber in a large pot or container with humus-rich, moisture-retentive soil, and keep the plant out of the wind. In that way, its deep-green leaves will remain handsome, and

54

pendent clusters of bright red flowers will be produced in autumn. The flowers are globular and about 1.5cm (5/8in) in diameter.

Berberidopsis will tolerate temperatures as low as -10°C (14°F) in open ground, but when it is grown in a pot you should take it indoors after the first night frosts and keep it in a cool, light place, where you only need to water it very sparingly.

☼ 0°C (32°F)

Berberidopsis corallina

Bidens ferulifolia

In 1992, a small shrub resembling a trailing form of *Coreopsis* was first introduced. The stems of this Central American plant spread rather untidily, which does not usually augur well for success in the world of ornamental plants. However, when you have seen what *Bidens* looks like in a handsome vase, you will be enchanted. The plant is experiencing a meteoric rise, and its semi-pendulous shoots with leaves resembling those of fennel are now trailing over vases and hanging baskets, and this rewarding plant with yellow flowers in summer has become the most popular species for balcony troughs in southern Germany and Austria.

Bidens ferulifolia is extremely strong, tolerates full sun as well as cooler positions. If you sow the small seeds indoors in February-March, the plants will bloom from June until far into autumn. It is possible to keep the plants through the winter, but growing them as annuals is simpler.

(1)

Bignonia buccinatoria

See: *Distictis buccinatoria*

Blechnum gibbum

Blechnum gibbum is actually a smallish tree fern which develops a short stem as it ages. The plant originally came from the southern islands of the Pacific and prefers a light position. If you keep the root ball thoroughly moist, the plant may even be put in a sunny position, but partial shade is best.

The most effective position for these tree ferns that I have ever seen was where they were

Blechnum gibbum

planted in stone urns flanking the front door of an attractive house.

The ferns need not be taken indoors until the first night frost, when they should be put in cool, light place. In that kind of situation, *Blechnum* will not need much watering during the winter, but occasional sprinkling with water will benefit the plant.

Should you be inclined to buy one of these magnificent ferns, then look out for them among the houseplants. Outdoor cultivation is healthier for the plant, as the humidity in heated living-rooms is too low, particularly in winter.

☼ 5°C (41°F)

Boronia heterophylla

Boronia's stems are almost vertical and its long narrow leaves contribute to its upright appearance. The leaves resemble those of rosemary, the difference being that the plant produces small globular flowers like those of blueberries. This remarkable little shrub, which grows to about 1m (3ft) tall came originally from Australia. The flowers are slightly fragrant and are used in the perfume industry. Plant the shrub in a smallish pot containing a mixture of sand and peat (or some other slightly acid soil).

Any moisture should be able to drain away easily. Put the pot in a light position, but not in full sun, and shelter it from easterly winds. Water moderately and cut shoots back hard if you prefer a bushier shrub.

The *Boronia* should be moved indoors in autumn, before the first night frost, and left to overwinter in a cool, light place. Water very moderately during this period.

☼ 5°C (41°F)

Boronia heterophylla

Bougainvillea

Bougainvilleas have a difficult time in northwest Europe, where they will do best in a large airy greenhouse or a winter garden. Another good way of cultivating them is in containers. Bougainvilleas should not be moved out of doors until fairly late in the season, some time in June or July, when the bracts surrounding the flowers begin to colour. Plants that are put out of doors too early in the season will only flower in fine summers.

Put the pot or other container out of doors in the sunniest and most sheltered spot you can find, preferably against a south-facing wall of the house. The soil should be well-drained, and should contain a lot of mineral constituents such as sand and clay. Water freely. The plant should be moved indoors before the first night frost. It can overwinter in a cool position, in which case it will shed its leaves. Alternatively, you may choose a warmer place so that the plant will retain its leaves. The latter method will provide greater certainty, as weak plants in particular are slow to sprout after a long leafless period, or do not sprout at all.

If the plant is overwintering in a warm place (12-20°C/53- 68°F), water moderately. A living-room is often too dry for bougainvilleas, so it is better to put it in a moderately heated bedroom, right in front of a sunny window.

If it is kept in a cool place (2-15°C/36-59°F) for the winter, the bougainvillea will not need any light. Make sure that the root ball does not dry out entirely during that period. From March-April, when the climber slowly begins to produce new shoots, you may give it slightly more water. New growth will not become more vigorous until May- June, when you should water freely and may also add some fertilizer. The following rule applies to both methods of overwintering: try to give the plant as much air as possible, and spray the leaves as frequently as possible in winter and spring to prevent infestation by red spider mite. The bougainvillea will be in flower when you buy it. The transition to the dry atmosphere of a living-room will often cause the flowers to drop. To prevent this, growers often plunge the plant into the rooting hormone Rhyzopon B, a chemical which

Bougainvillea

slows down flower loss. You can minimize the effect of the transition yourself by putting a newly purchased plant in an airy place with high humidity or by putting the plant out of doors straight away in summer.

It is possible, though not easy, to take cuttings from bougainvilleas. In spring or summer, take tip cuttings, about 10cm (4in) long, from non-flowering shoots, and put them in peaty soil. Cover the cuttings with glass or plastic and keep the soil temperature in the frame at 20°C (68°F). Do not stand the frame in the sun. The cuttings will take root faster if you first dip them in rooting powder.

● 2°C (36°F) or ○ 12°C (53°F)

Bougainvillea 'Lady Mary Bering'

Bougainvillea x *buttiana*

Many of the bushy types of bougainvillea, sold as *spectabilis*, are in fact crosses between *Bougainvillea glabra* and *Bougainvillea peruviana*.

The floral bracts may be bright red, or pink, salmon, orange, cream, or white. The many

Bougainvillea x *buttiana*

Bougainvillea x *buttiana*

cultivars are usually sold without names. It is best to let cultivars with variegated leaves overwinter in a warm place.

● 2°C (36°F) or ○ 12°C (53°F)

Bougainvillea x *buttiana* 'Pink Tip'

Bougainvillea glabra

The best-known bougainvillea originally came from Brazil, but is now to be seen as an ornamental plant in all Mediterranean countries. The bracts are usually a deep shade of magenta when they open, and steadily become lighter in time. The form with white flowers is less common.

Many cultivars have been developed from this

Bougainvillea glabra-hybrid

species, usually with magenta bracts. *Bougainvillea peruviana* has been crossed with most of the cultivars with pink to orange bracts, and this species belongs to the *Bougainvillea* x *buttiana*.
Bougainvillea glabra 'Sanderiana' is a compact bush with larger, bright mauve bracts, which remain on the plant like "dried flowers" after it has flowered.
Bougainvillea glabra 'Alexandra' was developed from the above cultivar. The bracts have a brighter, reddish violet colour. This plant, too, has a compact bushy shape.

● 2°C (36°F) of ○ 12°C (53°F)

Bougainvillea glabra 'Sanderiana'

Bougainvillea sanderiana

See: *Bougainvillea glabra* 'Sanderiana'

Bougainvillea spectabilis

Many bougainvillea hybrids are on sale as *spectabilis*, but this is rarely the correct name. *Bougainvillea spectabilis* is a fast-growing species from Brazil.
Its fairly lax stems are covered in spines which help the plant to scramble high up into the trees.
The plant will only survive the winter in a warm spot, and is in every sense more vulnerablevulnerable than those sold as *spectabilis* hybrids.
The latter plants are nearly always specimens of *Bougainvillea* x *buttiana*.

○ 12°C (53°F)

Bougainvillea x *buttiana*

Brachycome iberidifolia

SWAN RIVER DAISY

This Australian annual is covered in small, daisy-lke flowers. Their centres are yellow or brown, and the ribbon- shaped petals may be in every imaginable shade from violet to pink. *Brachycome* (often incorrectly labelled *Brachyscome*) is highly suitable for hanging baskets. Not only the flowers, but also the deeply divided leaves show up splendidly in them, and the plant is also fairly resistant to drought. It is about 30cm (12in) tall. Stand or hang the plant in a sunny position and water moderately. Sow indoors in March-April, or out of doors in May.

(1)

Brachycome iberidifolia

Browallia americana

Brachyscome

See: *Brachycome*

Brassica oleracea

ORNAMENTAL CABBAGE

Brassicas appear on the market as other pot plants begin to deteriorate. They were developed from the common cabbage.

The most bizarre shapes and colours were created by selection, and there are numerous, mainly Japanese, cultivars on sale. They have crenated or crinkled leaves with very diverse colours: white, green, pink to mauve by way of red, and are often bi-coloured.

Brassicas are usually grown as annuals: seeds sown indoors in March (or out of doors in April) will grow into decorative plants towards the end of summer, and display their best colours in full sun.

(1)

Browallia americana

The loose growth and abundant flowers of *Browallia americana* make it a highly suitable container plant for enthusiasts with sophisticated tastes. The flowering shoots clamber elegantly over the edges of pots or tubs, while the small violet to pink flowers, 1.5cm (_in) across, are suspended from the

Brassica oleracea

stems like so many butterflies. The light spots above the dark centres further enhance the subtle effect. Sow *Browallia americana* (or *Browallia viscosa* and *Browallia speciosa*, which closely resemble it) indoors in March. After the risk of night frosts has receded, the seedlings of these warmth-loving South African species may be taken out of doors. Stand the pot in a sunny position and follow the standard management procedure for annuals. It is easy to collect seeds from this plant.

(1)

Brugmansia arborea

ANGELS TRUMPETS

The name *arborea* refers to the tree-like growth of this species, which develops into a handsome rounded shape. This, and its velvety leaves, will make the plant steal the show on the patio. Relatively short, broad, white flowers with an overpowering fragrance are borne in late summer. The plant will flower abundantly if it is given plenty of water and fertilizer. Stand it in full sun or partial shade during the summer. Leave the plant out

Brugmansia arborea

of doors to harden off for as long as possible, but it is essential to move the container indoors by the time of the first night frost. Large plants may then be cut back hard to gain space. There are two ways in which these plants can overwinter: either in a cool (5-12°C/41-53°F), dark and almost dry place, where the plant will shed its leaves, or in a lighter, slightly more humid place at a temperature of approximately 12-15°C (53-59°F). In the warmer place, the *Brugmansia* will retain its leaves. Do not let the temperature rise above 15°C (59°F), as the plant would then continue to

grow and northern winters are too dark for that. It would result in lax growth which would need to be cut back in spring. All parts of all brugmansias are highly toxic.

● 5°C (41°F) of ○ 12°C (53°F)

Brugmansia cornigera

See: *Brugmansia arborea*

Brugmansia x flava

Hybrids are not always the result of human intervention. *Brugmansia arborea* and *Brugmansia sanguinea* both originally came from

Brugmansia x flava

the Andes Mountains and provided the natural hybrid *Brugmansia x flava* which, in fact has been cultivated for a very long time. The yellow flowers of x *flava* are not pendent, but are slanted downwards. Their strong greenish veining, the most characteristic of this species, is clearly visible along the sides of the calyx. The shape of the leaves varies, but is usually oval rather than elongated. For management, see *Brugmansia arborea*.

● 5°C (41°F) or ○ 12°C (53°F)

Brugmansia suaveolens

The wild *Brugmansia suaveolens* grows in south-east Brazil. It can rarely be seen in countries like Great Britain, where the plants sold under this name are nearly always hybrids. *Brugmansia versicolor* (from Ecuador) has often been crossed with them. The hybrid is backcrossed with *Brugmansia suaveolens* and is then called *Brugmansia x insignis*. The fragrant flowers of these dubious shrubs, which are also frequently sold incorrectly as *Brugmansia arborea*, are no less

Brugmansia suaveolens

Brugmansia suaveolens 'Klerx Variegata'

tinge at the base of the trumpet and the veining of the petals are characteristic features which distinguish this cultivar from others. For management, see *Brugmansia arborea*

● 5°C (41°F) or ○ 12°C (53°F)

Brugmansia suaveolens 'Klerx Variegata'

At some time, a shoot with variegated leaves grew out of the base of a common *Brugmansia suaveolens*, and this feature has been preserved ever since. The cultivar appears to retain its colours even after intensive propa-

beautiful for all that. They are trumpet- shaped and always have soft pastel colours such as buttery yellow, pale pink, salmon pink, or creamy white. For management, see *Brugmansia arborea*.

● 5°C or ○ 12°C (53°F)

Brugmansia suaveolens 'Guatemala'

The flowers of this cultivar gradually change from white at the base to pink. The greenish

Brugmansia suaveolens 'Guatemala'

gation by cuttings. The leaves are green with greyish-green spots and buttery yellow to creamy white veins and margins. The plant has a good compact shape.

This is a plant for genuine enthusiasts who can let the plant continue to grow in a light position in winter. Water moderately during that period and keep the temperature at a minimum of 15°C (59°F) so that the plant loses as few leaves as possible. It is a fact that, after losing its leaves, the plant is slow to start growing again in spring.

○ 15°C (59°F)

Brunfelsia pauciflora

YESTERDAY-TODAY-AND-TOMORROW

Anyone without a greenhouse or a conservatory will have difficulty in inducing *Brunfelsia* to flower. In late winter and early autumn, this spreading shrub from Brazil needs a tropical climate to develop buds: the right conditions for the plant are room temperature combined

Brunfelsia pauciflora

with high humidity. However, as soon as the buds begin to open in April, lower temperatures are required (about 13-18°C/55-64°F). In summer, while the plant is in flower, it will also grow well out of doors, but only if it is in a light, warm, sheltered, but slightly shady position. Water freely and give the plant adequate food when it is out of doors. As soon as night temperatures threaten to fall below 7°C (45°F), it is essential to move the frost-tender *Brunfelsia* indoors. Provide light, fairly dry, and relatively warm winter quarters (10-18°C/50-64°F) with relatively high humidity. Sprinkle the plant regularly.

○ 7°C (45°F)

Buxus sempervirens

COMMON BOX

Evergreen *Buxus* is excellent for topiary work. To achieve optimum results, decide early on what kind of shape you wish to create, and work towards it gradually.

Allow for the fact that the shrub is slow to recover from being cut back rigorously to thicker stems. The spheres, pyramids, rectangular blocks, and figures look splendid in traditional terracotta pots or other stylish containers.

Although box is fully hardy in open soil, you should protect a containerized shrub from the worst frost as well as from the sun and chill winds. Stand the pot against the house in winter, or push it, wrapped in straw, rush-matting, or other insulating material, in among other pots. The best position is out of the sun and sheltered from dry winds which would cause the moisture in the evergreen foliage to evaporate at a time when it cannot be replenished by the frozen roots.

During the summer, you can cultivate box in any kind of soil, provided no water is left in the pots. The shrub has a distinct preference for a light position.

❋

Buxus sempervirens

C

C

Caesalpinia ferrea

In eastern Brazil, where *Caesalpinia* originally came from, it grows into a plant over 10m (33ft) tall. This species is also frequently planted in other tropical countries because of its handsome, flaking, grey bark and decorative foliage. It is because of these transparent pale green leaves that *Caesalpinia ferrea* is sometimes sold as a container plant. The small yellow flowers appear only when the plant is in a very warm position. This species even prefers a slightly warmer position than that of *Caesalpinia gilliesii*, but apart from that, it should be cared for in the same way.

○ 8°C (46°F)

Caesalpinia ferrea

Caesalpinia gilliesii

The large yellow flowers borne by this shrub have red stamens, approximately 10cm (4in) long. In the south of South America, the species grows as a large shrub or small tree. When the plant is containerized, the long lax stems may be cut back immediately after it has flowered. This *Caesalpinia* will only flower out of doors in a warm and sunny position in July and August. Keep the soil continuously moist (but never soaking wet) in summer, and give the plant plenty of fertilizer, particularly in early summer. Although it will tolerate temperatures as low as -10°C (14°F) in open ground, a containerized specimen should be moved indoors before the first frost, and given a light position. If the leaves fall, it is also possible to keep it in a dark place throughout the winter. In either case, you should water the plant just enough in winter to prevent the soil in the container from drying out completely.

○ of ● 5°C (41°F)

Caesalpinia gilliesii

Calliandra

Calliandra's flowers seem to consist entirely of stamens, which are often red and highly conspicuous. However, many species of this shrub from America, Africa, and Asia have beautiful pinnate leaves, and are worth cultivating just for that reason.
There are about 200 different species of *Calliandra*, some with large leaflets, others with rows of small leaflets. There is little difference between then, and the number of leaflets varies. The flowers, too, resemble one another.
These evergreen plants require a light, fairly warm position in winter, preferably 12-16°C (53-60°F). In spring, red spider mite may be particularly troublesome. You can prevent infestation by letting in as much fresh air as possible and spraying the foliage.

You should water sparingly in winter. In summer, *Calliandra* likes a very warm position, preferably in a greenhouse or conservatory, or else in a sheltered spot out of doors. Grow the plant in light, sandy soil containing adequate nutrients, and water evenly.

○ 12°C (53°F)

Calliandra

Calliandra tweedii

The finely divided foliage of *Calliandra tweedii* is very soft and downy, just like the buds and flowers with their deep-red stamens, 3cm (1 1/4in) long. The flowers of this plant, which comes from Brazil, grow in clusters.

○ 12°C (53°F)

Calliandra tweedii

Callistemon citrinus

BOTTLEBRUSH

The flowers of the bottlebrush consist entirely of stamens. Those of *Callistemon citrinus* are red and point in all directions, which makes them resemble brushes. The fact that bottlebrushes do not develop petals appears to have something to do with their natural habitat in the dry regions of Australia. There, any moisture in the petals would rapidly evaporate, and that would mean excessive wastage. The coloured stamens have therefore taken over the function of flower petals and attract insects.

Bottlebrushes require sunny positions and a lot of fresh air. They are tolerant of wind, which makes them highly suitable for a windy balcony. They make undemanding container plants in that they are fairly impervious to disease and infestations, and also tolerate irregular care. Preferably plant the bottlebrush in slightly acid soil and water moderately in summer. You can leave the plant out of doors until late autumn, as it will tolerate several degrees of frost.

In winter, the plants require a light, cool position in fresh air. A temperature of 5-10°C (41-50°F) is ideal. Water *Callistemon citrinus* very sparingly, but make sure it does not dry out. From early spring until late summer you should cultivate the shrub in well-drained soil and water freely.

August is the best time for propagating this plant. Break off a sideshoot in such a way that a small piece of bark remains attached to the shoot. Provided with this 'heel', the cutting will root successfully in a sandy soil mixture at room temperature.

○ 0°C (32°F)

Callistemon citrinus

Callistemon 'Violaceus'

BOTTLEBRUSH

The flowers of *Callistemon* 'Violaceus' appear to be tinged with deep purple. As the nights turn colder later in the season, the rather small, sturdy, blueish-green leaves acquire a reddish-brown or purplish-brown tinge. Manage the plant in the same way as *Callistemon citrinus*.

☼ 0°C (32°)

Callistemon 'Violaceus'

Calycanthus fertilis *var.* laevigatus

ALLSPICE

With its large shiny leaves and remarkably shaped purple flowers, *Calycanthus* makes an exotic impression. The shrubs, however, are fully hardy. They originally came from China or the United States. Five of the six species, which are very similar to one another, grow in the US. The leaves have slightly different shapes and colours; the stems and leaves are either hairier or less so; and the colour of the flowers may vary slightly, but, apart from that, it makes little difference whether you buy *Calycanthus occidentalis*, *C. floridus*, or *C. fertilis*. *Calycanthus fertilis* var. *laevigatus* is distinguished by its leaves, which are also shiny green beneath. The flowers have the fragrance of ripening fruit. Put the plant in a large container with humus-rich soil in a sunny position. When the the plant has finished flowering in summer, stop giving it fertilizer, so that the stems have an opportunity to mature. Weak new shoots will be cut by frost. Keep the soil slightly moist at all times.

Calycanthus may be kept out of doors in winter, when the leaves will fall, so that there is no need to water the plant. There should be no water left in the container, and if there is a severe frost, the container should be insulated because containerized plants are always more tender than the same plants in open ground.

❋

Calycanthus fertilis var. *laevigatus*

Camellia japonica

COMMON CAMELLIA

The best-known camellias are the more than 2,000 hybrids developed from *Camellia japonica*. The colour of the flowers varies from red to pink to white, and includes every shade in between. The flowers sometimes have multi-coloured stripes or specks. The decorative stamens of single- flowered cultivars are

Camellia

Camellia japonica 'Elegans'

particularly striking, but there are also culti-vars with semi-double or fully double flowers.

Many of the modern cultivars will tolerate temperatures as low as -18°C (c.0°F).
Camellias in pots or containers, however, should be moved indoors if there is a frost, and then require as cool as possible a frost-free position which should also be light and airy. Because these shrubs retain their leaves in winter, the root ball should always be kept slightly moist. After a cold spell, the buds - which were formed the previous summer - will begin to open. Sometimes they will even open in early February. Leave the plant in a cool position, as a sudden rise in temperature and drop in humidity may cause the buds and flowers to fall. Sprinkling with decalcified

Camellia japonica 'Guilio Nuccio'

water (boiled, for instance) is recommended while the plant is in bud. As the buds begin to colour, you should water more freely, but never saturate the soil; you should also make sure that excess water can drain away. Cease watering when the shrub is in flower.

If there is no frost, camellias are best out of doors. In summer, the shrub needs a (half-) shady spot, sheltered from the wind. That kind of cool position is best for its growth. The pot-ting compost should on no account contain lime - rhododendron compost is excellent - and even during watering and feeding, it is most important that no lime gets into the soil. If you take these precaustions, the camellia can be left for years in the same large pot or container, as it greatly dislikes having its roots disturbed.
Camellias grow evenly in all directions, so that pruning is hardly necessary. If you do need to cut back, do so immediately after the plant has flowered, as camellias flower on the previous year's wood. Popular cultivars include the fol lowing:
Camellia japonica 'Elegans' - this vigorous container plant has large flowers; its pink petals often have white streaks;
Camellia japonica 'Guilio Nuccio' - with its beautifully arching, red to pinkish-red petals encircling the strongly contrasting yellow stamens, this is one of the loveliest cultivars;

Camellia 'Button Bows'

Camellia japonica 'Mathotiana Alba'

Camellia japonica 'Mathotiana Alba' - a spreading cultivar with magnificently formed, pure white flowers which remain at their best if you stand the container in a sheltered spot or indoors while they last.

☼ 0°C (32°F)

Camellia 'H. Gouillon'

Camellia sinensis

TEA SHRUB

Tea grows on shrubs. What you put in your teapot are snippets of the fermented leaves of *Camellia sinensis*, a shrub which originally came from China but is now cultivated in many mountainous subtropical regions. *Camellia sinensis* grows on cool, moist slopes where, however, it is never chilly. When grown as a container plant, the tea shrub will require a minimum temperature of 12°C (53°F) in summer and winter if it is to remain in good condition. As heated living-rooms are

too dry, and northern winters are too short, a greenhouse or conservatory is the ideal place for this plant. In summer, you should stand the container in partial shade in a spot where it is sheltered from the wind. Provide a large pot with lime-free soil which should be kept continuously moist in summer and moderately so in winter.

☼ 12°C (53°F)

Camellia sinensis

Camellia x williamsii

Camellia saluensis and *Camellia japonica* are the ancestors of *Camellia* x *williamsii*, from which a great many cultivars were subsequently developed. They are just as hardy,

Camellia x *williamsii* 'Jury's Yellow'

and sometimes even hardier, than *Camellia japonica* cultivars, and may be managed in the same way. See *Camellia japonica*.

Camellia x *williamsii* 'Jury's Yellow' is one of the few camellias with yellow flowers. Within a ring of white petals, it has a yellow pompon consisting of petals developed from stamens. This cultivar was produced in 1972, and makes an excellent container plant with abundant flowers borne over a long period, and compact growth.

☼ 0°C (32°F)

Campsis x *tagliabuana* 'Madame Galen'

TRUMPET FLOWER

Campsis x *tagliabuana* is a cross between the American trumpet creeper *Campsis radicans*, only just fully hardy in northern Europe, and the large-flowered but vulnerable Chinese *Campsis grandiflora*. Unlike the trumpet creeper, this hybrid does not attach itself to walls, but develops into a shrub, with very long shoots which can be tied to supports. The most popular cultivar is 'Madame Galen', whose lovely apricot-coloured flowers fade to red later on.

Although 'Madame Galen' will tolerate temperatures as low as -10°C (14°F) in open ground, it is better to grow the shrub in a large container with well-drained soil. If you use a

poor mixture of humus and sand, making sure that this remains thoroughly moist in summer, the plant will not develop excessive greenery, but will flower well. In a greenhouse, it will shoot up to a great height when planted in open soil.

Stand the container out of doors in as warm a spot as possible, preferably in full sun. If the leaves fall in autumn, side shoots may be cut back hard. As soon as the temperature drops to near freezing, you should move the container indoors and let the plant overwinter in a cool place, in the dark if necessary. Keep the soil almost dry.

● 0°C (32°F)

Canna x *generalis*

Cannas originally came from tropical America, where they flower almost all the year round. In more northerly European countries, the various cultivars are grown as summer bedding plants or in containers. The flowers are large and brightly coloured - red, orange, and yellow - although there are some in softer shades of pink or cream. Two-tone, speckled, and striped flowers also occur. They are borne at the tips of flower stems which grow up to 1-2m (3-6ft) tall. Large, lax, banana-shaped leaves are produced at the base of these shoots.

Campsis x *tagliabuana* 'Madame Galen'

Canna

In spring, stimulate the rhizomes' growth by putting them in a container in a warmer position (15-25°C/59-68°F), and watering the shoots more freely as they develop. After the last frost, the plants may be put out of doors again in a spot sheltered from the wind. Now you may give the plants plenty of water and fertilizer, as they will only flower well in very rich soil.

The container should be taken indoors again before the first night frost and left to overwinter in a place where it is not too cold, although it may be dark. As the foliage will then die down, you need only water very sparingly. Propagation is easiest by division of the rhizomes in early spring. However, as long as that is not essential, it is best to leave them alone as much as possible.

● 10°C (50°F)

Canna Indica group

See: *Canna* x *generalis*

Capsicum annuum

ORNAMENTAL PEPPER, CHILLI PEPPER

Chilli peppers and sweet peppers are descended from the wild *Capsicum annuum*, which presumably grew wild in South America at one time. The species has also become the parent of innumerable cultivars grown for ornamental purposes. In many florists and garden centres, you will, in early summer, be able to choose from a large selection of dwarf shrubs producing red, orange, yellow, or green to aubergine- or eggplant-coloured fruits developed from white flowers. Preferably find

Capsicum annuum

a spot out of doors in full sun for ornamental peppers, and water moderately. Move them indoors in autumn, where they will provide colour in a living-room for a little longer. It is possible, in theory, to let ornamental peppers overwinter, but buying new ones or growing them from seed provides better-looking plants, and capsicums are therefore cultivated mainly as annuals. Sow in early spring at a temperature of about 20°C (68°F).

(1)

Capsicum annuum 'Madame Jeanette'

CHILLI PEPPER

This cultivar combines beauty and usefulness. The plant, which grows to about 1m (3ft) tall, will develop yellow fruits in summer, even in a sheltered position on a balcony or patio - a wonderful sight. After you have thoroughly admired their appearance, you may pick the fruits and eat them. But beware - there is a tale that this cultivar is named after one of the hottest whores in South America! Its seeds are extremely pungent, and this pepper is usually included in recipes for that reason. It is removed before the dish is served, but will give it a unique flavour particularly useful in Surinam cookery. Grow this cultivar in the same way as the species.

(1)

Capsicum annuum 'Madame Jeanette'

Capsicum annuum 'Habanero'

CHILLI PEPPER

The cultivar 'Habanero' has a milder flavour than 'Madame Jeanette', but is only considered edible by those who like very spicy food. For anyone else, it is a beautiful ornamental plant, which will also manage to fruit in a sheltered position on a balcony or patio. The peppers have an irregular shape and turn bright orange in autumn. Grow this cultivar in the same way as the species.

(1)

Capsicum annuum 'Habanero'

Carica papaya

PAPAYA

Papayas are particularly suitable for lovers of exotic plants. This South American species produces fibrous stem, 1-3m (3-10ft) tall, with a tuft of large, shiny, palmate leaves at the top. Fruits will only develop in a hot environment, and if you have a male plant as well as a female one. Androgynous specimens also produce fruits, but such plants are extremely rare.

If you cultivate the papaya in a pot or container, the plant will not grow much beyond 1-1.5m (3-5ft) tall. The container may be moved out of doors as soon as the chance of night frosts has passed. Stand the pot in as warm a spot as possible, where there is not too much wind. Give it a rich, well-drained soil mixture, as the plant will certainly die if it is kept in wet soil for long. This will also occur if the plant is left out of doors when there is a frost. The papaya should therefore be taken indoors in good time to overwinter in a light position at a minimum temperature of 5°C (41°F), with the soil kept almost dry.

Instead of the genuine papaya, you can also grow a *Carica pentagona*.

This species is always propagated by cuttings and is rarely for sale. The *pentagona* remains smaller and tolerates more cold than the *papaya*.

Since adult plants do not live long, you should sow *Carica papaya* every three to five years. Sow under glass at a soil temperature of about 25°C (77°F), and use sandy, free-draining soil, which should really be sterilized first in order to kill germs.

☼ 5°C (41°F)

Carica papaya

Carissa grandiflora

See: *Carissa macrocarpa*

Carissa macrocarpa

NATAL PLUM

Because of its forked spines, this tough little shrub from South Africa is sometimes grown as hedge in its country of origin. Even the green leaves, which remain on the shrub in winter, are stiff and awkward. In summer,

delightfully fragrant flowers appear among the leaves and ultimately develop into orange-red fruits the size of a plum, hence its common name. The fruits are edible, but, even so, it is better to keep them for ornamental purposes, as they are easily confused with the deadly poisonous fruits of the closely related *Acokanthera*.

Carissa likes fresh air and prefers to be out of doors in summer. Water only when the soil feels dry, and protect the plant against prolonged rain. Use an airy, free-draining soil mixture and feed sparingly.

You should take the plant indoors and stand it in a light place as soon as the temperature drops below 5°C (41°F). Avoid a stuffy atmosphere and water sparingly during this period. Not much water will evaporate from the surface of the leaves between 5 and 12°C (41-53°F).

☼ 5°C (41°F)

Cassia corymbosa

From June to October, golden yellow flowers with remarkably bent pistil and unusual

Cassia corymbosa

stamens appear between the pinnate leaves of this Central American shrub. The plant will grow up to 2m (6ft) tall in a container, and tolerates hard pruning.

In summer, *Cassia* likes a sunny position out of doors and continuously moist soil, preferably containing some clay, sand, and sufficient nutrients. If you feed regularly, the plant will continue to grow and flower well. In winter, it should have a cool, light position, where it will not require much water.

At higher temperatures, you can keep the shrub growing in a very light location, and then it will continue to flower for some time during the winter. Cut back hard after the plant has flowered, so that it can branch out during the new season.

☼ 5°C (41°F)

Cassia didymobotrya

GOLDEN WONDER

Cassias should really be called *Senna*, but that name is hardly ever used any more. *Cassia (Senna) didymobotrya* produces flowers at the end of long stems which continue to grow while the plant is in flower. The leaves consist of innumerable leaflets on either side of the midrib. The species originally came from the countries around the Indian Ocean, but now it grows in all countries with a mild tropical or Mediterranean climate.

Cassia didymobotrya

Even though *Cassis didymobotrya* is less hardy than the other two species described here, it may still be put out of doors in a large pot or other container in summer. You should, however, take the plant, which grows about 2m (6ft) tall, indoors again as soon as the temperature falls below 10°C (50°F).

Immediately after it has flowered, you should cut back the flower stems to encourage new buds to form. For further management, see *Cassia corymbosa*.

☼ 10°C (50°F)

Cassia x floribunda

Cassia multiglandulosa and *Cassia septemtrionalis* are the parents of this hybrid, which looks very much like a smaller version of *Cassia corymbosa*. The hybrid, however, flowers more abundantly, and looks more graceful when grown in a container. For further management, see *Cassia corymbosa*.

☼ 5°C (41°F)

Cassia x floribunda

Catharanthus roseus

ROSE PERIWINKLE

The rose periwinkle's long and abundant flowering season makes it one of the most popular annual border plants. It originally came from Madagascar, and is also a rewarding summer-flowering plant for balcony and patio containers, as well as for window boxes. As soon as the danger of frost has receded, *Catharanthus* (until recently better known under its old name *Vinca Rosea*) may be put out of doors. It needs a sunny position and a lot of moisture. It is easiest to grow the perennial plant as an annual. Sow under glass in March-April.

(1)

Catharanthus roseus

Ceanothus x *delilianus* 'Gloire de Versailles'

Along the dry west coast of southern Canada, the United States and northern Mexico, ceanothuses grow in among the brushwood. Some species have pink or white flowers, but most of them are intensely blue. They flower in the latter part of summer and in early autumn, and so take over from the summer-flowering shrubs.
Ceanothuses are often bought for that reason. Unfortunately, the shrub usually causes disappointment, as the first really severe winter will kill it. Although the deciduous species are generally stronger than the evergreen kind, they are still vulnerable at temperatures below -10°C (14°F). Grow the ceanothus in a large pot and water regularly in summer, because a lot of water evaporates from the leaves even though the plant originally came from a dry region.
Leave the pot out of doors in the fresh air for as long as possible in autumn, but if the temperature falls below -5° (23°F), you should take it indoors.
Ceanothus 'Gloire de Versailles', a cultivar of *Ceanothus* x *delilianus*, is one of the more

robust types. In open ground, it will survive temperatures as low as -15°C (5°F). As the leaves fall in autumn, you can keep the plant in a dark place indoors. Choose a position that is as cool as possible and move the plant out of doors again as soon as the temperature rises above -5°C (23°F).
A lot of fresh new foliage will appear in spring. Pot-grown specimens will then need feeding to gain enough energy to flower. As propagating the plants either by cuttings or by seed is very complicated, that job is better left to professional nurserymen.

● -5°C (23°F)

Ceanothus x *delilianus* 'Gloire de Versailles'

Centradenia inaequilateralis

'Cascade' is the sole cultivar of this Mexican species offered for sale, and it looks suspiciously like *Heterocentron elegans*, another species from Mexico. You will consequently find the same plant labelled *Heterocentron* 'Cascade' at some nurseries. That, however, makes no difference as far as management is concerned. 'Cascade' does best as a hanging plant in full sun, in which case you should water moderately and use free-draining, nutritive soil. If you occasionally give it some fertilizer during the season, this hanging plant, which can also be grown as ground cover, will flower profusely. You may expect repeated waves of flowers from May to July, with a late flowering period continuing well into the autumn. Take the plant indoors before the first night frost, and then cut it back hard. In its pruned state, the plant will survive the winter very well in a cool and light position, with very little water. The cultivar can be propagated by cuttings in summer: take tip cuttings and insert them in a sandy substrate in a covered frame.

☼ 7°C (45°F)

Centradenia inaequilateralis 'Cascade'

Ceratostigma willmottianum

It is impossible to give an adequate description of the subtle shade of this perennial's mauvish blue flowers.

They appear quite late in summer, and the display subsequently continues with the leaves, which turn red from the tips in autumn. In China, the *Ceratostigma* may grow up to 1m (3ft) tall, but in colder countries the shrub dies down to its base in an average winter, and will need to start all over again.

Fill the pot with free-draining, humus-rich soil. Find a sunny to semi-shady position for the plant, and water moderately in summer. In winter, the pot may be dug in, plant and all, preferably in a dry spot in the garden.

❄

Cestrum

Several species of *Cestrum* from Central and South America provide a prolonged display of flowers. If warmth and moisture are adequate, the tubular flowers will appear all the year round, which makes cestrums highly popular among owners of conservatories or winter gardens.

Those without this kind of luxury accommodation will merely be able to enjoy the flowers, which subsequently develop into red to black fruits, in summer. Allow for the fact that these vigorous shrubs grow to about 2m (6ft) tall and must be taken indoors in winter. If you have a large living-room which is light and not too warm, and where humidity is not reduced excessively, you can let the *Cestrum* continue to flower there. Otherwise, a cool, light room (10-15°C/50-59°F) will do. The plant will retain its leaves during this dormant period, and you should therefore give it a few drops of water from time to time to compensate for transpiration from the leaves.

It is even possible for the plant to overwinter in the dark, but only at very low temperatures: between 0°C and about 5°C (32-41°F). It will then shed its leaves and should be kept entirely dry.

Pruning is possible in autumn, winter or early spring, but be careful: the entire plant is poisonous. The flowers produced on new shoots in summer, will appear in large numbers if you water the nutritive potting compost freely and feed regularly. Stand *Cestrum* in a warm position in summer, slightly sheltered from the fiercest midday sun. Propagation is by seed, which, however, often grow into hybrids (if there are other *Cestrum*

Ceratostigma willmottianum

74

species in the vicinity), or by cuttings. Take semi-ripe cuttings in early summer, and let them root at a soil temperature just over 20°C (68°F).

☼ 10°C (50°F) or ● 0°C (32°F)

Cestrum aurantiacum

This striking species from Guatamala has orange-yellow flowers which are borne from midsummer to far into autumn on specimens cultivated in containers. The plant sheds its leaves as soon as the temperature falls below 13°C (55°F), so it is best to overwinter it in a slightly warmer position. For further management, see *Cestrum*.

☼ 13°C (55°F)

Cestrum aurantiacum

Cestrum elegans

This is the best-known species, frequently offered for sale as *Cestrum purpureum*. The shrub, rigidly erect at first, has lance-shaped, slightly downy leaves. The stems eventually arch over under the weight of the racemes of red flowers.
For management, see *Cestrum*.

☼ 10°C (50°F) or ● 2°C (36°F)

Cestrum fasciculatum

This species closely resembles *Cestrum elegans*, except that it is somewhat broader and arches over right from the first. The flowers are slightly downy on the outside. For management, see *Cestrum*.

☼ 10°C (50°F) or ● 2°C (36°F)

Cestrum fasciculatum

Cestrum fasciculatum 'Newellii'

See: *Cestrum* x *newellii*

Cestrum elegans

Cestrum-hybrid resembling *aurantiacum* 'Album'

Cestrum-hybrid

Cestrums hybridize easily, and innumerable hybrids have therefore been created, sometimes accidentally, sometimes in a deliberate attempt by growers to extend their range with some lovely new cultivars. The broad-leafed plant with creamy flowers represents one such an attempt. It proved to be a failure, however, as the plant flowers for only four weeks and the grower will therefore not market it. In fact, it closely resembles the splendid and rewarding *Cestrum aurantiacum* 'Album'. For management, see *Cestrum*.

☼ 13°C (55°F)

Cestrum-hybrid *(cherry red)*

Cestrum x newellii

It is even more difficult to distinguish the red-flowered species from one another. The innumerable hybrids are sometimes merely indicated by the colour of their flowers, cherry red for instance. *Cestrum x newellii* is the best-known hybrid in this group. It is presumably a cross between *Cestrum elegans* and *Cestrum fasciculatum*. The deep-red flowers develop in large clusters at the tips of arching stems. For management, see *Cestrum*.

☼ 10°C (50°F) or ● 2°C (36°F)

Cestrum fasciculatum 'Newellii'

Cestrum nocturnum

At first sight, *Cestrum nocturnum* does not look very attractive. The greenish to greenish-white flowers are long but very narrow. They are produced in large numbers at the tips of vertical shoots. Their fragrance develops towards evening. Some people like the scent and stand *Cestrum nocturnum* among other container plants on the patio; others find it unpleasant.
For management, see *Cestrum*.

☼ 10°C (50°F) or ● 2°C (36°F)

Cestrum parqui

This species is rarely seen, presumably because of its short flowering period in June and July. Personally, I think it is the loveliest of all. Its modest, greenish- yellow flowers breathe the atmosphere of the Andes, and develop an exotic fragrance towards evening. The clusters are proudly upright at the ends of

vertical stems with strikingly elongated leaves. The plant is used for medicinal purposes but it can also be exceptionally poisonous.
For management, see *Cestrum*.

○ 10°C (50°F) or ● 0°C (32°F)

Cestrum parqui

Cestrum nocturnum

Cestrum purpureum

See: *Cestrum elegans*

Chaenorrhinum organifolium

Its low dense growth and profuse flowers make this *Chaenorrhinum organifolium* one of the most rewarding pot plants to have on the patio. The small flowers are particularly lovely: mauvish pink, attractively striped, and with yellowish white lips. If you stand the plant on a table, you will be able to enjoy it to the full. The cultivar most frequently for sale is 'Blue Dream'. *C. organifolium* likes a sunny position in well-drained soil. Although it grows as a perennial in Mediterranean countries, it is better to grow the plant as an annual in a colder climate. When it has finished flowering, you can harvest the dark brown seeds. If you sow them indoors in March-April, the plants will begin to flower by the end of May. If you do not wish to harvest the seeds, cut back the shoots that have finished flowering. The plant will then keep its compact shape and will also flower longer.

(1)

Chaenorrhinum organifolium 'Blue Dream'

Chamaecytisus palmensis

This species of broom grows in the gentle shade of native pines in La Palma (Canary Islands). The plant serves as an example of the low-growing species distinguished from the common broom by the Greek word *chamae* (low).
These species are highly suitable for rock gardens. They originally came from the

Balkans, Central Europe, North America, or Japan, and are fully hardy. Only the species from the Canary islands, including *Chamaecytisus proliferus* (which closely resembles *C. palmensis*), should be taken indoors in winter. If you wish to cultivate them in pots, plant them in sandy, lime-free soil which should be kept slightly moist throughout the growing season. A position in semi-shade is best. The plant should be taken indoors when the first night frost occurs. As the leaves remain on the shrub during the winter, the plant needs to overwinter in a light place where the atmosphere is not too dry. A conservatory or greenhouse is ideal. If you do not have either, put the plant in a cool room. Cut back in winter or immediately after flowering, or the shrub will become straggly. Prune in good time, as no species of broom will recover well after severe pruning. Old wood sprouts slowly or not at all.

The *chamaecytisus* species from the Canary Islands are usually not for sale, and are currently cultivated only by genuine enthusiasts. Winterhardy species such as *Chamaecytisus multiflorus* (syn. *C. albus*), *C. austriacus*, *C. hirsutus*, and the well- known *C. purpureus* are also suitable for cultivating in pots. They are available at nurseries and may remain out of doors in pots in winter, though it is sensible temporarily to move them indoors (to a light place) if temperatures fall below -10°C (14°F).

☼ 0°C (41°F)

Chamaecytisus x *spachianus*

See: *Genista* x *spachiana*

Chrysanthemum frutescens

See: *Argyranthemum frutescens*

Cibotium

Before the young fronds of *Cibotium* unfold, they are rolled up tightly at the top of the stem and thus resemble a bishop's crosier, hence the cibotium's Dutch common name 'bisschopsstaf'. All tree ferns, of which there are about 15 species, do best in a cool greenhouse or conservatory, where it is warm but airy. In summer, they also grow well out of doors in a (semi-) shady, warm position, sheltered against the wind. Temperatures between 15 and 30°C (59-86°F) are ideal. Keep the potting

Chamaecytisus palmensis

Cibotium

compost permanently moist, but not soaking wet, and sprinkle the plant in hot dry weather. You should take the *Cibotium* indoors again as soon as night temperatures have fallen below 5°C (41°F). When indoors, the plant should have a light, airy position sheltered from the hot midday sun; the temperature should preferably be kept between 7 and 15°C (45-59°F).

☼ 5°C (41°F)

Cistus

ROCK ROSE

Rock roses are back in fashion again after a long period of neglect. It was a strange occurrence, as these Mediterranean shrubs were among the first container plants to be cultivated. They probably lost favour because of their need for light in winter. Now *Cistus* is back in all its glory. Plant catalogues now include dozens of species and cultivars for growing in gardens - apparently they tolerate more frost than was previously thought. In a sunny, sheltered position, some species will withstand temperatures as low as -12°C (11°F). This, however, depends on the soil being thoroughly dry.

In places where more severe frosts occur, rock roses should be treated like container plants. That is not a drawback, as the low-growing shrubs look most attractive in terracotta pots.

Stand them in a warm and sunny position in summer, and water freely. Also make sure that the potting compost is well-drained. Compost containing some clay and mixed with coarse sand is most satisfactory. In winter, *Cistus* requires a light, cool (2-12°C/36-53°F), and, above all, airy position. During this period you should give the plant an airing as soon as the weather permits. It will require very little water at that time.

During the flowering season in spring and early summer, new flowers will open each morning. The petals, crumpled when they appear, look as though they are ironed smooth by the sun in the course of the morning. They fall in the afternoon, but fortunately new buds will open again next morning.

It is simple to sow *Cistus* species in spring, but, as they hybridize so easily, it is uncertain what kind of plants will emerge. Sowing has led to the creation of a huge number of hybrids, with predictable problems as far as nomenclature is concerned. Many species, in fact, appear to have been crossed previously. In summer, you can take cuttings by tearing short side shoots (maximum length: 10cm/4in) from larger stems (heel cuttings) but tip cuttings are also possible. If you water moderately, the cuttings will root quite easily in a mixture of peat and sand. Several popular species and cultivars are descibed below.

☼ 0°C (32°F)

Cistus 'Barnsley Pink'

See: *Cistus* 'Grayswood Pink'

Cistus 'Grayswood Pink'

This hybrid is a compact, neatly branching shrub, about 60cm (24in) in height and spread. Pale pink flowers appear between the velvety, greyish-green leaves in June and July. The cultivar closely resembles *Cistus* 'Silver Pink'.

For management, see *Cistus*.

☼ 0°C (32°F)

Cistus 'Grayswood Pink'

Cistus ladanifer

This variable species is native to countries round the western shores of the Mediterranean. Its white flowers often have red to brownish red markings at the base of each petal. One of the most valuable resins of antiquity, laudanum, was extracted from the sticky stems and foliage. It is a good remedy for constipation and baldness, and for stemming the flow of blood.

For management, see: *Cistus.*

☼ 0°C (32°F)

Cistus ladanifer hybrid

Cistus monspeliensis

The elongated leaves of *Cistus monspeliensis* curl over at the edges. In the Canary Islands

Cistus monspeliensis

and western Mediterranean countries, large shrubs, 1.5m (5ft) tall, cover vast tracts of land. You can smell the resin secreted by young stems everywhere you go. The species has been used remarkably often for developing new cultivars.

In a container, *Cistus monspeliensis* has a rather vertical growth, which may be partly corrected by tipping. This should be done early in the spring, as the ivory-white flowers are produced at the tips of young shoots in May-June.

For further management, see: *Cistus.*

☼ 0°C (32°F)

Cistus x pulverulentus

The white-woolly *Cistus albidus* and the equally hairy *Cistus crispus* were the ancestors of this hybrid, from which the popular cultivar *Cistus* 'Sunset' was developed. 'Sunset' can have a height and spread of about 50cm (20in). The plant will stay compact and has sinuate, woolly leaves. Large, deep pink flowers are borne from May to July.

For management, see *Cistus.*

☼ 0°C (32°F)

Cistus x *pulverulentus* 'Sunset'

[MT0371]

Cistus symphytifolius

The large-flowered *Cistus symphytifolius* originally came from the Canary Islands. It is available only from specialized nurseries, the reason for its lack of popularity presumably being its rather straggly growth. This is unfortunate, because its usually sinuate leaves, of which only the undersides are hairy, and crimson flowers, 5cm (2in) across, make it a truly lovely species.

☼ 5°C (41°F)

Cistus symphytifolius

x *Citrofortunella microcarpa*

CALAMONDIN, DWARF ORANGE

This is the dwarf orange tree often available at florists. It is a cross between *Citrus reticulata* and *Fortunella margarita*. The result is a compact little bush with small yellow or orange fruits which remain on the tree for a long time. If the plant is kept indoors, new flowers are produced throughout the year, and are followed by the fruits.

In summer, stand the small shrub out of doors in a warm and sunny position, but protect it from the fiercest midday sunshine. Keep the soil, which should be slightly acid, permanently moist, but never really wet. Give the plant lime-deficient rain water or boiled tap water.

In autumn, you should move x *Citrofortunella* to a cool, light indoor location, or to a conservatory or greenhouse. The ideal winter temperature is between 5 and 15°C (41- 50°F). The plant will not need much water during

x *Citrofortunella microcarpa*

this period, but make sure that the potting compost does not dry up entirely. Too much moisture, excessively dry compost, or too dark a position may cause the leaves to fall.

The variegated form of this species, x *Citrofortunella microcarpa* 'Variegata' needs even more light and warmth if it is to grow and flower satisfactorily.

☼ 5°C (41°F)

x *Citrofortunella microcarpa* 'Variegata'

Citrus limon

LEMON

Cultivating this large container plant is very easy. Put a few lemon pips in a pot, stand it in a living-room, and the result will be seedlings with shiny green leaves.

Citrus limon

Move the small plants out of doors at the end of May and do not let the potting compost dry up or become very wet. The larger the pot, the faster they will grow. As soon as the night temperatures drop to below 5°C (41°F), the small lemon tree should be taken indoors. Not to a warm, dry living-room, but to a light position in a cool space where temperatures are preferably between 10 and 15°C (50-59°F).

Citrus limon

Give it just enough water to prevent the potting compost from drying up altogether.

Plants cultivated in this way rapidly grow into 2m (6ft) tall shrubs. They will need regular pruning to keep them in check. White flowers with a strong sweet fragrance, followed by lemons, will eventually appear on the tree. Fructification, however, will be slow in the case of plants grown from pips.

If you wish to produce fruits, you should buy one of the following cultivars, which will also remain smaller:

Citrus limon x *meyeri* 'Meyer' - little more than 1m (3ft) tall, with 8cm (3in) fruits;

Citrus limon 'Oscar' - small and profusely flowering;

Citrus limon 'Ponderosa', or *Citrus ponderosa* - compact with very large fruits.

For ornamental purposes, *Citrus limon* 'Quatre Saisons' is a magnificent species, with large, deep-green shiny leaves and wonderfully fragrant creamy flowers which emerge from pink buds. Small lemons are formed at the end of the summer.

☼ 5°C

Citrus limon 'Quatre Saison'

Citrus sinensis

SWEET ORANGE

The German and Dutch names for orange literally mean "apple from China", the country where the species presumably originated. Centuries before the beginning of the Christian era, the Chinese were engaged in crossing citrus species, from which innumerable orange cultivars were developed. After they had spread to other subtropical regions, even more hybrids were developed, and the total number is now estimated at about 200.The plants are usually grafted on to the bitter orange *Poncirus trifoliata*, which tolerates temperatures as low as -15°C (5°F). The grafted plants, however, should be taken indoors when the first frost occurs and should then be managed like *Citrus limon*. Orange trees may be grown from pips in the same way as lemons.

☼ 5°C (41°F)

Citrus sinensis

Citrus fruits

Nearly all citrus fruits are hybrids with untraceable origins.
The following summary may provide some idea of what is on sale under the various names.
x *Citrofortunella microcarpa*, calamondin, dwarf orange;
x *Citrofortunella mitis*, see x *Citrofortunella microcarpa*;
Citrus aurantifolia, lime, descended from, among others, *Citrus medica*;
Citrus aurantium, Seville orange;
Citrus aurantium var. *myrtifolia*, chinotto, used in the same way as lemons;
Citrus deliciosa, see *Citrus reticulata*;
Citrus 'Fortunella', see *Fortunella margarita*;
Citrus grandis, see *Citrus maxima*;
Citrus hystrix; known in Indonesian cookery as Djeruk Purut;
Citrus limon, lemon;
Citrus madurensis, see *Fortunella japonica*;
Citrus maxima, pomelo, shaddock;
Citrus medica, citron;
Citrus meyeri (syn. *Citrus* 'Meyer'),

lemandarin, a cross between a lemon and a mandarin; *Citrus mitis*, see x *Citrofortunella microcarpa*;
Citrus microcarpa, see x *Citrofortunella microcarpa*;
Citrus nobilis; tangerine, presumably a cross between *Citrus reticulata* and *Citrus sinensis*;
Citrus x *paradisi*, grapefruit;
Citrus reticulata, mandarin;
Citrus sinensis, sweet orange;
Citrus x *tangelo*, ugli fruit, a cross between *Citrus sinensis* and *Citrus* x *paradisi*;
Fortunella japonica, Marumi kumquat;
Fortunella japonica 'Variegata', a form of Marumi kumquat with variegated leaves;
Fortunella margarita, Nagami kumquat.

Clerodendrum paniculatum

In south-east Asia, this shrub grows as tall as a man and is planted in front of houses and temples. It is called Pagoda tree in those countries. Its Dutch name 'Kansenboom' (Chance tree) is a literal translation of its botanical name.
Some species contain medicinal substances which, it appears, have a varying effect on patients.
Clerodendrum paniculatum has not long been available as a houseplant.
The cultivar often on sale is called 'Starshine'. As this plant needs high humidity and a great deal of light, it is really more suitable for a conservatory or greenhouse. Find a warm and sheltered spot for it out of doors at the height of summer.
Put the clerodendrum in a large pot with nutritive soil and water freely while it is growing.

Clerodendrum paniculatum

It may be kept in a living-room in winter, provided the atmosphere is neither too dry nor too warm. Alternatively, you should stand it in a cool room and water sparingly. If you prune the shrub lightly after it has flowered, it will produce good new growth in spring.

☼ 10°C (50°F)

Clerodendrum ugandense

BLUE GLORY BOWER

This delightful plant from Central Africa has only recently become available. It has a bushy growth and graceful mauve to light blue flowers resembling butterflies, with their stamens representing antennae.
The flowers soon fall if the plant is kept in a living-room.
At the height of summer, the plant prefers to be out of doors in the warmest spot you can find. In a conservatory or greenhouse, *Clerodendrum ugandense* can be relied upon to flower profusely over a long period.
Water freely in summer, but very moderately in winter. As the clerodendron retains its leaves in winter, it should be kept in a light location in a cool room during that season.

☼ 5°C (41°F)

Clerodendrum ugandense

Clitoria ternatea

The worthy botanist Linnaeus considered that the flower of this plant from tropical southeast Asia resembled a clitoris. It winds its way casually among the shrubs in its native environment, and in more northerly climates does very well in warm and sunny areas indoors. It

is grown from seed, which needs a temperature of at least 20°C (68°F) in order to germinate. Seedlings may be moved out of doors in midsummer. Put them in a large pot filled with nutritive, airy soil. They will, however, grow faster in a greenhouse or conservatory, or in a sunny spot by a window. That would also be an ideal place for them to overwinter, as clitorias cannot withstand low temperatures. Seed is available in small quantities only.

☼ 10°C (50°F)

Clitoria ternatea

Clivia miniata

KAFFIR LILY

There is something rather grand about a clivia. Its long, dark green leaves show up splendidly in a pot or urn at the entrance to an impressive house, particularly in the kind of shady position that it prefers (although it will tolerate sunshine out of doors).Plant the clivia in slightly acid but nutritive soil and leave it there for years - if need be until the root ball cracks the pot. Add a top dressing of compost and/or well- rotted cow manure every spring.
In autumn, the plant may remain out of doors until temperatures fall below 5°C (41°F). Let the plant harden off thoroughly, then put it in a cool place (8-15°C/46-59°F). In spring, you will see a flower stem appearing at the centre of the plant. Wait until it is at least 10cm (4in) tall, and then stand the clivia in a slightly warmer position. Gradually water more freely. While it is in flower, and also afterwards during the summer, the plant may have plenty of water and plant food, but you should never let the soil become thoroughly wet. Offsets

will eventually develop at the base of the plant, and these can be potted up separately. Propagating by seed is also possible, but in that case it will be many years before you have another flowering plant.

☼ 5°C (41°F)

Clivia miniata

Clivia nobilis

This plant is rarely for sale. It flowers profusely and has pendent orange-red flowers

Clivia nobilis

borne on a relatively slender stem. Even the rough-edged leaves are fairly slender. Manage the plant in the same way as *Clivia miniata*.

☼ 5°C (41°F)

Cneorum tricoccon

DWARF OLIVE

The leaves of this small shrub, which comes from the coastal regions of western Mediterranean countries, resemble those of ordinary olives, except that they are much smaller. Everything about this dwarf olive is in fact small: the plant's height and spread do not exceed 50cm (20in), and its bright yellow flowers are no more than about 1cm (1/2in) in diameter. The flowers appear in early summer and are followed by small bright red fruits which eventually turn black. Stand the shrub in full sun and keep the potting compost fairly moist. It is essential for the soil to be well-drained; it should preferably contain some clay. Keep the dwarf olive in a cool but frost-free position in winter. Make sure that its position is light enough, so that the leaves will remain on the plant. Water still more sparingly at the time. Propagation is possible by seed or by letting semi-ripe cuttings take root in sandy soil and a humid atmosphere in late summer.

☼ 0°C (32°F)

Cneorum tricoccon

Coffea arabica

COFFEE PLANT

The narrow terraces where the first coffee was presumably cultivated are still to be seen in the mountains of Yemen.
Coffea arabica originally came from Ethiopia, but was first actually cultivated in the Arabian Yemen. Later on, the Dutch smuggled the unroasted fruits to the Dutch East Indies and then to South America, where most of the coffee is produced nowadays.
If you wish to grow the plant at home, you will need packaged, fresh, unroasted coffee beans. The seeds will require a soil temperature between 20 and 25°C (68-77°F) in order to germinate; in a humid atmosphere, their growth is slow. The seedlings, which produce glossy green leaves, do best in a warm but airy atmosphere. Find them a light position, not in bright sunlight, and moist fertile soil.

These requirements mean that, in summer, it is best to stand the coffee plant in a greenhouse or in a warm and sheltered position where it is not too sunny. Water freely and feed regularly.
In autumn, when the night temperatures drop to below 10°C (50°F), the plant should be taken indoors. The ideal winter temperature is between 12 and 16°C (53-61°F).
While it is overwintering, the plant will require a light position, very little water, and as much ventilation as possible.

☼ 12°C (53°F)

Convolvulus cneorum

The leaves of this convolvulus are covered in short silvery grey hairs. They protect the plant, which grows in sunny positions along the Mediterranean coasts, against glaring sunshine. Funnel-shaped, pink-tinged white flowers appear at the ends of shoots in summer, and look magnificent in a stone pot or trough.

Grow the convolvulus in very well-drained, poor, and calcareous soil, and leave it to dry out entirely before watering again. It should not be given fertilizer, otherwise this low, spreading (and sometimes trailing) shrub will lose its silvery appearance.
Convolvulus cneorum retains its leaves in winter and will survive a light to moderate frost in (dry) open ground. When grown in a pot, however, it should overwinter in a light, cool, but frost-free place. Water sparingly or not at all during this period.

☼ 0°C (32°F)

Coffea arabica

Convolvulus cneorum

Convolvulus floridus

This convolvulus grows up to several metres tall (6ft and over) in the Canary Islands. The leaves of this sturdy shrub, like those of *C. cneorum*, are covered in silvery hairs. Large clusters of small white flowers, about 1cm (_in) in diameter, are produced at the ends of stems in summer. As far as I know, this species is not even available from specialized growers in Europe. That is a pity, because, in view of the prevailing climate in its natural environment, it might be an excellent container plant. Poor soil, moderate watering, and a light position in winter might encourage it to flower really well.

☼ 0°C (32°F)

Convolvulus floridus

Convolvulus mauritanicus

See: *Convolvulus sabatius*

Convolvulus minor

See: *Convolvulus tricolor*

Convolvulus sabatius

The stems of this convolvulus are thinner and more pendulous than those of *Convolvulus cneorum*. Leafy shoots produce ever-lengthening stems bearing small lilac blue flowers from May until well into October. Pinching out will make the plant bushier.

In baskets, however, the trailing growth of this convolvulus is an advantage. It will steal the show in daytime, but the flowers, 2cm (3/4in) in diameter, close in the evening.

Grow the convolvulus in well-drained soil in a sunny to half-shady position. Although the species can survive the winter in a cool but light position with scarcely any water, it is usually grown from seed which easily germinates at room temperature in early spring.

☼ 0°C (32°F) or (1)

Convolvulus sabatius

Convolvulus tricolor

This species is sometimes confused with the climbing convolvulus *Ipomoea tricolor* which grows up to 3m (10ft) tall. With its herb-like growth, the maximum height of *C. tricolor* is

50cm (20in). This summer-flowering border plant also does very well in containers. The potting compost may be slightly richer than that used for other species of convolvulus, but fertilizers should be avoided as they will lead to the production of more foliage and fewer flowers. The plant's botanical name refers to its tricolor flowers with yellow centres, white rings, and blue borders.

This convolvulus is grown as an annual. Sow indoors at room temperature in February-March, or out of doors in April- May. In a sunny position, it will flower from July until well into September. Growing the plant in rather poor soil will stimulate the production of flowers. Moderate watering is sufficient.

There are innumerable lovely cultivars, all with yellow and white centres.

The borders, however, vary in colour: bright blue for 'Blue Ensign'; mauvish blue for 'Blue Tilt'; light blue for 'Cambridge Blue'; crimson for 'Crimson Monarch'; lavender pink for 'Lavender Rosette'; and dark blue for 'Royal Ensign'.

(1)

Convolvulus tricolor 'Blue Tilt'

Coprosma x *kirkii*

Coprosma x *kirkii* is a natural cross between two shrubs from New Zealand. The leaves are its main decorative feature, as the flowers and fruits are small and insignificant. The popular cultivar 'Variegata' has green- to greyish-green-marbled leaves with creamy white margins.

The shrub grows and spreads slowly, which makes this *Coprosma* most suitable as basic planting for a container including more striking species.

The leaf colours will develop best in a sunny position. The plant does not need much water, provided you make sure that the potting compost does not dry up completely.

Coprosma species retain their leaves in winter if they are kept in a light, cool, and frost-free position. Water very sparingly at that time.

If you wish to progate the plant, you can do so by taking small heel cuttings from a fairly thick stem.

Insert the cuttings in sandy soil at a temperature of at least 20°C (68°F). They will quickly root in this way.

☼ 0°C (32°F)

Coprosma x *kirkii* 'Variegata'

Coreopsis ferulifolia

See: *Bidens ferulifolia*

Corokia

The young shoots of this shrub do not always grow outwards like those of most other shrubs, but sometimes kink and turn inwards again. They get enough light as leaves are sparse. It is thought that this characteristic growth pattern is a form of protection against grazing animals in its country of origin, New Zealand.

Corokias make unusual container plants, not only because of their small star-shaped yellow flowers in spring, but also because of their shape and greyish downy stems and leaves which remain on the plant throughout the year. In countries like Great Britain the shrub rarely produces its decorative orange to deep red berries after it has flowered. Its ultimate

Corokia cotoneaster

height and spread are 1.5m (5ft). In summer, you should put the corokia in a container with well-drained soil in an airy position in partial shade, or in full sun if need be. Keep the soil constantly moist throughout the summer. The shrubs can withstand a few degrees of forst, but should be taken indoors in winter. Put them in a cool (2-10°C/36-50°F), light, airy position. Water sufficiently to prevent the soil from drying up entirely.

The three species of *Corokia* vary considerably. Different leaf shapes occur within a sin-

Corokia buddleioides

gle species, but the flowers of the various species closely resemble one another. Hybridization has also occurred in natural conditions, so that it is often difficult to decide to which species a particular type belongs.

Corokia buddleioides grows a little taller than the other species. Its silver-haired stems have lancet-shaped leaves, which are sometimes short, but may also grow to about 12cm (5in) long. The flowers are produced in panicles at the ends of stems.

Corokia cotoneaster is the genuine wire-netting bush, with spoon-shaped or round leaves which, depending on the cultivar, are deep green to bronze in colour. The flowers are borne singly.

Corokia x *virgata* is a natural cross between the above species. The plant has many varying characteristics, and countless cultivars have been developed from it.

Corokia macrocarpa creates a silvery impression when it produces new growth. This is because of its fine hairs and greyish-green foliage. As far as I know, this species is not available on the market.

○ 2°C (36°F)

Crassula ovata

MONEY TREE

This is one of the easiest container plants to manage. It does not harm *Crassula ovata* at all if you occasionally forget to water it. Waterlogged soil, however, is potentially fatal, and it is therefore sensible to give the plant a sandy soil mixture and to stand it in the sun (or partial shade) in summer.

In a good, sunny position, the plant will branch out vigorously.

If it is really happy, it will produce clusters of small, star-shaped, white and pale pink flowers.

If you think the plant is growing too big, just take cuttings and grow new specimens. Propagation is simple: break off older leaves from the stem and insert them in the soil at the base of the stem. Young plants will grow out of them after a while.

The crassula should be kept in a light and frost-free position.

At low temperatures, it scarcely needs watering, but water moderately if the plant is kept in a living-room.

○ 5°C (41°F)

Crassula portulacea

See: *Crassula ovata*

Crassula ovata

Crinodendron hookerianum

LANTERN TREE

The glossy, leathery, dark green leaves of this Chilean shrub suggest how it should be managed: more or less like a rhododendron. This means that it should be placed in a sheltered, light, but (semi-)shady position, in slightly acid soil (definitely lime-free), which is kept moist.

In open ground, *Crinodendron* will withstand a minimum temperature of -10°C (50°F), but a plant grown in a container should be taken indoors at the time of the first frost.

In winter, the plant prefers a light and cool position, so that it retains its leaves.

Make sure the soil is kept moderately, but uniformly, moist.

The buds develop in autumn and winter and will begin to open from early spring onwards. When the plant is in full bloom in spring, rows of red lantern-shaped flowers hang from the stems.

Although propagation is slow, it is not impossible.

Put semi-ripe cuttings in a sandy soil mixture, cover the frame with glass or plastic, and keep it at room temperature.

☼ 0°C (32°F)

Crinodendron hookerianum

Crinum asiaticum

This crinum comes from tropical Asia, and needs more heat than the more familiar *Crinum* x *powellii*.

The reason why *Crinum asiaticum* is so rarely for sale may be that it flowers best under glass. In a greenhouse or conservatory, this huge plant will definitely steal the show.

The leaves, over 1m (3ft) long, arch over gracefully.

Flower stems emerge from older leaf sheaths and, when in flower, may grow to up to 1m (3ft) tall. These stems will continue to produce delightfully fragrant white flowers throughout the summer months.

For the management of this poisonous plant, see *Crinum* x *powellii*.

☼ 5°C (41°F)

Crinum x powellii

One of the most rewarding of all container plants was produced by crossing two South African species: *Crinum bulbispermum* and *Crinum moorei*. In a sunny position, round flower stems are produced, bearing widely funnel-shaped pink flowers which can grow up to 10cm (4in) long. Their flowering period, however, is considerably shorter than that of *Crinum asiaticum*. Plant the long, and up to 15cm (6in) wide bulb in a rich but free-draining soil mixture in spring. The neck of the bulb should be just on the surface. Do not water until the leaves appear. Leaves may grow up to 1m (3ft) long, and the longer they become, the more freely you should water them. Find a sunny spot for the pot or container in summer, and give the plant plenty of water and fertilizer. Leave the plant out of doors after it has flowered, but give it less water and no food. It will retain its leaves in winter, and therefore needs a position which is not too dark, and just enough water to prevent the leaves from dying down, which, however, frequently occurs in early spring. This is an indication that you should stop watering. After its period of rest, the bulb will sprout and you may start watering again. Transplant crinums as rarely as possible. Leave them in their pots for as long as possible, and, if you give them a top dressing of dried cow manure or other nutritive fertilizer, they will continue to produce an ever- increasing profusion of flowers.

☼ 5°C (41°F)

Crinum x powellii

Crotalaria agatiflora

CANARY-BIRD BUSH

Racemes of greenish-yellow butterfly-shaped flowers are suspended from the long stems of *Crotalaria agatiflora* in summer. After pollination, long smooth hollow pods are produced. If you shake the ripe fruits, you will hear the seeds rattling. The name *Crotalaria* comes from the Greek word *krotalon*, which means castanets.

The canary-bird bush (so named because it looks as though a swarm of canaries has alighted there) originally came from the fresh but warm air of East Africa. Stand the shrub in

Crinum asiaticum

Crotalaria agatiflora

full sun and fill the pot with very free-draining soil. The plant does not need very much water, and in winter it requires even less. It may be cut back hard in autumn. As the crotalaria is evergreen, it should be kept in a light position to overwinter. Give it as much fresh air as possible during that period.

There are over 500 Crotalaria species. *Crotalaria capensis*, *Crotalaria laburnifolia*, and *Crotalaria semperflorens* are also suitable for growing as container plants.

☼ 10°C (50°F)

Cuphea ignea

CIGAR FLOWER

The cigar flower is a familiar border plant which flowers throughout the summer.

Tubular red flowers with a strongly contrasting white spot at the aubergine- (eggplant-) coloured mouths are produced continually at the tips of this miniature shrub. It originally came from Mexico and is eminently suitable for growing in flower troughs on a sunny balcony, or in a low pot at the base of larger container plants.

Although it is possible to let the plant overwinter in a cool, light position, and then take cuttings in spring, it is better to grow the cigar plant like an annual. It can also be propagated by seed, which you should sow indoors in March-April.

Do not move the plants out of doors until after the last night frost.

(1)

Cuphea ignea

Cuphea pallida

Cuphea pallida

The long slender shoots of *Cuphea pallida* form broad loose tufts of leaves and flowers. The mauvish pink flowers measure approximately 2cm (3/4in) in diameter, and open in late summer and autumn. Fill the container with normal potting compost, stand the plant in a sunny to semi-shady position and give it normal amounts of water. In addition to the above species, there are several comparable cupheas which are also very suitable for growing in containers.

Although it is possible to let the plants overwinter, it is easier to grow them like annuals, as described for *Cuphea ignea*.

Cuphea lanceolata - sticky stems, over 50cm (20in) long, bear deep purple flowers; the cultivar 'Purpurea' produces mauvish purple flowers and grows a little taller;

Cuphea llavea - shoots up to 90cm (36in) tall bear bright red flowers; the subspecies *miniata* is smaller in every respect;

Cuphea llava miniata 'Firefly' - see *Cuphea x purpurea* 'Firefly';

Cuphea platycentra - see *Cuphea ignea;*

Cuphea procumbens - the sticky stems, about 50cm (20in) tall, bear purplish pink flowers;

Cuphea x purpurea - a cross between *Cuphea llavea* and *Cuphea procumbens*. The result of this hybridization is a plant with shoots about 1m (3ft) long, bearing flowers in mixed colours: from bright red to pink to mauve. Sometimes cultivars are sold by colour, for instance 'Firefly' which has bright orange-red flowers.

(1)

Cyathea

TREE FERN

There are over 300 species of *Cyathea*; those from subtropical regions are particularly suitable for countries like the Netherlands. In winter, the tropical species require night temperatures above 15°C (59°F). *Cyathea cooperi* from Australia is closely related to the familiar *Cyathea australis*, which can remain out of doors in the south-west of the British Isles even in winter.

Cyathea cooperi

If you wish to grow this tree fern as a container plant, use a large pot or tub, as it will eventually grow many metres (yards) tall, with an equal spread. The plant should be taken indoors even before temperatures fall to below 5°C (41°F); it should then be put in a cool, light position. The plant does not need much water while it is dormant.

In summer, *Cyathea cooperi* is one of the few tree ferns which may have a position in full sun, provided the soil is kept permanently moist. It does better, however, in semi- shade, and in hot weather you should sprinkle the leaves occasionally to prevent them from drying out.

Repot the *Cyathea* regularly, or cover the top of the container with a nutritive mixture of compost and dried cow manure.

☼ 5°C (41°F)

Cycas revoluta

JAPANESE SAGO PALM

Sago palms are genuinely ancient plants which should not really be called palms. In the Triassic period, about two hundred million years ago, there were many species of *Cicadaceae*. Now there are about nine left, including the *Cycas revoluta* from Japan and Taiwan.

The species is cultivated in Java because of the edible pith (sago) in its trunk.

As a houseplant or a container plant, *Cycas revoluta* will grow steadily but slowly. Pinnate leaves develop regularly at the top of a hairy, scaly, ovoid trunk. New leaves are still soft and vulnerable as they unfold, but they subsequently become strong and hard, with pointed tips.

The sago palm cannot flower until it is older. The species has male and female plants. The former have a cone in the centre of the plant, whereas the female plants have a jumble of ovaries.

After pollination, these ovaries grow into felt-like orange yellow seeds, about the size of a shelled broad bean. Because the seeds are exposed in the centre of the palm, the plant is called a gymnosperm.

Stand the *Cycas revoluta* out of doors in a warm position which gives it some protection against bright sunshine. Water moderately, but regularly, so that the soil remains uniformly moist.

The plant should only be given liquid fertilizer when new leaves unfold.

Do not be too quick to repot the sago palm and do not disturb the top layer of soil, as that is where there are important, fragile roots. In winter, the plant prefers a cool, light position indoors, where it should not be warmer than 15°C (59°F).

If you wish to propagate the plant, you should

Cycas revoluta (female plant)

do so from seed. Sago palms, however, grow slowly, and the seedlings therefore remain small for a long time.

☼ 5°C (41°F)

Cymbalaria muralis

IVY-LEAFED TOADFLAX, KENILWORTH IVY

Ivy-leafed toadflax grows wild on rocky slopes in southern and central Europe, and also feels very much at home against the damp old walls of city ramparts, canals, and buildings in more northerly countries. The plant is self- seeding: the stem with the fruit capsule turns towards the wall and presses the seeds into a crack.

In open ground, ivy-leafed toadflax does not usually survive the combination of cold and damp in winter. In a dry rock garden, or in a

Cymbalaria muralis

Cymbalaria muralis 'Albiflora'

pot or hanging basket with very well-drained soil, all is usually well. In very severe frost, however, it is better to take the plant indoors.

In summer, ivy-leafed toadflax requires a shady to half- shady position and potting soil that is kept uniformly moist. If the soil dries out too much, or the plant is exposed to excessive sunlight, it will stop growing. A vigorous plant produces long untidy runners covered in miniature leaves and miniature flowers, which continue to appear throughout the summer.

Propagation is by division; by letting shoots develop roots and potting them up separately; by putting cuttings in water or moist soil; or by seed.

There are some beautiful white-flowered cultivars of ivy- leafed toadflax on sale. These include: Cymbalaria muralis 'Albiflora' (also called Cymbalaria muralis albiflora), which bears fairy-like white flowers with yellow lips, and Cymbalaria muralis 'Globosa Alba', which is very compact.

✽

Cymbalaria pallida

IVY-LEAFED TOADFLAX

In addition to the native ivy-leafed toadflax, countless other species and cultivars grow in southern Europe.

The colour of the flowers is somewhat variable, and there are also transitional forms, all of which has led to confusion in naming them.

It is quite possible that different suppliers will offer you the same kind of plant, but under a different name. This applies not only to Cymbalaria pallida from Central Italy, but also to Cymbalaria aequitriloba, which is found throughout southern Europe; to Cymbalaria hepaticifolia, which comes from Corsica; and to the originally Italian Cymbalaria pilosa.

Cymbalaria pallida is distinguishable from Cymbalaria hepaticifolia by hairy leaves; from Cymbalaria aequitriloba by much longer honey guides; and from Cymbalaria pilosa by having far fewer leaf lobes - Cymbalaria pallida has five at the most, but usually three, the central lobe being consider-ably larger than the others.

For management, see Cymbalaria muralis, with the difference that Cymbalaria pallida prefers a sunny position.

✽

Cymbidium

Orchids are generally believed to be plants which will only thrive in a hothouse or a living-room. There are, however, species which prefer cooler conditions, and *Cymbidium* is one of them. The numerous hybrids of this species are often sold as houseplants, but fail to flower more than once. This is caused by excessively high summer temperatures. Buds will only be formed in summer if temperatures are not too high; these buds will open in the following winter. Containerized specimens need light, well-drained orchid compost. If the plants are kept out of doors in summer, they should be watered freely and occasionaly given some orchid fertilizer or greatly diluted houseplant fertilizer.

The plant should be taken indoors as soon as temperatures fall below 8°C (46°F) in autumn. Stand it in a cool position until the flower stem becomes clearly visible. You should then find a warmer position for the *Cymbidium*, for instance in a living-room.

☼ 8°C (46°F)

Cytisus x racemosus

See: *Genista* x *spachiana*

Cymbalaria pallida

D

d

Datura arborea

See: *Brugmansia arborea*

Datura flava

See: *Brugmansia* x *flava*

Datura metel

ANGELS' TRUMPETS

Unlike the trees and shrubs referred to as angels' trumpets (see *Brugmansia*), the herbaceous species are annuals. They are sown indoors in March-April, or outdoors in May. The velvety grey leaves of *Datura metel* grow on stems up to 50cm (20in) tall; in summer, the funnel-shaped flowers, up to 20cm (8in) long, rise above them. The flowers are usually white, but there are numerous cultivars with yellow, pink, or blue blooms. Pollination is followed by the development of spiny oval capsules with abundant seed. It does not spread like the common *Datura stramonium*, but it is highly germinative.

(1)

Datura suaveolens

See: *Brugmansia suaveolens*

Diascia

All the fifty or so *Diascia* species originally came from South Africa, and like a sunny position, where they will flower all through the summer and autumn. As the perennial species do not survive an average winter, they are propagated by cuttings taken in late summer and kept in a cool and light location throughout the winter. Sowing is often easier still, but that should be done in early spring (between February and early April), or the new plants will not flower until the end of the

Preceding page: *Datura metel*

summer. Diascias are rewarding pot plants, provided they are give warmth and light soil. The flowers are borne at the tips of long stems which become rather straggly but should not be cut back. The plants are usually sold simply as Diascias without the name of the species. Suitable species for pots or containers include:
Diascia barberae - up to 30cm (12in) tall, with abundant salmon-pink flowers;
Diascia fetcaniensis - forms a fairly compact plant up to 20cm (8in) tall; produces a profusion of deep pink flowers.

(1)

Diascia

Dicksonia

TREE FERN

Dicksonia is the most impressive of all tree ferns. The plants originally came from Tasmania and Australia, but now adorn a great many gardens in subtropical countries because of their magnificent appearance. *Dicksonia antarctica* is cultivated in New Zealand and is then exported to Europe in a very strange manner: as a trunk without fronds or roots. In

Dicksonia antarctica

a relatively small container, however, the trunk will develop roots within a few weeks, with new, fresh green fronds appearing at the top at about the same time.

Dicksonia antarctica will withstand a few degrees of frost; nevertheless, it should be kept indoors in winter in a cool, well-ventilated and light place, where the humidity should not be reduced unduly. The edges of the fronds will turn an ugly shade of brown if the atmosphere is too dry. In summer, the fern

Diascia fetcaniensis

should be put out of doors again, preferably in a spot sheltered from harsh sunlight. Cultivate the tree fern in a relatively small tub filled with light, humus-rich, slightly acid soil.

Water freely in summer to compensate for the high level of transpiration through the leaves. The potting compost should be kept uniformly moist in winter.

○ 5°C (41°F)

Dicliptera suberecta

With its greyish, felt-like leaves and the tubular orange flowers that appear at the ends of stems in summer, this small shrub from Uruguay is a real delight. Put it out of doors in a warm, sunny or semi-shady position in late spring. Give it humus-rich, free-draining soil, plenty of water, and feed it regularly. As soon as outdoor temperatures drop below 7°C (45°F) at night, the *Dicliptera* should be taken indoors. As the plant will probably still be flowering at that time, it may be kept in a living-room for a while. It retains its leaves in winter, so you should find a light location which should not be either too dry or too cold (7-15°C/45-59°F). If you cut back the plant hard after it has flowered, it will remain bushy. Lax growth may also be pruned in spring, as *Dicliptera* produces flowers at the tips of new stems. The shrub develops a lot of underground runners, which can easily be potted up separately.

○ 7°C (45°F)

Dicliptera suberecta

Diospyros kaki

CHINESE PERSIMMON, KAKI, PERSIMMON

Anyone who has tasted a persimmon is unlikely to forget its flavour. The fruits are eaten when they are overripe as the tannin, which makes people's teeth feel rough, will have broken down by then. When thoroughly ripe, persimmons are orange red, sweet, juicy, with gelatinous sections. The cultivar 'Sharon', referred to as Sharon fruit, is yellowish orange, firmer and therefore easier to transport (from the regions where it is cultivated in Israel), but its flavour is less intense. The tree originally came from China, and more than a thousand cultivars have been registered in China and Japan alone. Anyone with enough space to house the small tree in winter, will find that it makes a magnificent container plant. It grows slowly and prefers lime-free soil in a warm and sunny position. The leaves turn lovely shades of yellow to orange to red in autumn, and then fall. In a warm position, the tree will bear yellow flowers in July, followed by fruits the size of tomatoes which remain on the trees after the leaves have fallen. If you wish to eat the fruits when they have ripened, you should then keep the leafless plant in a light position indoors. After the fruit has been picked, the plant may be kept in a darker position if need be. Remember that low winter temperatures are essential for the development of new buds.

○ of ● 5°C (41°F)

Diospyros kaki

Dipladenia

See: *Mandevilla*

Distictis buccinatoria

MEXICAN BLOOD FLOWER

The sturdy stems of this evergreen Mexican climber require space and good support because they grow fast. It is therefore mostly found growing up the walls of large greenhouses, winter gardens or conservatories. The plants grow vigorously, even in containers, and in summer the tips of stems are adorned with large trumpet-shaped, orange-red flowers. Water freely in summer and feed regularly. In winter, the plant prefers a cool, well-ventilated, light position. Watering is scarcely required. In early spring, this *Distictis* may be cut back hard. When the new shoots are well developed, you should take the container out of doors as soon as possible, as the plant likes fresh air and will withstand a few degrees of frost if need be.

○ 0°C (32°F)

Distictus buccinatoria

Dodonaea viscosa

In summer, large clusters of winged seeds are suspended between the sticky leaves of *Dodonaea viscosa*. The purple seed capsules are used in dried flower arrangements. *Dodonaea* is scarcely familiar as a container plant yet, which is a pity, since it is easy to cultivate and highly decorative.

If sown in spring, the seedlings will develop into flowering shrubs within a few years. Propagation by cuttings is also possible if you let young stems develop roots in heated soil (20°C/68°F) in summer.

Dodonaea prefers an airy, sunny position in

summer, conditions resembling those in Central America and the other subtropical countries where it is indigenous.

In its native environment, the plant is cultivated because of its useful characteristics: the roots hold the soil together; the wood is very hard and durable; it makes a good windbreak when grown as a hedge; and its fruits can be a substitute for hops in beer brewing (in Australia).

Give *Dodonaea* light, well-drained soil and water freely in summer.

A cool, light position will be adequate in winter. Frequent pruning will give the shrub an attractive bushy shape.

Growing it as a standard plant is also possible, but start early, because this shrub cannot be pruned back to old wood.

Dodonaea viscosa 'Purpurea' has purple fruits as well as leaves of the same colour, especially when the shrub is placed in full sun.

☼ 2°C (36°F)

Dodonaea viscosa 'Purpurea'

Dombeya wallichii

Dombeya wallichii's ball-like clusters of pink flowers turn brown and remain on the shrub for a long time, just like those of hydrangeas.
The plant originally came from Madagascar and the areas of continental Africa nearest to

Dombeya wallichii

the island. In subtropical regions, the plant's flowering season is in winter, and large, slightly hairy leaves adorn the wood.

The leaves resemble those of *Sparmannia africana*, African hemp.

When containerized, *Dombeya* needs to be sheltered from the wind and full sun, but should be in the warmest part of the garden, or alternatively in a conservatory or greenhouse. Water freely in summer, but make sure the shrub is planted in light potting compost, so that excess water can drain away easily. Water less in late summer and stop feeding the plant.

The shrub should be taken indoors quite early to overwinter in a light, moderately cool place (12-16°C/53-60°F). It will need scarcely any water at that time.

☼ 10°C (50°F)

Dracaena draco

DRAGON TREE

If you make a cut in the trunk of *Dracaena draco*, the tree will exude a sticky red sap which gives it its name (the Greek word *drakaina* means dragon). The true dragon tree grows in the Canary Islands, but, unfortunately, it has become very rare as a result of the red resin being collected. Ancient specimens still survive here and there (the oldest one, which was blown down in 1868, was estimated to be 6,000 years old, but was probably much younger).

The tree reaches a certain height before beginning to branch out. *Dracaena draca* first develops on a single stem until the rosette of strong, pointed leaves begins to flower. Subsequently, the tree ramifies continually after each flowering season, ultimately achieving a spreading umbrella-like shape.

As a container plant, the dragon tree is easy to manage, but, because of its slow growth, it is only available from specialized container plant nurseries.

You would normally purchase a rosette with lancet-shaped leaves a few centimetres (an inch or so) long. It will be years before the rosette is supported by a stem. In summer, the dragon tree prefers a warm and sunny position.

Keep the potting compost uniformly moist throughout this period. In winter, the tree requires a cool and light, but frost-free location. Stand the pot on a cold windowsill, use polystyrene foam to protect it from the cold window, and occasionally give it a little water to compensate for transpiration through the leaves.

☼ 0°C (32°F)

Dracaena draco

Dracocephalum moldavica

DRAGON'S HEAD

From July until well into the autumn, beautiful lilac-blue lipped flowers appear between the fragrant leaves of the dragon's head, and attract many insects. This herbaceous plant may grow to about 30cm (12in) tall in a pot.

Sow this species from eastern and central Europe indoors in March, or out of doors from April onwards (the plants withstand temperatures as low as -15°C/5°F). Apart from that, the plant has no special requirements.

The cultivar *Dracocephalum moldavicum* 'Album' has pure white flowers.

(1)

Dracocephalum moldavica 'Blue Dragon'

Dregea corrugata

See: *Dregea sinensis*

Dregea sinensis

Dregea's small, creamy white and pink flowers (1.5cm/5/8in across) are rather like those of the wax flower. They both belong to the *Asclepiadaceae*, one of the most highly developed families in the plant world.

Dregea sinensis is better known by its old name *Wattakaka sinensis*. The shoots, which have oblong green leaves, greyish green beneath, twist upwards for as much 2m (6ft), and therefore need support. The plant is most suitable for greenhouses, conservatories, and winter gardens, but can grow quite well in a sheltered, not exccessively sunny spot out of doors in summer. Water freely during the growing season. The soil should be very well-drained.

The plants need a dry place in which to over-winter. As *Dregea* requires a high degree of moisture even in winter, heated living-rooms are unsuitable. A cool, but not chilly, location (10-17°C/50-62°F) is best.

○ 10°C (50°F)

Dunalia australis

See: *Acnistus australis*

Dunalia tubilosa

See: *Acnistus australis*

Duranta erecta

PIGEON BERRY, SKYFLOWER

The individual flowers of *Duranta erecta* (usually called *Duranta repens*) are about

Duranta erecta (vruchten)

1cm (1/2in) wide. They grow in elongated spikes. Orange yellow berries are produced after the flowers, and the plant therefore

Dregea sinensis

remains a delight to behold from early summer until far into autumn. The colour of the flowers varies considerably: it is usually lilac blue, sometimes tending more towards blue or purple, and occasionally pearly white.

In the wild, the shrub grows to about 5m (16ft) tall with an equal spread. In a container, such growth can be curbed by pruning. This should be done early in the season, or else in autumn, as the flowers develop at the tips of young shoots. The new shoots arch over gracefully, which gives the whole shrub a light and airy appearance.

Duranta erecta needs sun and warmth in summer, and is best cultivated in a greenhouse or conservatory.

At the height of summer, the plant will also do well in a sheltered position out of doors. In all events water freely.

There are two methods for letting the plant overwinter. If you wish it to retain its leaves, the area where it is kept should not be dark, nor should the temperature fall below 10°C (50°F). The alternative is a cool, dark position (minimum temperature 5°C/41°F), in which case the plant will lose its leaves, and the potting compost should be kept almost entirely dry.

Water very sparingly if you adopt the first method (retaining the leaves).

Propagation may be effected in summer by cuttings or in spring by seed, which should germinate at room temperature.

○ 10°C (50°F) or ● 5°C (41°F)

Duranta erecta

Duranta plumieri

See: *Duranta erecta*

Duranta repens

See: *Duranta erecta*

Duranta erecta

E

e

Echeveria

The leaves of echeverias are swollen with the moisture that will sustain them in times of drought. The rosetted plants originally grew in the mountainous regions of Central America (especially Mexico). A layer of wax or a hairy surface protects them from glaring sunlight. You should therefore put echeverias in the sunniest spot you can find, sheltered from rain.

Water regularly, preferably at soil level in order to prevent the moisture touching the leaves. Let the soil dry up completely before watering again.

Echeveria

Long flower stems with small yellow, orange, or red flowers grow out of the sides of the rosettes, particularly during the darker months. In winter, echeverias prefer a light, cool position, where they will need very little water.

The lowest leaves eventually drop off, so that the rosettes are supported by bare stems. The rosettes may now be cut off, left to dry for several days, and then planted in sandy soil. Broken-off leaves may be propagated in the same way.

Echeverias are nearly always sold without further description. There are about 150 spe-

Preceding page: *Erythrina crista-galli*

cies and countless available hybrids, and it is therefore difficult to tell them apart.

☀ 5°C (41°F)

Echeveria kircheriana

Echium candicans

Several close relatives *of Echium vulgare* (Viper's bugloss) are very suitable for cultivating in containers. In Madeira, the Canary Islands, and the Azores, these plants are shrubby, and grow about 2m (6ft) tall. Because of its sturdy shape and magnificent flowers, *Echium candicans* is often called "Pride of Madeira". Bees, bumblebees, hoverflies, and butterflies are attracted to the flower spikes that appear at the ends of grey-leafed stems. The flowers of all shrub-like species of *Echium* occur in shades of lilac to sky-blue, and gradually fade to pink. White or white-striped flowers also occur.

The shrubs grow on damp slopes, often in partial shade.

Even in northwest Europe, some protection against the fiercest midday sunshine is desirable. The containers, however, should be placed in as warm a position as possible. Water freely in summer; excess water, however, should be able to drain away easily. You should therefore use a humus-rich, and extremely porous soil mixture to prevent the plant's sensitive roots from rotting. In winter, shrub echiums require a light, cool position where it should not be warmer than 14°C (57°F). They consume hardly any water while they are overwintering.

☼ 5°C (41°F)

Echium candicans

Echium webbii

Echium webbii closely resembles *Echium candicans*. It is indigenous to the Canary Island La Palma, where it grows on wooded slopes, shaded by *Pinus canariensis*. The rocky ground there is covered with decaying pine needles, and it is therefore best to give the plant slightly acid potting compost. For further management, see *Echium candicans*.

☼ 5°C (41°F)

Encephalartos lehmannii

Like the cycas palm, the *Encephalartos* belongs to the ancient plant order of *Cycadaceae*. Each plant in that order is either male or

female, and all belong to the group of plants that existed on earth before there were insects, and were pollinated by the wind.
Encephalartos grows wild in central and southern Africa. The South African species *Encephalartos lehmannii* is one of the easiest to cultivate.

Encephalartos lehmannii

Choose a large container, so that the swollen underground parts of the tree have plenty of space, and fill it with light, mineral, slightly acid soil. Full sun is essential for preserving the grey waxy covering of the leaves. For the same reason, no fertilizer and not much water should be given. In winter, a light, cool position and totally dry conditions are essential for ensuring that this unusual plant has a long life.
Encephalartos is propagated by seed. This is a task for a genuine enthusiast, who should let the large red seeds germinate in warm, moist sand, and only pot them up carefully when roots have developed. As sowing and germi-

Echium webbii

nating is a slow process, many plants were taken from the wild in former days. This is one of the reasons why *Encephalartos* is threatened with extinction in its native environment. The international trade has now been prohibited, and amateur gardeners cannot be regarded as genuine enthusiasts unless they buy cultivated plants only.

☼ 5°C (41°F)

Ensete ventricosum

See: *Musa ensete*

Epilobium glabellum

WILLOW HERB

In New Zealand, this small herb grows in moist places beside streams and on shady slopes; it dislikes full sun. White flowers are borne continually on the ends of stems from June until late summer. The flowers measure 1-2cm across (1/4-3/4in) across.

Epilobium glabellum

The plant will flower longer if you pick the oblong capsules. The willow herb does best in fertile, clayey, but free-draining soil, which should be kept cool and moist in summer.
Although this lovely ground cover, which trails gracefully over the rim of its container, is

frost-hardy, it is advisable to move container-ized specimens indoors in frosty weather. You should take them out of doors again as soon as the thaw sets in.
The most suitable place to keep the plants is in an unheated greenhouse or cold frame. Digging them in, pot and all, is also possible. Propagation is by seed in spring.

❄

Erica arborea

TREE HEATH

Tree heath is common in the western regions of the Mediterranean, in the mountains of East Africa, in Arabia and Asia Minor, and in Madeira and the Canary Islands. The related species *Erica azorica* grows in the Azores. It takes many years for the shrubs to grow several metres tall (6ft and over); their trunks become twisted and orange brown in colour. The highly fire-resistant wood of the roots is used for making tobacco pipes.
The plant grows quite slowly in a pot or tub, but in spite of this will flower profusely in early spring, when its stems are covered in countless minuscule white flowers. Plant the shrub in slightly acid, humus-rich soil, which should be kept uniformly moist in summer. Tree heath likes a warm and sunny position, but also fresh air, and it is therefore advisable

Erica arborea

to keep it out of doors rather than in a green-house. In winter, however, the plant must be moved indoors, but, even there, it will require an airy, cool, and very light position.

Keep the temperature below 15°C (59°F), or it will begin to grow, and consequently fail to flower in spring. Water sparingly at this time, but do not let the soil dry out entirely.

☼ 5°C (41°F)

Erigeron karvinskianus

FLEABANE

There are very few potted plants that will give you greater enjoyment than this daisy-like fleabane. From June onwards, the delicate flower stems will arch over the edge of the container, and continue to flower contin-uously until well into October. Although this plant, which grows 20cm (8in) tall, will be killed by frost during an average winter, its seeds will germinate all over the place in the garden, particularly in between paving slabs. The seedlings will flower the same summer.

If you wish to be assured of new plants, then sow the seeds directly in the container, in-doors in March-April, or out of doors in April-May. The seedlings do not require any special care. The pink to white flowers, 2cm (3/4in) across, will automatically appear in full sun or partial shade.

(1)

Erigeron karvinskianus

Erigeron mucronatus

See: *Erigeron karvinskianus*

Eriobotrya japonica

LOQUAT

In southern countries, the loquat is to be found in many a kitchen garden. The low, compact tree is full of leaves. Clusters of orange-yellow fruits with a fresh, sweet fla-vour are formed at the ends of brownish woolly shoots. Each fruit contains a single large stone, which is easily removed from the very juicy flesh.

Unfortunately, you may need to travel to taste the fruits, as they rarely develop in colder climates. Nor do they keep well, so this delicacy is rarely imported. Only after very hot summers will fruits be formed in autumn, and they will need to ripen in a greenhouse before they can be harvested in spring. In countries such as Britain and the Netherlands, the tree is therefore grown mainly for its decorative appearance rather than its fruits.

In open ground, the loquat will withstand a considerable amount of frost, but a con-tainerized specimen should be moved indoors before the frosts begin. If winter temperatures do not drop below 10°C (50°F) for any length of time, the tree will retain its leaves, and therefore needs a light place in which to overwinter. A cool, well-ventilated winter gar-den, where there is no risk of fungus disease, would be ideal.

The tree may be moved out of doors again in early spring, and placed in a sheltered position

Eriobotrya japonica

to prevent the foliage from being damaged. The leaves are bright green above and felty white beneath, sometimes with a tinge of pink. Do not water until the soil has entirely dried up.

Sow stones indoors, or take cuttings from non-flowering tips of stems in spring.

○ 10°C (50°F)

Erysimum 'Bowles Mauve'

It is easy to detect that this greyish-green cultivar of *Erysimum linifolium* is related to wallflowers. It is a perennial which originally came from Spain and Portugal, and does not flower until the year after it was sown. Then, however, flowering will begin early in the season.

The loose, arching shoots on which the deep mauve flowers are borne appear in April. Cut back the shoots after they have flowered to achieve a more compact shape, but refrain from doing so if you want to treat the plant as a biennial.

Put the plant in light, sandy soil; stand it in a sunny position and water moderately. In winter, the plant can be dug into the garden in its pot in a fairly dry spot.

Propagation is by division; by seed sown in spring for flowering the following year; or by heel cuttings torn from the shoots in summer,

Erysimum 'Bowles Mauve'

which will take root in sandy soil that is kept fairly dry.

❄

Erythrina abyssinica

FLAME CORAL TREE

The coral tree grows over 10m (33ft) tall in the highlands of East Africa, and the foothills of the Himalayas. The red flowers are borne in spring at the ends of branches that are still bare. The large oval leaves unfold after the tree has flowered.

To see this splendid sight, you will probably need to travel to the regions where the tree is indigenous, or to southern countries where the flame coral tree is planted for ornamental purposes. It should be possible, however, to grow the tree in a container, particularly because the tree can overwinter without leaves at low temperatures.

● 5°C (41°F)

Erythrina abyssinica

Erythrina crista-galli

COCKSPUR CORAL-TREE

This plant is still only to be seen in the homes of genuine enthusiasts, although it is one of the least demanding of all container plants. Halfway through the summer, the tips of the coral-tree's branches are weighed down by the racemes of scarlet flowers. During this period, the South American plant needs as much

warmth as possible and plenty of water and food.

The stems automatically die off in autumn. The leaves fall, and the plant should be taken indoors as soon as the frosts begin. After the stems have largely withered, the plant should be cut back to ground level. In that way, it will

not take up much space, and will survive the winter if kept entirely dry. The shrub should have a cool position in winter (below 10°C/50°F), or it will fail to flower profusely the following season. Do not water until the new shoots begin to develop in spring.

If you propagate from seed, the seedlings will start flowering after about three years. Heel cuttings, taken from a principal stem in summer, will quickly root in sandy soil at room temperature.

● 0°C (32°F)

Eschscholzia californica

CALIFORNIAN POPPY

Eschscholzias are extremely simple to cultivate, and should be sown directly in a container in autumn or early spring. They are, however, rather difficult to prick out because of their tap roots.

Plants sown in autumn need some protection against frost, for instance by putting the pot in a cold frame or greenhouse.

By midsummer, the eschscholzias' orange flowers will appear among the feathery foliage. In a sunny position, and with regular watering, the plants will continue to flower until far into the autumn, with the 'caps' continually

Eschscholzia californica 'Purple Gleam'

dropping off the buds to reveal the calyces. Besides the orange-flowered species, there are countless cultivars with delicate colours: 'Alba' has creamy white flowers, as does 'Milky White', though they have orange centres; 'Purple Gleam' has light carmine flowers, and the double flowers of 'Rose Bush' are also carmine.

(1)

Eschscholzia californica

Eucomis bicolor

PINEAPPLE FLOWER

The bulb of this *Eucomis* is planted in April, with its apex just on the surface of a large pot containing nutritive soil. Start watering as soon as the bulb begins to sprout. Water freely throughout the season and feed regularly. Stand the pot containing this South African bulb in a greenhouse or conservatory, or out of doors on a patio. The plant likes a warm spot, but prefers not to be in full sun.

In July, you will be amazed by the plant's characteristic florescence. Numerous star-shaped green flowers with purple-edged petals appear. The flower spike is topped with a tuft of leaves. After it has flowered, the bulb gradually begins a period of dormancy. As soon as the leaves turn yellow, you should move the pot to a frost-free indoor location,

and then forget about it until the following spring.

● 5°C (41°F)

Eucomis bicolor

Euonymus japonicus

JAPANESE SPINDLE

The many cultivars of *Euonymus japonicus* are usually sold as garden plants because of their ability to withstand temperatures as low

Euonymus japonicus 'Argenteo Variegatus'

Euphorbia polychroma

as -15°C (5°F). In a pot, however, the root ball is more sensitive. The plant should therefore be moved indoors in winter, where an unheated greenhouse or conservatory, or a light position in an unheated room will be adequate. Take the euonymus out into the fresh air again after every period of frost. It should remain out of doors in early spring, where, in normal soil and with normal watering, it will grow steadily in either a sunny or a shady position. The popular cultivars have variegated leaves: *Euonymus japonicus* 'Argenteo Variegatus' (white-edged leaves); *Euonymus japonicus* 'Aureomarginatus' (gold-edged yellowish-green leaves);
Euonymus japonicus 'Luna' (new name 'Aureus', green-edged butter-yellow leaves);
Euonymus japonicus 'Marieke' (new name 'Ovatus Aureus', green to greyish-green leaves with pale yellow edges); *Euonymus japonicus* 'Microphyllus' (small slender leaves with several variegated patterns).

○ -5°C (23°F)

Euonymus japonicus 'Ovatus Aureus'

Euphorbia epithymoides

See: *Euphorbia polychroma*

Euphorbia polychroma

POLYCHROME MILKWEED, SPURGE

The compact growth of the polychrome euphorbia makes it a rewarding container plant. The ends of the longish shoots turn golden yellow in May. The flowers, surrounded by golden yellow bracts, look good until the end of July. This colourful euphorbia dies down to soil level in winter. The species originally came from the cold regions of southeast Europe and Asia Minor, and, because it is fully hardy, the containerized plant may be buried in the garden at this time. Propagate the plant by dividing the clump, but be careful with the white sap, which is poisonous. Two other species of euphorbia, both with golden-yellow flowers, are suitable for cultivating in containers: *Euphorbia nicaeensis*, which grows to 70cm (28in) tall, and the rather more vigorous *Euphorbia villosa*.

❋

Euryops athanasiae

See: *Euryops speciosissimus*

Euryops pectinatus

Even without its daisy-like flowers, this South African plant is a joy to behold because of its velvety, greyish-green, deeply divided leaves. Florists sometimes incorporate its fern-like foliage in their bouquets. From May onwards, the woolly-haired buds open to display golden-yellow flowers at the tips of the fairly long flower stems that issue from the top shoots. For management, see *Euryops speciosissimus*.

○ 5°C (41°F)

Euryops pectinatus

Euryops speciosissimus

This yellow-flowered shrub has many different names. At specialized container plant nurs-

Euryops speciosissimus

Euryops originally came from South Africa and likes a warm and sunny position. Allow for the fact that in such an environment the plant will consume a lot of water. In a shadier position, less water will be required, but make sure the root ball does not dry out. Also add plenty of fertilizer to keep the plant flowering for as long as possible.

Although the shrubs can withstand a few degrees of frost, they should be taken indoors before the first night frost. In a light position, they will then continue to flower for a while. Overwintering in a cool, fresh, light place is also possible. The shrub may then be cut back hard. Remove fallen leaves to prevent fungus diseases.

☼ 5°C (41°F)

eries, it is sometimes on sale under its old name *Euryops athanasiae*. At florists, it is often called yellow marguerite, with the incorrect Latin name *Chrysanthemum* (or *Argyranthemum*) *frutescens* attached to it. Whatever it is called, it is one of the most rewarding of all container plants. Depending on how it is pruned, this *Euryops* will flower profusely throughout the summer, and reach a height and spread of 50cm-1.5m (20in-5ft).

Euryops speciosissimus 'Sunshine'

'Sunshine' is one of the many hybrids developed from *Euryops speciosissimus*. This cultivar begins to flower early in spring, and continues until late autumn.

☼ 5°C (41°F)

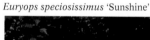

Euryops speciosissimus 'Sunshine'

F

f

Farfugium japonicum

Anyone with a shady garden, for instance a town garden in between tall buildings, would do well to grow this old-fashioned houseplant. Its leaves, over 10cm (4in) wide, grow close to the ground, are tolerant of shade, and can withstand cool, wet weather.

It looks very attractive in a pot on a shady, mossy patio, particularly when combined with ferns.

You need not take the plant indoors until it turns frosty; it may then be kept as a house-plant on a windowsill facing east or north. Keep the humus-rich soil uniformly moist out of doors, and on the dry side in winter.

There are countless variegated cultivars of the green-leafed species, including *Farfugium japonicum* 'Argentea' (also called 'Variegata'), with greyish-green and cream-coloured spots, and *Farfugium japonicum* 'Aureo-maculata', with yellow spots.

☼ 0°C (32°F)

Farfugium japonicum 'Aureo-maculata'

Fatsia japonica

JAPANESE ARALIA

In places where it never freezes more than a few degrees, fatsias may remain out of doors, either in open ground or in a container. In some countries in northwest Europe, fatsias are familiar houseplants, although it is really better to grow them as container plants.

Because of its handsome palm-shaped leaves, a fatsia is one of the most decorative plants to have on your patio.

Stand the plant in a light, but not excessively sunny spot, for instance on a shady patio. Water very freely in summer, but slightly less in winter, provided the plant is kept in a cool room. It is also possible for it to overwinter as a houseplant, but then the humidity should not be allowed to fall too low.

It is easy to propagate fatsias in summer. Cut off a top shoot through a leaf node. Remove the large leaves, but not the very newest, and put the cutting in moist soil, preferably under glass. Try out an old, unsightly plant in the garden. Dig it in and note how many winters it will survive.

☼ 0°C (32°F)

Fatsia japonica

Feijoa sellowiana

PINEAPPLE GUAVA

In the tropics, *Feijoa sellowiana* (better known as *Acca sellowiana*) is cultivated for its fruits, which are related to guavas and are called 'guajave' in Brazil. These fruits, which are made into a refreshing drink, are now available at some greengrocers and super-markets.

Fruits the size of pigeon's eggs develop even when the plant is grown in a container, but they do not ripen until winter.

In countries further north, people are more specifically interested in its highly decorative leaves (green above, with delicately white-haired undersides), and the memorable beauty of its flowers, which energe from feltlike white buds.

A tuft of striking, bright red stamens projects beyond the white to pale-pink petals - a wonderful sight!

If you take good care of the shrub, it will flower from May until well into autumn. Good management in this instance means: a sunny, warm position, average amounts of water and food, and humus-rich soil.

Repot the pineapple guava as rarely as possible; it is preferable to plant it in a fairly deep pot when it is young, and then to spread a layer of humus and old cow manure over the soil every year.

The original soil should not be disturbed, as that is something the surface roots cannot tolerate.

In winter, the plant should be given just enough water to prevent the root ball drying out. Its position should be as light as possible to enable the plant to hold its leaves.

Keep the temperature between 2 and 12°C (36 and 53°F). In a very light location, the *Feijoa* may also overwinter at room temperature, but do not, in that case, forget to give the plant slightly more water.

○ 2°C (36°F)

Felicia amelloides 'Aurea'

Felicia amelloides

BLUE MARGUERITE

This South African mini-shrub can withstand a few degrees of frost. It is a most convenient

Feijoa sellowiana

Felicia amelloides

container plant, which is best grown as an annual, but can survive the winter.

The pretty blue to lilac flowers with yellow centres appear from midsummer until far into autumn. Some people call them blue daisies, but that name is also used for the blue-flowered *Bellis*. In summer, *Felicia amelloides* prefers a light position in semi-shade or full sun, but it dislikes blazing hot conditions. Prevent the soil from drying out.

The evergreen shrub may be kept in a light position in a cool room in winter. Water sparingly and cut back straggly shoots hard in spring. The variegated cultivars of *Felicia amelloides* such as 'Aurea' (golden yellow and green leaves), and 'Santa Anita Variegata' (variegated speckles) need slightly more sun and warmth than the species.

○ 0°C (32°F)

Ficus carica

FIG

Figs can grow in sheltered positions in open ground, for instance against a sunny wall. In southern countries, *Ficus carica* grows into a low, spreading tree, but against a wall it develops into a thinly branching shrub. In a container, the fig will remain somewhat smaller and more graceful, particularly as you can prune it in such a way that about five main branches remain. The leaves are strong and beautifully lobed, and, in a very sunny position may even develop false fruits (the fruit is actually a swollen receptacle). *Ficus carica* should be cultivated in a very large container with light, highly nutritive soil. In summer, the shrub needs a great deal of water

Ficus carica

and a lot of fertilizer. In winter, the fig should be stored in a frost-free location, and kept almost dry, in the dark if need be, in which case the leaves will fall. If it is growing healthily, the fig should be repotted every three years or so, when you should, if possible, renew all the soil, or in any case as much as possible. There is no objection to shortening a few thick roots to provide room for a more spreading root system. There are countless fig cultivars suitable for growing in containers, for instance *Ficus carica* 'Brown Turkey' and *Ficus carica* 'White Marseilles'.

● 0°C (32°F)

Fremontia californica

See: *Fremontodendron californicum*

Fremontodendron californicum

FLANNEL FLOWER

Stems and leaves of flannel flowers are covered in specks with coarse, light brown hairs. This characteristic feature gave rise to its English name, which has been translated literally into several languages, the botanical name being something of a tongue twister. The flannel flower has become increasingly popular in recent years. If you don't let the plant have a period of dormancy, it will bear very large, saucer-shaped, shiny yellow flowers, followed by oblong fruits, all the year round. The flowers are produced one after the other, with new buds appearing continually on vertical stems just below the top of the shrub. It is because of that vertical growth that the shrub, which comes from the southwest of the United States, does not keep its looks for long. Pruning does not really produce a more handsome shape, and it causes a reduction in bud production. It is therefore preferable to renew the plant regularly. It is possible to take tip cuttings, but because they do not root quickly, it is advisable to propagate the plant by seed. It is easier still to buy a new plant. The flannel flower likes a warm and sunny position in summer. Even then you should only water moderately - wet soil leads to root rot - and not add any fertilizer. In winter, you should keep the potting soil even drier, and find a cool, light position indoors for the plant. The flannel flower is evergreen in theory, but, in spite of that, it often sheds some of its beautifully shaped leaves. Fortunately, that is not a problem, as leaves will sprout again in the same places in very early spring. In areas where the temperature does not fall below -12°C (8°F), the *Fremontodendron* will survive the winter out of doors in open ground. *Fremontodendron californicum* and *Fremontodendron mexicanum* were crossed to produce the cultivar *Fremontodendron* 'California Glory', which is more vigorous still, and bears even larger flowers (up to 10cm/4in in diameter).

☼ 0°C (32°F)

Fremontodendron californicum

Fuchsia

Fuchsias evoke the very atmosphere of the tropics. Even so, most species grow in relatively cool and moist places such as the slopes of the Andes Mountains. In those areas, hummingbirds are responsible for pollination, and the flowers owe their beautiful shades of red to them. Insects cannot distinguish red, but birds can, and the flowers are irresistibly attractive to these birds. They hover just below the flowers, and use their long beaks to draw nectar from them, during which operation the flowers are pollinated. In northwest Europe, bumblebees ensure pollination. If their elongated proboscis cannot reach the nectar from below, they gnaw a hole in the side of the flower.

Over 8,000 registered cultivars have been developed from the more than a hundred wild species, which grow in New Zealand and Tahiti as well as in Latin America. About 2,000 of them are cultivated, and the strongest are available in the plant trade. As fuchsias do not like a stuffy atmosphere, it is best to grow them out of doors in summer.

After any risk of a night frost has passed, the fuchsias may be taken out of doors. Most species and cultivars do best in partial shade. Water moderately in spring, and freely in summer; the root ball should never be left to dry out. The soil should be humus-rich, moisture-retentive and nutritive; it should really be renewed each spring. During the growing season, the plant needs feeding regularly. Requirements for overwintering vary depending on the species.

Fuchsia fulgens var. *fulgens*

The herbaceous stems of this Mexican species can grow up to 2m (6ft) long in a single season. The plant will flower with increasing profusion throughout the season, bearing clusters of red flowers which grow to more than 5cm (2in) long. It may be placed in a slightly sunnier spot than usual for fuchsias, and the soil should be left to dry out before it is watered again. This procedure will imitate the dry Mexican climate. The soil holds the thickened roots, which develop into a radical tuber as they age. After the leaves and stems have died off, the tuber may be left to overwinter in a dry, dark position at a minimum temperature of 7°C (45°F). The plant will continue to grow and flower in winter if you keep it in a light location where the temperature does not drop below 2°C (36°F).

● 7°C (45°F) or ☼ 2°C (36°F)

Fuchsia fulgens var. *fulgens*

Fuchsia 'Gartenmeister Bontstedt'

Fuchsias from the Triphylla group make excellent container plants. 'Gartenmeister Bontstedt' is one of the oldest hybrids (1905), and grows into a vigorous, bushy plant. It flowers late and continues well into autumn. If the shrub is kept in full sun, stems and leaves will turn partially wine red.

The plant needs a light, cool position in winter. Digging it in is unsuitable.

☼ 5°C (41°F)

Fuchsia 'Gartenmeister Bontstedt'

Fuchsia 'Golden La Campanella'

Fuchsias are usually grown for their flowers, but the 'Golden La Campanella' (developed in 1980) is an exception. Its greyish-geen leaves have buttery yellow to creamy white margins. Like all variegated forms, it has a moderate growth rate. Digging the plant in for the winter is impossible.

It will need a light location, where it is not too cold. It is best to take cuttings in late summer in case the adult plant does not survive the winter.

It is easy to take cuttings by selecting tips with several pairs of leaves. Cut off the bottom leaves and put the cutting in a small pot with wet propagating compost. Use a thin stick to prick a small hole in the soil before inserting the cutting.

☼ 5°C (41°F)

Fuchsia 'Golondrina'

For people without green fingers, *Fuchsia* 'Golondrina' is a real boon. This cultivar is one of the strongest fuchsias in existence, and it also flowers profusely. The lax stems make the plant highly suitable for hanging baskets. In a maritime climate, 'Golondrina' is fully hardy. After the stems have died off, the roots should be covered with a thick layer of insulating material such as the leaves of trees.

It is possible for the plant to overwinter in a light, frost-free place, but you may also dig it in if you are short of space. Remove all leaves and flowers from the plant and cut it back hard. Remove it from its pot, shake all the soil off its roots, and then tie a label to a strong stem. Lay the plant, and any other fuchsias that may be treated in the same way, in a hole in the garden, fill it with peat dust, and cover it with plastic. Finally deposit the removed compost on top of the plastic. (Storing fuch-

Fuchsia 'Golondrina'

Fuchsia 'Golden La Campanella'

sias in a pit is possible only if the underground water level is low!) Alternatively, you may use a discarded box freezer filled with peat dust for storing fuchsias.

Stand the freezer in a frost-free location and leave the lid slightly open.

● 2°C (36°F)

Fuchsia 'Happy'

'Happy's' flowers slant cheerfully upwards. This kind of growth greatly appeals to a large body of enthusiasts. The popular *Fuchsia* 'Walz Jubelteen' grows in the same way, as does *Fuchsia* 'Estelle Marie', a real fuchsia for advanced devotees!

Fuchsia 'Happy' was developed in the Scilly Isles, and is fully hardy there and in other parts of Cornwall. Containerized specimens should be taken indoors in winter. Alternatively, however, you may take the plant out of the compost and store it in a pit (see *Fuchsia* 'Golondrina')

○ or ● 2°C (36°F)

Fuchsia 'Happy'

Fuchsia 'Harry Gray'

White-flowered fuchsias are, on the whole, less hardy than coloured forms. 'Harry Gray' flowers early, producing a profusion of pink-

tinged white flowers. It is best to cultivate it as a hanging plant, while bearing in mind that it does not tolerate any sun. Its flowers show up magnificently in a shady or half-shady position.

This plant is unsuitable for storing in a pit.

○ 5°C (41°F)

Fuchsia 'Harry Gray'

Fuchsia hartwegii

Vigorous growth, velvety green leaves produced in whorls round the stem, and orange-

Fuchsia hartwegii

red flowers make *Fuchsia hartwegii* a magnificent container plant. Until recently, this cultivar was grown only by real enthusiasts, which is strange, as it is easy to manage. In Columbia, the species grows mainly at levels between 2,000 and 3,000m (6,000 and 10,000ft), and it is therefore well able to withstand cool, damp summers. In winter it prefers a cool, light location. This species should not be stored in a pit.

☼ 5°C (41°F)

Fuchsia 'Lady Isobel Barnett'

Many fuchsias have strongly contrasting colours. 'Lady Isobel Barnet', which was developed from *Fuchsia* 'Caroline' and *Fuchsia* 'Derby Belle' in 1971, has very subtle shades: pinkish red and lilac pink. This bushy plant flowers profusely over a long period and is also easy to cultivate. You can let it over-winter in a cool and light location, but it is also possible to store it in a pit (see *Fuchsia* 'Golondrina').

☼ 2°C (36°F)

Fuchsia 'Lady Isobel Barnett'

Fuchsia magellanica

When you find a fuchsia growing in open ground in a garden, it is nearly always *Fuchsia magellanica* var. *ricartonii*. The species comes from the southern Andes and Tierra del Fuego, where winter frosts are severe. During that season, the plants die down to soil level. In countries with a milder climate such as Ireland, stems and leaves remain on the plants even in winter. As a container plant, this vigorous shrub is grown in a large pot. Stand it in partial shade, so that the soil remains cool, and enjoy the numerous slender flowers that are borne from the second half of the summer until far into autumn. In winter, you may stand the pot in a cool and light position indoors. In that case, the shrub will not die down, and will grow even larger the following year: up to about 1.5m (5ft) in height and spread. It is also possible to lower the pot into a deep hole in the garden and cover it with a thick layer of leaves or straw. The final option is to store it in a pit (see *Fuchsia* 'Golondrina'). A great many lovely cultivars have been developed from *Fuchsia magellanica*, including some with variegated leaves. The names given to them, however, are highly confusing. A deviant form is described as a subspecies or variety on one occasion, and as a cultivar the next. The cultivar *Fuchsia magellanica* 'Aurea' has golden yellow foliage.

☼ or ● 0°C (32°F)

Fuchsia magellanica 'Aurea'

Fuchsia paniculata

LILAC FUCHSIA

The flowers of *Fuchsia paniculata* are borne in lilac-purple plumes. They might easily be mistaken for those of a lilac, a late-flowering one, however, as this fuchsia does not begin to flower until early summer or even later after a cold spring.

Although the species is relatively simple to

cultivate, it is rarely sold as a container plant. A half-shady to sunny position in summer is adequate. Water freely at this stage, and give the plant some fertilizer from time to time.

In winter, you should move it to a cool, light location indoors, where you need only sprinkle the stems with a plant spray. The species originally came from Central America, as did *Fuchsia arborescens*, which closely resembles it and may be cared for in exactly the same way.

☼ 5°C (41°F)

Fuchsia paniculata

Fuchsia procumbens

The relatively unknown *Fuchsia procumbens* is a real maverick. The plant develops a mat of thin, juicy stems with small delicate leaves. Its small yellow flowers, an unusual colour for fuchsias, are borne in summer and are 1.5cm (5/8in) long. *Fuchsia procumbens* comes from New Zealand, and grows there in damp and shady places.

Grow the little plant in a shady spot in humus-rich, moisture-retentive soil. The stems will trail over the rim of the pot or hanging basket.

The plant should be taken indoors after the first night frost, and left to overwinter in a light, cool, and dry location.

The runners root of their own accord and it is therefore very easy to cultivate new plants. Reddish berries, about 2cm (3/4in) long, are formed after the plant has flowered. The highly germinative seeds contained in the berries should be sown in spring.

☼ 0°C (32°F)

Fuchsia procumbens

Fuchsia 'Ringwood Market'

Fuchsia 'Ringwood Market' was developed from *Fuchsia* 'Tristesse' and *Fuchsia* 'Susan Ford' in 1976. The pendulous flowers are bi-coloured, with bright red sepals and lavender-blue petals (the latter colour gradually turns lilac pink as it fades). This colour change also occurs in the case of other fuchsias, so that a single plant may have flowers in varying shades.

The semi-trailing *Fuchsia* 'Ringwood Market' has a bushy shape and produces a profusion of flowers from June onwards. It does best in partial shade out of doors, and should be managed like *Fuchsia* 'Golondrina' in winter.

● 2°C (36°F)

Fuchsia 'Ringwood Market'

G

_g_

Gardenia augusta

Cape jasmine is still known in the flower trade by its obsolete name _Gardenia jasminoides_. You will find it on display as a small, shiny green shrub in the houseplant section. It will often be in flower, producing intensely fragrant, creamy-white, fully double blooms. It is also possible to cultivate this Asian shrub as a container plant. It should, however, be moved indoors as soon as temperatures begin to fall below 10°C (50°F).

Provided the humidity is not reduced excessively, the plant may be kept in a living-room during the winter. Otherwise, this evergreen shrub should be placed in a light location at a temperature between 12 and 16°C (53 and 60°F), and watered very moderately. In summer, the Cape jasmine needs a lot of moisture, but because it does not tolerate hard, limy water, you will need to use rain water or boiled main water. The shrub likes a warm position, but preferably not in full sun. The fragrant flowers are produced from halfway through the summer until well into autumn. When the shrub has grown quite tall (it can reach 1.5m/5ft after many years), you may also cut off the flowers on a short stem and enjoy them indoors. One bloom is enough to fill an entire room with its sweet, heavy fragrance.

○ 10°C (50°F)

Gardenia grandiflora

See: _Gardenia augusta_

Gardenia jasminoides

See: _Gardenia augusta_

Gardenia augusta

Gaultheria procumbens

In September, this low-growing evergreen gaultheria flaunts its red berries, which developed out of whitish balloon-shaped flowers. In the garden, the shrub is used as ground cover in neutral to acid soil. The plant is particularly convenient as underplanting for trees, or combined with heather, but because it is fully hardy, this prostrate shrub is also very suitable for growing in a pot in winter. Plant it in one of the (frost-resistant) pots that become available when flowering annuals are past their prime, and preferably stand the pot in a sheltered spot to prevent the leathery leaves from drying out too much. For the same reason, you will also need to give the plant some rain water or boiled main water from time to time in winter - if there is no frost.

❄

Gaultheria procumbens

Genista x spachiana

In the old days, when our living-rooms were cooler and damper, this genista was an excellent houseplant.
In spring and early summer, its arching branches were covered in yellow flowers. Nowadays, however, it is too hot and too dry for this graceful little shrub in centrally heated rooms.
The two species from which this hybrid was developed (*Genista stenopetala* and *Genista canariensis*), originally came from the Canary Islands, where they grow on mountain slopes in places where moisture from the ocean often condenses into mist and low-hanging cloud.
It is therefore far better to move the *Genista*

out of doors in summer, where it will benefit from the dew every morning and will subsequently tolerate full sun without any problems arising.
A position in partial shade, however, is preferable, because the plant will then lose less moisture by evaporation. For the same reason, it is advisable to grow the plant in a plastic pot, as that will retain moisture more effectively than one of earthenware.
Genista x *spachiana* will withstand several degrees of frost, but it is preferable to move the plant indoors before the temperature falls to that level.
As the plant holds its leaves in winter, it will need a well-lit location, where the atmosphere is not too dry. A conservatory or greenhouse would be an ideal place for it to overwinter, but a cool room is an excellent alternative. Prune in winter or immediately after flowering to prevent straggly growth. Cut back in good time, because *Genista* takes time to recover from hard pruning. Old wood will sprout very slowly or not at all.

☼ 0°C (32°F)

Genista x *spachiana*

Geranium clarkei 'Kashmir White'

CRANESBILL

This geranium from Kashmir, about 50cm (20in) tall, bears white flowers above finely divided leaves. The flowers are excellent for combining with almost any other potted plant.

The plant looks equally lovely on its own, and close-up, as its petals are beautifully veined with purple. This easy-to-manage plant flowers all summer and well into autumn, though not profusely.

Geranium clarkei will grow either in half-shade or in full sun. In the latter case, water freely in summer.

It is better not to feed it, as that will result in weak plants. Planted in the garden, the species, which dies down to the soil in winter, is fully hardy, but if the plant is grown in a pot, protection from temperatures below -10°C (14°F) is advisable.

❋

Geranium clarkei 'Kashmir White' *with* Artemisia

Geranium ibericum 'Genyel'

CRANESBILL

The purplish blue flowers of this geranium from Asia Minor appear above velvety divided leaves in summer, mainly in June. The plant resembles the more familiar *Geranium platypetalum*, which comes from the same region. Both species start off as compact spheres, and grow to a maximum height of 50cm (20in), with a good spread. Manage them in the same way as *Geranium clarkei*. They are slightly hardier, and can withstand greater drought.

❋

Geranium macrorrhizum

CRANESBILL

This is definitely one of the easiest and most rewarding pot plants in existence. It makes excellent ground cover in the garden, even in poor, dry soil. Containerized specimens are also worth cultivating for their fragrant leaves, which turn wonderful colours in autumn, as well as for their flowers in late spring.

Depending on the cultivar, these are white (*Geranium macrorrhizum* 'Album'); pale pink ('Ingwersen's Variety'); deep pink ('Spessart'); or magenta ('Bevan's Variety' and 'Czakor'). There is also a variegated form, 'Variegatum', which has green leaves with cream blotches and purplish pink flowers.

These very strong plants have no special requirements.

❋

Geranium macrorrhizum 'Album'

Geranium rectum album

See: *Geranium clarkei* 'Kashmir White'

Geranium ibericum 'Genyel'

Gladiolus callianthus

Gladiolus callianthus

This gladiolus is also popular with those who do not really like gladioli. The flowers, which last for weeks at the end of summer, have a very natural look: white with aubergine-coloured centres. They arch over gracefully above the more than 1m (3ft) tall, sword-shaped leaves.

The corms may be planted in a border in May, but *Gladiolus callianthus* shows up better in a large pot or tub. Make sure that excess water can always drain away easily from the highly nutritive, moisture-retentive soil in which the leaves will develop sufficient strength for the production of flowers. Stand the container in a sunny or semi-shady position, and never let the soil dry out.

Gradually water less after the plant has flowered; the foliage will die down naturally. Take the plants indoors before the first frost, remove the corms from the pot and keep them cool and dry until the following spring.

A great many cormlets will develop round the old corms in summer, and these may be used for propagation.

It will be several years before the young corms have reached an appropriate size for flowering.

● 0°C (32°F)

Gloriosa rothschildiana

See: *Gloriosa superba* 'Rothschildiana'

Gloriosa superba 'Rothschildiana'

GLORY LILY

The glory lily needs high temperatures in spring to encourage growth. Cultivation in a greenhouse or conservatory is therefore most suitable, but, in summer, it is better for this climber to be out of doors in a warm, slightly shady to sunny position, where it is less likely to be affected by aphids than when under glass.

Plant the glory lily in a large pot or container with nutritive, moisture-retentive soil. Make sure, however, that the tubers do not become waterlogged. Large new flowers, over 10cm (4in) in diameter, are borne continually from late spring until early autumn.

As soon as temperatures fall below 10°C (50°F), it is time to move this tropical plant indoors. Let the soil dry out. Leaves and stems will die down, but the tubers in the soil will stay alive. Let the plants overwinter at room temperature and disturb them as little as

Gloriosa superba 'Rothschildiana'

possible. The growing point is particularly vulnerable during this period. You will need to renew the potting compost after a few years, as the glory lily likes highly nutritive soil; it is therefore wise to give it plenty of fertilizer during the growing season.

To propagate *Gloriosa*, sow indoors early in spring. Tubers are on sale occasionally, and they bring about faster results if planted in warm, steamy soil in April. The stem, which is leafless at first, does not start climbing until the leaf tips begin to grip. Prior to that stage, you can tie the stems. Be careful - all parts of the glory lily are poisonous.

● 10°C (50°F)

Gomphocarpus fruticosus

See: *Asclepias fruticosa*

Grevillea banksii

SILK OAK

The grevillea's pinnate leaves are covered in very fine down and are particularly tough. The underside of the leaves, where the stomata are situated, is slightly dented. All such details are adaptations to the arid climate of Australia. Characteristic reddish flowers are borne on the 1.5m (5ft) tall shrubs in summer. The flowers are adapted to pollination by birds, and *Meliphagidae* (honey-eating birds) in particular are enticed into Australian gardens in this way.
Grevillea banksii has been cultivated for a long time, but even this best-known species is rarely seen in countries like the Netherlands. This is a pity, as the shrub is highly decorative and relatively easy to manage. Put the shrub in a warm and sunny position in summer, and keep the soil moderately moist with rain water or softened water. Prune slightly if necessary. In winter, the plant requires a light, cool and

Grevillea banksii

airy position and little water. During this period, however, you should make sure that the root ball of this evergreen plant does not dry out entirely.

○ 5°C (41°F)

Grevillea juniperina

The needle-like leaves of *Grevillea juniperina* closely resemble those of another species from eastern Australia: *Grevillea rosmarinifolia*. The leaves of the latter, however, are greyish green like those of rosemary, whereas *G. juniperina* has green leaves.
In summer, the small shrub bears clusters of flowers among its leaves. Containerized plants can easily be kept at a height of 1m (3ft) by regular pruning.
Management is the same as for *Grevillea banksii*.

○ 5°C (41°F)

Grevillea robusta

SILK OAK

The Australian silk oak is cultivated because of its fern-like foliage. In Australia itself, this species develops into a tree some 30m (100ft) tall. Do not be alarmed - in a large pot or tub, the shrub is quite manageable and may be

Grevillea juniperina

Grevillea robusta

Griselinia littoralis 'Variegata'

kept in the required shape by pruning. The yellow-ochre, brush-like flowers rarely appear in northern European countries, so that the leaves are the plant's sole decorative feature.

The Australian silk oak is well-known as a houseplant, but needs a lot of fresh air, and should therefore be kept in cool areas only. In summer, a sheltered, semi-shady spot out of doors is best.

Keep the soil uniformly moist with decalcified water. In winter, the best place for the plant is a light, but not excessively sunny, position indoors, preferably with a temperature between 5 and 15°C (41 and 59°F).

Water very sparingly while the plant is dormant. If the shrub overwinters in a dark place, it will shed its leaves, but new foliage will develop in spring.

○ or ● 5°C (41°F)

Grevillea x semperflorens

This cross between *Grevillea thelemanniana* and *Grevillea juniperina f. sulphurea* has long arching stems on which magnificent creamy pink flowers with long pinkish red styles ending in pale green stigmas are borne in late summer. The leaves are clearly greyish green beneath, needle-shaped, and very often forked. Do not prune the long stems; they will continue to arch over gracefully and translucently.

For management, see *Grevillea banksii.*

○ 5°C (41°F)

Griselinia littoralis

This New Zealand shrub grows vigorously out of doors, even in the shade. You should not expect much of the flowers, which are small and not very beautiful. The apple-green foliage, however, is a joy to behold, and creates suitable background for more exuberant container plants.

Griselinia littoralis is undemanding. It makes little difference whether its position is sunny or shady, cool or warm, whether you water freely or sparingly. Do not take the plant indoors in autumn until the frosts become quite severe. This plant can easily withstand a few degrees of frost. Provide a cool, light, airy position in winter, and water just enough to prevent the soil from drying out. Pruning is unnecessary. The shrubs grow slowly, particularly the variegated forms such as *Griselinia littoralis* 'Variegata'. Like other variegated species, this slow-growing plant needs more light and warmth to stay healthy.

○ 0°C (32°F)

Grevillea x semperflorens

H _____ *h*

Haemanthus coccineus

BLOOD LILY

This magnificent species is rarely on sale. In autumn, it bears cup-shaped red bracts filled with the actual flowers, of which only the yellow stamens are visible.

Two or three leaves with beautiful markings appear immediately after the plant has flowered, and remain on the plant during the winter. For management, see *Haemanthus multiflorus*.

☼ 10°C (50°F)

Haemanthus coccineus

Haemanthus multiflorus

BLOOD FLOWER

Haemanthus multiflorus (which is really called *Scadoxus multiflorus* nowadays, but is rarely sold under that name) flowers in the shelter of shrubs in the East African island of Zanzibar, where it is warm and fairly dry. The pinkish red flowers grow in large spherical umbels, 20-30cm (8-12in) in diameter. The projecting stamens are their most striking feature and resemble the hairs of powder brushes.

The leaves are formed either during or after the summer flowering period and often remain on the plant until spring. Plant the bulb with its apex just below the sandy soil, or buy a flowering plant. It will do best out of doors in a very warm and light position which is not too sunny, and requires plenty of water and plant food while it is in full growth.

The plant becomes dormant as soon as its leaves turn yellow. The bulb's need for water is minimal, and you may keep it in a pot in a cool, dark place. Until the leaves die down, however, the plant needs a light position, and some water from time to time. Leave the bulb in its pot for as long as possible as it does not like being disturbed.

● or ☼ 10°C (50°F)

Haemanthus multiflorus

Hebe

Hebes are often found among the garden plants at garden centres. They frequently, however, turn out to be frost- tender, particularly in wet soil and in freezing easterly winds.

129

Hebe 'Inspiration'

The variegated species in particular are very vulnerable, and it is therefore better to grow them as container plants. An unheated greenhouse or conservatory, or a cool room, is the best kind of place in winter. As hebes are evergreen, they need to overwinter in a light location.

In summer, the small shrubs like to be in the fresh air, in a position varying between semi-shade and full sun. Water freely, especially in full sun, and never let the soil dry out. In nutritive soil, they will bear spikes of blue, mauve, pink, or white flowers for several weeks from early summer.

Hebe x *andersonii* is a cross between *Hebe salicifolia* and *Hebe speciosa*; it grows over 1.5m (5ft) tall, with an equal spread. Hybridization has resulted in the development of many forms, all pf which belong to the *Hebe* Andersonii group. One of these selections, 'Variegata', eventually grows up to 2m (6ft) tall, and has green to greyish-green leaves with ivory-white margins. *Hebe* 'Inspiration' is one of the countless cultivars with untraceable ancestry. It has variegated, greyish-green and green leaves with very broad, yellow margins.

☼ 0°C (50°F)

Hedera helix

IVY

Ivy is one of Europe's strongest plants. Its evergreen leaves cover forest floors and trees all over the continent, from Scandinavia to Russia. Even in a container, this immensely strong plant will withstand the severest of winters. As a forest plant, *Hedera* likes cool, moist soil, and it is therefore preferable not to stand the pot in full sun. Keep the soil well watered.

Ivy is highly suitable for a cool, north-facing balcony, or a shady patio.

The plant attaches itself to trees, walls, rush-matting, fences, mesh, etc. by its adventitious rootlets.

If you plant ivy in a trough with a piece of wire mesh, it will develop into a green dividing screen as tall and as wide as the mesh itself. If the trough is movable, you can stand this green divider screen wherever you like.

Ivy may also be used for topiary, a craft dating back to ancient Greece and mentioned in the first century B.C.

It has become so popular that you can buy ivy in a pot with pre-formed metal supports. By training and pruning the ivy carefully, you can fill the form with dark green leaves.

If you would prefer something rather more frivolous, choose a variegated ivy.

Hedera helix

Crossing common ivy with *Hedera algeriensis*, *Hedera colchica*, or *Hedera hibernica* has led to the development of vast numbers of cultivars. There are specialized growers who sell nothing but species of ivy; genuine enthusiasts meet at ivy associations. The hobby has gone to great lengths, especially in the United States.

Huge structures of wire mesh are filled with fertilizer and moist sphagnum moss. Cuttings of ivy species are inserted and gradually cover the entire frame with ivy leaves in every imaginable shade.

✳

Hedychium

GARLAND FLOWER, GINGER LILY

Ginger lilies are particularly suitable for cultivating in containers. With the exception of *Hedychium gardnerianum*, however, they are rarely for sale. In spite of that, the plant is described here to encourage growers, as there is nothing to prevent its wider distribution.

Ginger lilies grow rapidly in spring, when they develop broad, ribbon-shaped leaves on round stems. They begin to flower in late summer and early autumn, when many plants are well past their prime. The flowers are overwhelmingly beautiful, and have a wonderful fragrance. They appear in spikes which grow up to 30cm (12in) tall and 10cm (4in) wide. You can tell by their fleshy rhizomes that they are members of the ginger family as they closely resemble large ginger roots.

The vigorous species of *Hedychium* grow mainly in the Himalayas, where the plants die down to the soil in the cold season. The same occurs under a milder climate if you store the plant in a dry and cool location during winter. Leave it out of doors for as long as possible and do not move it indoors until the first night frost. Then cut all stems to just above soil level. Leave the rhizomes in the pot, and put that in a cool place, in the dark if you wish.

In early spring, pot up the rhizomes in fresh, fertile soil in a wide pot or tub (the plant produces a lot of foliage, and is therefore likely to be blown over in a narrow pot).

You should then find an outdoor position for the ginger lily as soon as the danger of frost has passed. Water freely in summer and feed adequately.

● 0°C (32°F)

Hedychium coccineum

RED GINGER LILY

This plant grows as tall as a man, and has pale red flowers, an unusually striking colour for a ginger lily. This shade is somewhat variable, which has led to the identification of subspecies that do not differ much from one another: *Hedychium coccineum carneum* has

Hedychium coccineum

flesh-coloured flowers; those of *Hedychium coccineum angustifolium* are brick red; and those of *Hedychium coccineum aurantiacum* are orange.

Hedychium coccineum (including the subspecies) needs more warmth to produce flowers, and is therefore best cultivated in a greenhouse or conservatory.

● 5°C (41°F)

Hedychium ellipticum

The graceful white flowers of this species from northern India are borne at right angles to the stem. They open in succession, starting at the

The roots of *Hedychium ellipticum*

Hedychium ellipticum

bottom of a spike which grows to about 10cm (4in) long. The plant itself may grow to 2m (6ft) tall.

● 0°C (32°F)

Hedychium flavum

YELLOW GINGER LILY

The yellow ginger lily closely resembles *Hedychium gardnerianum*, and also comes from the cool mountain regions of northern India.

● 0°C (32°F)

Hedychium flavum

Hedychium forrestii

The elegant white flowers of this species appear to be upside down. The lip is raised, while two other, narrow petals point downwards. Between the two, there is a style with a pale pink stigma. This species does not grow quite as tall as the other ginger lilies. It comes from Yun-nan, a mountainous province in southwest China. Manage it in the same way as the Indian species.

● 0°C (32°F)

Hedychium forrestii

Hedychium gardnerianum

This is the most familiar ginger lily. In certain subtropical regions such as the Azores, it was introduced as an ornamental plant at some time, but it soon became naturalized, and is now a nuisance. In countries like the Netherlands, it develops into one of the most rewarding container plants. Large, sweet-smelling, golden-yellow flower spikes are borne in late summer on stems up to 2m (6ft) tall. This species is the one most frequently available from container plant specialists. The other species, which all come from the mountainous regions around the Himalayas, are just as easy to cultivate.

● 0°C (32°F)

Helianthemum 'Snow Queen'

ROCK ROSE

Helianthemums grow on the sunny slopes of mountains in America, Europe, Africa, and Asia. Several species from southern Europe, North Africa, and Asia Minor are the ancestors of the innumerable hybrids available

Hedychium gardnerianum

Plant them in sandy soil, and ensure perfect drainage. Water moderately in summer and do not feed the plants. The trailing shrubs bear small crumpled flowers closely resembling those of *Cistus*. Although they are smaller, they are produced in far greater profusion. Cut back the stems after they have flowered. This will render the shrubs more compact, and the new shoots will often flower again in late summer. An unheated greenhouse or cold frame would be an ideal light and dry place where the evergreen plants could overwinter without suffering too much from frost. The cultivar 'Snow Queen' is also sold under its synonym 'The Bride'. The magnificent greyish-green leaves and relatively large white flowers with vibrant yellow centres are produced on long, more or less pendulous stems.

❄

Helianthemum 'The Bride'

See: *Helianthemum* 'Snow Queen'

Helianthemum 'Wisley Pink'

ROCK ROSE

'Wisley Pink' is one of the helianthemum's most popular cultivars. The profusion of flow-

as garden plants. They will easily survive temperatures as low as -10°C (14°F), or even lower, but only in a dry position. As garden plants, they are therefore suitable only for dry places such as rock gardens, or at the foot of a south- or east-facing wall. In other gardens, they do very well when grown in containers.

Helianthemum 'Snow Queen' with ivy-leafed toadflax

Helianthemum 'Wisley Pink'

ers that it bears is undoubtedly one of the reasons for that. Its oblong leaves are greyish green, with grey, woolly undersides. The flowers produced in such abundance in summer vary considerably in colour. On some bushes they are pale pink, on others deep pink to pinkish red.

For management, see *Helianthemum* 'Snow Queen'.

✳

Helichrysum microphyllum

See: *Plectostachys serphyllifolia*

Helichrysum petiolare

The small grey-woolly leaves of this South African prostrate plant have become very popular in recent years.

Its shoots are suspended from countless hanging baskets, or trail over the rims of troughs and pots. No wonder, since this is an extremely rewarding plant which can easily withstand fierce sunlight, and continues to grow imperturbably if you occasionally forget to water it.

Helichrysum is not grown on its own, but is always combined with flowering plants to provide colour, as the grey-woolly shoots

normally do not flower. They often grow too long in the course of summer, but may be kept in check by trimming.

In warm summers, buds sometimes appear on the ends of the shoots.

They are usually removed, as *Helichrysum* is not grown for its flowers. It is better to wait until the clusters of small, golden yellow flowers open before cutting them off. The flowers have a delightful honeyed fragrance, and if you hang up the stems to dry, your home will be filled with the scent. The dried flowers keep very well.

Helichrysum petiolare

As *Helichrysum* can barely withstand frost, it is best to take heel cuttings and let them overwinter in a cool, light place. That will ensure that you have new plants every year.

☼ 0°C (32°F)

Helichrysum petiolare 'Gold'

Countless variegated forms have been developed from the common species.
The dark green leaves of *Helichrysum petiolare* 'Gold' has creamy yellow blotches. 'Limelight' (also called 'Aureum') has yellowish green blotches; 'Silver' has white blotches which, because of their hairiness, look silvery; and 'Variegatum' is cream with grey blotches.
The cultivars need even more light than the species, and are more tender. Apart from that, they may be treated just like *Helichrysum petiolare*.

☼ 5°C (41°F)

Helichrysum petiolare 'Gold'

Helichrysum petiolatum

See: *Helichrysum petiolare*

Heliconia

LOBSTER CLAWS

These relatives of the banana grow best in a tropical or temperate greenhouse. In summer, they flower beautifully in a large pot or tub in a light and sheltered position (in gentle sun or

Heliconia rostrata

partial shade) out of doors. Give the plant plenty of water and food.
In winter, keep the plants fairly dry in a light location at a minimum temperature of 15°C (59°F).
Heliconia psittacorum (Parrot's flower, Parrot's plantain) produces large banana-like leaves which can grow to 2m (6ft) long, and in summer bears graceful flowers in all kinds of colours, but usually orange. Over 1,000 cultivars have been described.

Heliconia psittacorum

Heliconia rostrata has even larger banana-like leaves. In warm conditions, a long, pendent inflorescence emerges from the false stem, its red and yellow bracts being particularly striking.

Heliconias are not yet standard items at garden centres, and will therefore remain plants for enthusiasts for the time being.

☼ 15°C (59°F)

Heliotropium arborescens

HELIOTROPE

Heliotropes are a familiar sight in flower beds, and may produce mauve flowers all through the summer. They have a delightful vanilla-like fragrance, especially towards evening and in the early in the morning. Because they are used mainly for bedding purposes, these plants are treated with growth inhibitors. They are on sale in May, and are best treated as annuals.

Heliotropium arborescens

Heliotropes are also back in fashion as container plants. If treated as perennials, the plants may eventually grow between 1 and 2m (3 and 6ft) tall, and they need to overwinter in a light, cool, and almost dry place. Give these Peruvian shrubs an airing as often as possible during that period, but avoid exposing them to frost, as they are decidedly frost-tender.

After the last night frost, you should find a warm and sunny position for the heliotropes, and give them plenty of water and fertilizer while they are in full growth.

The result should be months of flowers and countless butterflies attracted by their fragrance.

Sow heliotrope indoors in spring, but it is also possible to take cuttings in summer. Take tip cuttings and put them in warm, moist, sandy soil. The innumerable forms on the market are usually sold without names. The cultivar 'Chatsworth' has purple flowers; those of 'Marine' are dark blue.

☼ 2°C (36°F)

Heliotropium corymbosum

See: *Heliotropium arborescens*

Heliotropium peruvianum

See: *Heliotropium arborescens*

Heterocentron

See: *Centradenia*

Hibiscus geranioides

This tree hibiscus is reminiscent of *Anisodontea* in the way it grows. The branches spread in all directions, and create a translucent impression enhanced by the delicate old-rose flowers on the outer half of the stems.

By pruning early in spring, you can achieve a more compact shape, but, if you have enough space, it is more attractive to let them grow unrestrictedly.

Find the plant a warm and sunny position in summer and water normally. In winter, it prefers a light and frost-free location. The lighter its position, the more leaves will remain on the plant. The fallen leaves are replaced in spring, and the stems do not therefore remain permanently bare.

☼ 5°C (41°F)

Hibiscus huegelii

See: *Alyogyne huegelii*

Hibiscus rosa-sinensis

ROSE OF CHINA

This hibiscus is a flower for home-loving people. Only if it is looked after regularly, will

Hibiscus rosa-sinensis continue to grow well. Its root ball must remain permanently moist, but must never become waterlogged, and the plant prefers to grow in a moist atmosphere at room temperature. Feed regularly while it is in full growth.

If you take good care of this hibiscus, new flowers, up to 12cm (5in) in diameter, will open daily. They feel velvety to the touch and are bright crimson. The stamens and pistil have fused to form a long column which protrudes well beyond the calyx.

There are numerous cultivars of *rosa-sinensis*, with salmon-pink, white, yellow, orange, or cream flowers. Others may be double, splashed with another colour, and/or have undulate leaves.

In China, the hibiscus grows into a shrub about 2m (6ft) tall, but in western European countries the plants for sale are kept compact with chemical inhibitors. These substances eventually disappear, and the plant will grow into a small shrub which you can enjoy indoors or on your patio. Give it a warm and sunny position on the patio, or stand it by a window - which should not be too sunny - in your living-room. You should move it indoors as soon as the temperature drops to below 7°C (45°F). It will often continue to flower exuberantly, and you will be able to enjoy it right through the winter. Even so, it is advisable to water more moderately in winter, so that the plant begins a period of dormancy. You may then move it from the dry, heated living-room to a cooler room where the temperature preferably varies between 10 and 15°C (50 and 59°F), and where the humidity is higher.

Do not take the hibiscus out of doors again until late spring, as cold is one of the causes of

Hibiscus rosa-sinensis (cultivar)

Hibiscus rosa-sinensis (cultivar)

bud drop. This, however, may also occur if the atmosphere is too dry, or if the plant is turned in relation to the light when it is indoors.

☼ 7°C (45°F)

Hibiscus schizopetalus

The origins of this hibiscus from East Africa are obscure, but it is presumably a very ancient hybrid of, among other species, the Asian *Hibiscus rosa-sinensis*. Its growth is looser and more horizontal than that of the genuine, bushy, Chinese rose. The main difference between the two species is that *Hibiscus schizopetalus*' petals have fused to become tubular.

The genuine original *Hibiscus schizopetalus* flowers very moderately, but its countless cultivars indulge their devotees with a profusion of flowers. Curious forms have been developed, including some with variegated leaves, and others with flowers that appear to consist of layers of petticoats.

Hibiscus schizopetalus likes a mild climate. Night temperatures should not fall below 10°C (50°F), or the plant is likely to drop its buds. In summer, it prefers a position in cool shade, where the maximum temperature does not exceed 25°C (77°F). Water regularly, as dehydration also leads to bud drop and infestation by pests such as woolly aphids, greenfly, and scale insects.

Hibiscus schizopetalus (varigated cultivar)

Hosta x *fortunei* 'Albo-marginata'

Try to keep the plant growing as a houseplant in winter.
Water regularly, but do not feed. A light position away from strong sunlight is preferable. If you can meet those conditions, the hibiscus will continue to flower during the winter.

☼ 10°C (50°F)

Hosta

FUNKIA, PLANTAIN LILY

Hostas belong to the group of garden plants which grow well in any kind of soil that is not too dry. They tolerate damp and shady conditions, and are therefore often grown by the waterside.
Their beauty as container plants is less well known.
If you do not stand the pots in hot sun, normal watering is quite enough to enable you to admire the plant's magnificent leaves. Some people even go so far as to cut off the flowers to prevent attention being distracted from the foliage. The leaves, however, attract slugs and snails.
Fill the pots with humus-rich, moisture-retentive soil, preferably leaf mould, and stand the pot in a cool and shady spot in among shrubs, under trees, or against a north-facing wall in summer.
The plant dies down to the ground in winter, while the fleshy roots remain in the pot, where they will need some protection against the severest frosts.

You should therefore stand the pot in an unheated greenhouse or cold frame, dig it in, or wrap it up well and put it close to the house.
Hosta fortunei is the best-known plantain lily; many different forms are available. It is probably not a natural species, but a group of garden plants that have been cultivated for centuries. One of them is 'Albo marginata', which has leaves with clear white margins. *Hosta sieboldiana* (syn. *Hosta glauca*) is the species that does most credit to its name plantain lily. The large, deeply ribbed leaves have a greyish-green to blueish-grey bloom, and white to mauve flowers.

Hydrangea anomala petiolaris

See: *Hydrangea petiolaris*

Hydrangea macrophylla

Countless hybrids and groups with untraceable origins are marketed under the name of *Hydrangea macrophylla*. The plants, which were sent to Europe in the late-eighteenth century, had been growing in Japanese and Chinese gardens for centuries, and were also hybridized there. The number of groups is now huge.

Hosta sieboldiana

You may choose between white, pink, purple, blue to mauve flowers, either with domed heads (hortensias), or flat heads with a ring of sterile decoys surrounding the actual flowers (lacecaps).

The colour of the flowers depends partly on the presence of aluminium in the soil, and on its acidity. In the case of some groups (but not all), the colour may change because of the presence of free aluminium ions, which can only be absorbed by the plants if they are growing in acid soil. If your blue-flowered hydrangea eventually turns pink, the amount of absorbed aluminium is too low. This usually suggests that the soil has an excessively high pH (degree of acidity) and sometimes a lack of aluminium. You can solve the latter problem by adding aluminium sulphate to the soil: mix 5 grammes (7 grains) of sulphate with 1 litre (1 3/4 pints) of water. For blue-flowered hydrangeas, the pH should not exceed 5.5.

Plant the blue specimens in rhododendron compost, or in a home-made mixture of conifer compost, or peat with 25 per cent sand or loam.

Always water with softened water or rain water, and only feed in spring until the plant flowers in June. The new shoots will subsequently develop, and should be hardened off quite soon afterwards.

Stand the containerized hydrangea in a cool and shady place in spring. Any pruning should be done immediately after it has flowered, as the new shoots that will produce buds the following year appear soon afterwards.

Move the hydrangea to a sunnier spot at this stage, as that will encourage it to flower more profusely.

These plants absorb a lot of water during the growing season, and should be watered daily. They shed their leaves in autumn, and containerized hydrangeas should be taken indoors before the first night frost (specimens in open ground are hardier). More leaves are shed, and the shrub can best spend the winter in a dark place.

Keep the temperature very low - below 10°C (50°F). Find a lighter position for the plant as soon as the buds begin to form in early spring.

● 0°C (32°F)

Hydrangea macrophylla

Hydrangea petiolaris

CLIMBING HYDRANGEA

When grown in the garden, climbing hydrangeas work their way up very high walls over a number of years. They do so by means of suckering roots attached to woody branches. The flower heads appear at the tips of stems in June. The fertile flowers are

enclosed in a ring of sterile decoys. The dried flowers remain on the plant until well into the winter - a splendid sight.

Climbing hydrangeas originally came from very cold regions such as northern Japan and Sachalin, and are therefore fully hardy. The roots will not even need protecting in a large container, in which the plant will do extremely well.

Hydrangeas grow slowly and remain more compact in a container than in open ground. Containerized specimens consequently need only slight supports up to 2m (6ft) in height. Do not stand the container in full sun, as hydrangeas like cool, slightly acid woodland soil which needs regular watering. Make sure that drainage is adequate. The plant is a real joy in shady positions, especially in a sheltered town garden.

❊

Hymenocallis x festalis

In spring, when the large bulb of the hymenocallis has just been potted up, nothing shows above ground.

It is therefore best to stand the pot among other container plants, preferably somewhere near the patio. The reason for this is that, in the course of summer, very remarkable white flowers with a delightfully sweet fragrance will emerge from a tuft of oblong, apple-green leaves.

The corolla, which resembles those of narcissi, is surrounded by long, curled, strap-shaped leaves. These festive streamers give the flowers their spidery appearance.

This ancient, but still relatively unfamiliar cross between *Hymenocallis longipetala* and *Hymenocallis narcissiflora* is sold as a bulb in spring. Plant in nutritive but very well-drained soil, and water more freely as the leaves grow taller in spring. Stand the pot in a sunny or half-shady position.

While it is in flower, and also afterwards, the hymenocallis will need a lot of watering to store up strength for the following year.

Stop watering in autumn when the leaves turn yellow, and be sure to take the plant indoors before the first night frost. The leafless bulb may overwinter in a cool, airy place, in the dark if need be. Repot the bulb in fresh soil in late winter, and put it in a lighter position. The *Hymenocallis*, often still sold under its old name *Ismene* should not be taken out of doors until the risk of night frosts has passed.

Propagate the plant by seed or by detaching offsets.

● 0°C (32°F)

Hymenocallis x festalis

I

i

Impatiens hawkeri

BUSY LIZZIE, BALSAM

The numerous cultivars of *Impatiens hawkeri* are referred to collectively as New Guinea hybrids, the species having originated there. The foliage of these sturdy plants, which can grow to a height of about 60cm (24in), is often dark. The bright-coloured flowers with their strikingly long nectar guides often contrast sharply with the leaves. The hybrids are usually displayed in mixed consignments collectively labelled New Guinea on the suppliers' stands.

Impatiens hawkeri New Guinea hybrids

Treat them like annual container plants and put them in a semi-shady but warm position. If you keep them growing by watering freely, they will continue flowering from the beginning of the summer until the first night frost. Much water is required as a great deal of moisture is evaporated from the surface of the juicy stems and large leaves, but make sure the roots do not become waterlogged, or they will rot and the impatiens will die. There is no need to feed the plants.

If the summer is excessively wet, flowers and buds may be affected by grey mould. If that occurs, the mouldy parts of the plant should be removed. For propagation, see *Impatiens walleriana*.

(1)

Impatiens linearifolia

See: *Impatiens hawkeri*

Impatiens niamniamensis

This species has succulent stems which can grow to 1m (3ft) long. They produce not only oblong leaves, but also thin stems with a pendent flower at each tip (like a parrot on a perch). The greenish yellow to whitish petals are scarcely noticeable, in contrast with the greatly enlarged sepal, which forms a kind of horn and ends in an inverted nectar guide. It may be red, pinkish red, or red and yellow. The final colour combination is the most

Impatiens niamniamensis

popular one; available cultivars bear such names as 'Arared' and 'Congo Cockatoo'.

Impatiens niamniamensis comes from tropical East Africa, and likes a warm position, sheltered from the wind and fierce midday sunlight. It is a perennial, but in colder countries it is grown as an annual and managed in the same way as the other species of *Impatiens*.

(1)

Impatiens, New Guinea hybrids

See: *Impatiens hawkeri*

Impatiens walleriana

BUSY LIZZIE, BALSAM

The cultivars of this East African balsam are sold mainly as garden annuals. They are, however, very suitable for hanging baskets and troughs for patios and balconies, and for pots in conservatories and living-rooms. In places like Madeira, where frost does not occur, busy lizzies grow into shrubs about 1m (3ft) tall.

Many of the plants sold in other countries are deliberately cultivated as dwarf forms, and subsequently kept small with growth inhibitors. Cultivars belonging to the F1-Explore

Impatiens walleriana F1-Explore series

series, for instance, do not grow taller than 10cm (4in).

In the kind of climate prevailing in countries like the Netherlands, it makes little sense to grow balsam as a perennial. The lack of light in winter causes straggly growth and leaf fall, so that the plants look very much the worse for wear in spring. It is, however, worth keeping your best specimens of *I. walleriana* and *I. hawkeri* through the winter and taking cuttings from them in early spring. They will easily grow roots in water, and can then be potted up. Apart from these exceptions, it is best to sow impatiens under cover in spring.

For general management, see *Impatiens hawkeri*.

(1)

Impatiens walleriana

Iochroma

Iochromas come from the mountainous regions of Latin America, where the air is fresh, but plants are not exposed to prolonged periods of cold weather. Because of their great need for fresh air, iochromas are unsuitable for cultivating as houseplants, but they are an excellent choice for well-ventilated greenhouses, winter gardens, or conservatories.

In summer, iochromas prefer to be out of doors in a warm and sunny position where their fragile stems cannot be damaged by wind. In that kind of warm and sheltered position, the plants need a lot of water and food if they are to continue growing well and to flower in midsummer.

As soon as night temperatures drop below 5°C (41°F), iochomas should be moved to a light and airy place where they can overwinter at temperatures between 10 and 15°C (50 and 59°F). In that way, the plants will hold their leaves, and will only need watering to compensate for what they lose as a result of transpiration. In emergencies, the technique of letting plants overwinter in the dark may be applied. The leaves will then fall, and the plants should not be given any more water. As a result of this treatment, the iochromas will be a little slower in beginning to grow again in spring. Hard pruning in spring and autumn will keep the shrubs a manageable size. Take tip cuttings from non-flowering shoots in summer. They will root easily under glas at a soil temperature of about 20°C (68°F).

○ 5°C (41°F)

Iochroma coccineum

RED IOCHROMA

Red is a rare colour for flowers, because insects cannot see it. Birds, however, are attracted by red, and the red iochromas of Central America are therefore pollinated by hummingbirds. The pendent tubular flowers grow in clusters of between five and eight specimens. For management, see *Iochroma*.

○ 5°C (41°F)

Iochroma cyaneum

BLUE IOCHROMA

The blue iochroma (the literal translation of *Iochroma cyaneum*), flowers more profusely than the other species, and is also the one

Iochroma cyaneum

grown most frequently as a container plant. Even so, the flowers of this species from the northwest Andes are not always blue. When grown from seed, plants are produced which may have lilac, purplish red, or even pinkish red flowers. Nurserymen propagate them by cuttings, and market them under names such as *Iochroma cyaneum* 'Purple' or 'Cherry Red'. For management, see *Iochroma. Iochroma cyaneum*).

○ 5°C (41°F)

Iochroma grandiflorum

LARGE-FLOWERED IOCHROMA

Iochrima grandiflorum comes from Ecuador, grows to over 1m (3ft) tall, and is therefore about half the size of the two other species. The rather more horizontal stems have large,

Iochroma coccineum

Iochroma grandiflorum

very felty leaves, and, at the tips, modest clusters of lilac to crimson flowers, each of which may grow to 7cm (3in) long. It is a graceful species for the genuine enthusiast.
For management, see *Iochroma*.

☼ 5°C (41°F)

Iochroma lanceolatum

See: *Iochroma cyaneum*

Iochroma tubilosum

See: *Iochroma cyaneum*

Ipomoea acuminata

See: *Ipomoea indica*

Ipomoea indica

MORNING GLORY

The mauve, pink, or blue flowers of morning glory are short-lived. They open early in the morning and close up for good the same afternoon.
Devotees of this plant scarcely notice this phenomenon, since new flowers are produced in profusion every day.
In addition to *Ipomoea indica*, there are very similar, more familiar species, which need less warmth; they include *Ipomoea tricolor* (often incorrectly referred to as *Ipomoea violacea*, another species which is rarely cultivated), and *Ipomoea purpurea* (with its well-known large-flowered blue cultivar 'Heavenly Blue').
Ipomoea nil requires a somewhat warmer position. Its flowers vary in colour, but always have white throats.
Choosing a handsome species is further complicated by the large number of cultivars, the confused nomenclature, and the very varying colour of the flowers.
Seed merchants have the unfortunate habit of selling mixed seeds in single packets, and flowers produced in this way will vary in colour and rarely be beautiful. Morning glory is very easy to cultivate.

The plant is frost-tender, and should therefore be sown under cover (*Ipomoea purpurea* and *Ipomoea tricolor* may also be sown out of doors after the last night frost). It is best to pre-soak the seeds in tepid water for 24 hours. All the plant needs is nutritive soil, plenty of water, a warm position, and something round which it can twine.

Use trellis, twigs, string or mesh, and make sure that there is enough of it to let the plant climb to 2m (6ft).
If you sow a seed every 10-20cm (4-8in), the leaves will eventually cover the entire frame, and the wealth of flowers is usually much admired.
The large black seeds, three of which are contained in each round capsule, may be

Ipomoea indica

harvested as soon as the capsule turns a straw-coloured shade of brown.

(1)

Ipomoea learii

See: *Ipomoea indica*

Ipomoea lobata

The flowers of *Ipomoea lobata* fade from red to white, and are quite different from those of other species of morning glory. They are tubular and slightly curved. The colour of each flower changes from orange red to white during its short life.

Ipomoea lobata

The flowers are not produced singly like those of other species.

Instead, they are borne on short stems in racemes of about 25 blooms, the lowest one being the first to open.

Although this Mexican perennial grows very tall in the wild, it is quite low-growing when containerized, and therefore needs less support than other species of *Ipomoea*.

For further management, see *Ipomoea indica.*

(1)

Ipomoea quamoclit

Ipomoea quamoclit

CYPRESS VINE

The twining shoots of *Ipomoea quamoclit* grow calmly up a framework of string or twigs. This makes it a very suitable species for cultivating in pots or containers. The magnificent, deeply lobed leaves and relatively small, but subtle red flowers are produced on the stems. If you sow the small seeds under cover in early spring, the flowers will appear by early summer. It is important to grow this species in a warm and sunny position.For further management, see *Ipomoea indica*.

(1)

Ipomoea versicolor

See: *Ipomoea lobata*

Ismene festalis

See: *Hymenocallis* x *festalis*

Isotoma axillaris

See: *Laurentia axillaris*

J, K   *j, k*

Jacaranda acutifolia

See: *Jacaranda mimosifolia*

Jacaranda mimosifolia

JACARANDA

In southern countries where frosts are unknown, jacarandas are favourite trees and
adorn the streets in spring with the trusses of
flowers varying from mauve to blue that are
borne on their bare branches. The leaves,
large and doubly pinnate, resemble those of
giant ferns, and appear after the tree has
flowered. If the magnificent leaves are your
main interest, the jacaranda will make an
excellent container plant. In theory, flowers
will also appear on shrubs growing to a height
of about 1.5m (5ft), but this only occurs in
favourable conditions, for instance in winter
gardens.
In summer, the jacaranda prefers a sheltered,
sunny spot. It will need a lot of water and
nutritive soil, preferably containing clay.
Good drainage is essential.
There are two ways of helping the shrub or
tree to survive the winter.
If you want the tree to hold its leaves, choose
a light place and keep the minimum temperature at 10°C (41°F). You may, however,
treat *J. mimosifolia* like a deciduous container plant, in which case you should cease
to water it in autumn, after which the leaves
will turn yellow and fall. As soon as the
temperature drops below 5°C (41°F), the tree
should be taken indoors to a dark but airy
position.
The jacaranda may be cut back hard in winter
if required. This reduces the likelihood of the
tree flowering, but it enhances its appeal as a
foliage plant.

☼ 10°C (50°F) or ● 5°C (41°F)

Jacaranda ovalifolia

See: *Jacaranda mimosifolia*

Preceding page: *Jacaranda mimosifolia*

Jacobinia carnea

See: *Justicia carnea*

Jasminum

JASMINE

The approximately 200 species of jasmine,
which grow mainly in tropical Asia and Africa,
include several highly rewarding container
plants. The twining stems produce evergreen
leaves and clusters of star-shaped flowers,
often with a wonderful fragrance. Some species are cultivated especially for the perfume
industry.
As the jasmine species hold their leaves in
winter, they will need a light location. The
minimum temperature during that period will
vary according to the species.
In summer, the various species of jasmine
prefer to be out of doors in large pots or tubs.
Find them a sunny spot with some protection
against the hottest midday sun. The very
vigorous species will consume a great deal of
water and food. In autumn, make sure that the
root balls are dry before moving the plants
indoors.
If the shoots fail to climb in the required
direction, you may lend a hand by training
them. Cut back old straggly shoots as far as
possible after flowering; this will enable the
plant to keep its characteristic shape. If you
cut off the shoots halfway, you will be left
with a shrubby plant full of unsightly pruned
stumps.
In spring and summer, you may take semi-ripe
cuttings from non-flowering shoots, and let
them root in sandy soil at about 20°C (68°F).

☼ 5°C (41°F)

Jasminum azoricum

JASMINE

Jasminum azoricum comes from the Azores,
the group of islands in the Atlantic where the
surrounding ocean has a moderating effect on
the climate and there are no frosts at sea level.
In a container, the twining climber will grow

Jasminum azoricum

rapidly to a height of 1.5 to 2m (5 to 6ft).It bears clusters of fragrant white flowers, up to 2cm (3/4in) across, from July to September. *Jasminum azoricum* closely resembles *Jasminum officinale* (Common jasmine, Jessamine), which also bears fragrant white flowers in late summer. It is easy, however, to tell them apart. *Jasminum azoricum* has leaves consisting of three leaflets, with the largest one in the centre, whereas those of *Jasminum officinale* consist of at least five leaflets.

For management, see *Jasminum*.

☼ 5°C (41°F)

Jasminum humile

YELLOW JASMINE

The yellow jasmine grows more like a shrub than a climber, although it has long lax shoots. This untidy bush may ultimately grow about 5m (16ft) tall, although this can be prevented by pruning. The species grows naturally in a very extensive area stretching from Asia Minor to Burma, and many different forms are known. Some authorities also regard the yellow-flowered species *Jasminum odoratissimum* from Madeira and the Canary Islands as belonging to *Jasminum humile*. The yellow flowers of *Jasminum humile* are borne in small, almost umbellate clusters in summer.

They have scarcely any fragrance. The cultivar 'Revolutum', however, which is most frequently for sale, has fragrant flowers. For management, see *Jasminum*.

☼ 5°C (41°F)

Jasminum nitidum

The flowers of this shrubby jasmine are relatively large, and are distinguished by their large number of petals.
The red-tinged green calyx at the base of the flower tube is strikingly star-shaped.
The plant begins to flower in midsummer, and continues until well into the autumn, even after this rather tender plant has been moved indoors early in the season.

☼ 10°C (50°F)

Jasminum nitidum

Jasminum humile 'Revolutum'

Jasminum polyanthum

Jasminum polyanthum is on sale as a flowering houseplant in winter. To achieve this effect, however, growers are obliged to force the evergreen climber from western China, as its natural flowering period is in summer. The strong sweet fragrance of its flowers will scent the entire house. It is an excellent species to grow as a container plant on a patio.

When cultivated as a houseplant, *Jasminum*

Jasminum polyanthum

polyanthum begins to grow frenziedly after flowering, and you will rarely succeed in making it flower again. This may be possible, however, if you manage it like a container plant. Let it continue to grow (without flowering) throughout the summer, and then cut it back as required in autumn. Let it overwinter in a cold, light place without giving it much water. Make sure that the temperature falls to below 10°C (50°F) from time to time. That is the secret for encouraging the plant to flower again!

☼ 0°C (32°F)

Jasminum sambac

ARABIAN JASMINE

The Arabian jasmine is thought to have come originally from India and is regarded as belonging to the tropical flora. Its wonderfully fragrant creamy white flowers are used in oriental cookery, and also for making tea. Arabian jasmine flowers from spring until far into autumn, though not profusely. This climber grows relatively slowly, and is therefore easier to keep in check than some of the

Jasminum sambac

other species of jasmine. Because of its tropical origins, however, it should overwinter in a fairly warm location.

☼ 10°C (50°F)

Juanulloa aurantiaca

See: *Juanulloa mexicana*

Juanulloa mexicana

In Central and South America, *Juanulloa mexicana*'s clusters of orange flowers are borne high up in the trees. The low-growing shrub is not rooted in the soil, but in the tree itself. It was thought at one time that the shrub was parasitic, hence its obsolete name *Juanulloa parasitica*. Its roots, however, merely clasp the host tree: the plant is in fact an epiphyte.

As a container plant, *Juanulloa* should be cultivated in ordinary humus-rich potting compost. In summer, stand the pot in the warmest place possible, where it is both sunny and sheltered, or the tropical plant will not come into flower in time in late summer. The flowers are borne on short stems; the oblong orange buds are slightly ribbed, thus causing five longitudinal grooves to be formed. The buds split open at the tips, thus releasing the tubular orange flowers which, judging by their shape and colour, need to be pollinated by birds. It remains to be seen whether the *Juanulloa* is here to stay as a container plant. If enthusiasts are not sufficiently successful in making their plants flower exuberantly, the *juanulloa* will be returned to the hothouses where the species has been flowering since 1840.

Water freely in summer, but ensure perfect

Juanulloa mexicana

Justicia carnea

drainage. Temperatures below 10°C (50°F) are undesirable, and this evergreen plant, with leaves from 10 to 20 (4 to 8in) long, should be taken indoors early. Let it overwinter in a light place and preferably keep the temperature at about 15°C (59°F). The plant needs very little water in winter, and the shoots may be cut back to about two pairs of leaves in spring.

☼ 10°C (50°F)

Juanulloa parasitica

See: *Juanulloa mexicana*

Justicia carnea

KING'S CROWN

Keeping the houseplant *Justicia carnea* (usually sold as *Jacobinia carnea*) out of doors in summer has become common practice recently. The atmosphere in living-rooms is often too dry for this ornamental shrub from South America, where it grows about 2m (6ft) tall. The word *carnea* refers to the flesh-coloured flowers which are borne from midsummer until well into autumn. By taking cuttings in autumn, growers manage to market flowering plants from April onwards.

By June, it is safe to move *Justicia* out of doors. It prefers a warm position, but not in burning hot sun. If you water freely, and feed the plant regularly, the shoots will rapidly form a dense bush with glossy dark green leaves. Stop feeding the plant after it has flowered. It will then harden off, but should be moved indoors when the nights turn colder. In winter, *Justicia* prefers to be kept almost dry in a light location, preferably at a

temperature around 15°C (59°F). If it sheds a lot of leaves, and consequently becomes permanently bare lower down, it is best to renew the plant very early in spring. Take semi-ripe tip cuttings in February or March, insert them in warm, moist soil, and cover with plastic sheeting. The young plant may flower the same year.In addition to the species with pink- to flesh-coloured flowers, there is also a pure white form, which is not, however, sold under a separate name.

☼ 10°C (50°F)

Justicia ovatica

See: *Dicliptera suberecta*

Justicia suberecta

See: *Dicliptera suberecta*

Kalanchoe manginii

In Madagascar, *Kalanchoe manginii* creeps along the ground. Its short shoots sometimes end in a stem with pendent bell-shaped flowers. The other stems produce complete little plants at their tips, so that an entire mat of *Kalanchoe* is eventually formed.

The cultivar *Kalanchoe manginii* 'Tessa' was developed from the wild species, and is a popular plant for a light position in a living-room or on a patio. In summer, it can only be admired as a foliage plant, as the flowers do not appear until there are fewer than 12 hours of daylight. This 'short-day' plant therefore does not flower until autumn, winter, or early spring. Hang it in your living-room while it is in flower. Afterwards, 'Tessa' will benefit from a period of rest, when it will need hardly any water, and should be put in a cool and light location. After a few months, you may reactivate the plant by giving it more water and warmth.

☼ 5°C (41°F)

Kennedia coccinea

The fast-growing shoots of this Australian climber become woody and can eventually carry the entire plant. Cultivated in this way, it will grow into an airy shrub or small tree about 2m (6ft) tall, with arching stems. Its ternate, greyish-green leaves are sufficient reason for acquiring this container plant. In summer, moreover, it will bear magnificent bright red flowers, which you can admire at eye level. Transparent drops of nectar are suspended from the flower stems and reflect the sun. This sweet secretion is intended to keep ants away from the flowers, because the nectar inside them is reserved for the flying insects that will ensure effective cross-pollination by taking the pollen to other plants further away. Ants are kept happy with the sweet bogus nectar. Cultivate *Kennedia* in a large pot with sandy soil and include a support. Stand the pot in a warm and sunny

Kennedia coccinea

position in summer, and water moderately. The plant should overwinter in a light, airy, cool location and should be given very little water, although the soil should never dry out entirely. In summer, propagate kennedias by taking cuttings which will root in soil at room temperature within several weeks.

Alternatively, propagate by seed. In that case, you should first scrape a weak spot in the thick testa or immerse the seeds in boiling water. They should then be left to swell up in the cooling water for 24 hours. Preferably sow in spring at a soil temperature around 20°C (68°F).

☼ 5°C (41°F)

Kalanchoe manginii 'Tessa'

L

l

Lagerstroemia indica

CRAPE MYRTLE

With their slender stems and wavy petals with contrasting yellow stamens, the flowers of *Lagerstroemia indica* have a fairy-tale quality. In a greenhouse or conservatory, this old-fashioned container plant will flower profusely in late summer. If grown out of doors, it will require a warm position, and will not begin to flower until August. Even so, you will be able to enjoy the flowers over a long period, as this plant from eastern Asia will tolerate light frost and need not be moved indoors until late in the year. The shrub will shed its leaves in autumn and should then be cut back hard. If you keep the plant in a cold and dark location in winter, and give it scarcely any water, it will survive in very good condition. Shoots produced indoors in spring are often lax and are best removed in late spring. After it has been taken out of doors again in spring, the *Lagerstroemia* will begin its race against the clock. At first, provide extra food in well-drained soil, which should preferably contain considerable amounts of sand and clay. From the end of June, you should cease to add any nitrogenous fertilizer, as that will stimulate vigorous growth rather than flowers. The species bears pink flowers, those of the countless cultivars may be brick red, deep red, purple, lavender, or white.

● –5°C (23°F)

Lagerstroemia indica

Preceding page: *Lantana camara*

Lagunaria patersonii

NORFOLK ISLAND HIBISCUS, QUEENSLAND PYRAMIDAL TREE

This magnificent ornamental tree adorns the parks of Madeira and the Canary Islands. Its flowers are borne successively for months on end, and closely resemble those of the hibiscus, a plant to which it is closely related. Its English name refers to the Pacific island east of Australia, one of the places where it grew originally. This wonderful container plant may be kept bushy by pruning: restrict its height to about 1.5m (5ft) and its spread to 1m (3ft).

Lagunaria patersonii

The plant holds its leathery leaves in winter, and a well-lit location is therefore required. It should also be cool and airy (5-10°C/41-50°F), which creates problems for many devotees. Higher temperatures combined with a stuffy atmosphere will cause infestation by red spider mite.
Water very sparingly in winter; sprinkle the plants in spring.

A warm and sunny position is ideal in summer. Water regularly but sparingly.

☼ 2°C (36°F)

Lantana camara

Lantana camara really is one of the easiest container plants to cultivate. It originally came from tropical America.
It was grown as an ornamental garden plant in other hot regions, but often became rampant, and in some places even developed into a real nuisance.

Lantana camara

In some countries, only cultivars of the species are available, and they should really be called the *Lantana Camara* group.
They develop into shrubs about 1.5m (5ft) tall, with a spread of around 1m (3ft), but it is also possible so to prune them that they grow into small trees.
Tip-prune excessively tall main shoots, and remove side shoots; any regrowth along the stem should be removed consistently. If you persevere, the young stem will grow bushy at the top, especially if you tip-prune the young shoots a few more times.
Lantana grows so fast that a cutting which rooted in spring may flower during the summer of the same year.
Plenty of water and ample fertilizer in well-drained soil are all that it requires.
The tubular flowers emerge from a single head in groups of about twenty.
They may be white, yellow, orange, red, pink or lilac pink, often two of these colours combined.

Lantana camara

The flowers change colour as they mature: orange will turn deep red, and yellow frequently turns pink. It is perhaps because of the plant's unpredictable nature that the various colour forms are not usually sold as named cultivars.
Lantanas may be taken out of doors after the final night frost, preferably to a sunny position. Move them indoors again just before the first night frost, so that the plants can harden off out of doors for as long as possible. A light location and preferably a temperature around 10°C (50°F) are adequate for the winter.

If you store the plant in the dark, a large proportion of the leaves will fall, and it will be slow to recover in spring. Rigorous pruning in

Lantana camara

154

early spring will ensure a bushier plant in summer.

○ or ● 2°C (36°F)

Lantana camara 'Aloha'

Lantana camara and *Lantana montevidensis* were the principal species used for the development of cultivars.

'Aloha' is classified as belonging to the Camara group, but is considerably smaller and more pendulous, like *Lantana montevidensis*.

The magnificent green and yellowish-green foliage shows up particularly well in hanging baskets.

Make sure that the leaves of this cultivar remain on the plant in winter.

For further maintenance, see *Lantana camara*.

○ 5°C (41°F)

Lantana camara 'Aloha'

Lantana montevidensis

Lantana montevidensis' flowers only change colour when cold autumn nights make them turn pinker.

In normal circumstances, the flower heads are lilac to violet in colour, often with a contrasting light spot in the centre of each small flower.

The flowers, like those of *Lantana camara*, attract butterflies, and this light honey guide helps their probosces in their search for nectar.

Lantana montevidensis is a spreading rather than an upright shrub, with soft, pendulous

Lantana montevidensis

stems. The plant is usually suspended in a large pot or basket, or placed on a pedestal, to display its trailing growth to better advantage. When given sufficient moisture and food, the plant will flower all summer.

For management, see *Lantana camara*.

○ or ● 5°C (41°F)

Lantana sellowiana

See: *Lantana montevidensis*

Lapageria rosea

CHILEAN BELLFLOWER, COPIHUE

Lapageria is the national flower of Chile, where the climber grows on damp wooded slopes in the middle of the country. There, on the western side of the Andes, the air is fresh, and the plant therefore prefers an outdoor position in summer. Specimens cultivated in greenhouses often need airing to prevent infestation by red spider mite or woolly aphid. The plant likes a light, but not excessively sunny position out of doors - full morning or evening sun is ideal. In the middle of the day, the climber (which, because of its slow growth, may be trained up a modest trellis) prefers to be lightly shaded by trees, shrubs, or other container plants. In such a position, *Lapageria* will also be sheltered from the wind, and the humidity will remain high. Ideal summer temperatures are between 15 and 25°C (15 and 77°F).

The plant requires light, humus-rich soil, preferably containing some clay as well as sand and peat. Do not water until the soil has dried out entirely, and feed in spring and early

Lapageria rosea

The small *Laurentia*, which is also called *Solenopsis* or *Isotoma*, will probably manage to do so. The plant remains compact, and has dense foliage consisting of characteristic, small oblong leaves. The complete clump grows about 10cm (4in) tall, with a spread of 15cm (6in). During its long flowering period (from early June until the first severe frost) fresh mauvish-blue flowers appear continually between the leaves. They are longer than they are wide, with a long flower tube and five petals which appear to form a small star (hence its name 'Blue Stars'). The small plants are not very striking in a summer border, but

Laurentia axillaris 'Blue Stars'

summer only. If the plant is managed in this way, magnificent oblong flowers will develop between the glossy green foliage in late summer and autumn. The flowers consist of six pinkish-red petals, often flecked, and 7 to 10cm (2 3/4 to 4in) long! After a hot summer, oblong yellow fruits are produced; they are edible, about 4cm (1 3/4in) long, and contain a lot of seeds. Although *Lapageria* will tolerate several degrees of frost in open ground, a containerized specimen should be moved indoors well before the frosts begin. The plant holds its leaves, and therefore requires a light location. It dislikes a dry atmosphere, and therefore prefers a fairly cool position, at a temperature between 5 and 14°C (41 and 57°F). The plants needs scarcely any water during the winter. The genus *Lapageria* consists of only one species, *rosea*, of which there is a white-flowered variety: *Lapageria rosea* var. *alba*. Many cultivars with flowers in various colours have also been developed, especially in Chile. The best-known examples are 'Flesh Pink', with flesh-coloured flowers, and 'Nash Court', which bears carmine flowers with darker venation.

☼ 5°C (41°F)

Laurentia axillaris 'Blue Stars'

Whenever a new plant is brought on to the market, it is always necessary to wait and see whether it will live up to expectations.

they show up all the more in a balcony trough, a pot, or a hanging basket. This perennial is grown as an annual because it is frost-tender. If you would like it to flower early (from May onwards), you should sow in June-July of the previous year. The seedlings may overwinter out of doors in a mild winter (with some cover if it is frosty), but it is better to keep them in a cool, light place, preferably a greenhouse or conservatory. If you prefer them to flower in late summer, sow in January-February. Most enthusiasts will buy *Laurentia* as an annual, even though it is possible to help it survive the winter in a light and cool location. Water *Laurentia* freely while it is in full growth, but make sure that excess water can drain away satisfactorily. A plant in moist soil may be placed in full sun, though some afternoon shade is preferable.

(1)

Laurus azorica

LAUREL

The remains of a type of forest that became extinct on the continent of Europe during the Ice Age, live on in Madeira, the Canary Islands, and the Azores. This is the *Laurussilva*, the laurel wood which, in addition to *Laurus azorica*, contains countless trees, perennials and mosses which have survived only in the damp mountain forests of those islands. Because of the moderating effect of the surrounding ocean, frosts do not occur. *Laurus azorica* prefers a half-shady, sheltered position out of doors in summer. It will grow very well in standard potting compost with normal amounts of water, and does not need feeding. Take the evergreen shrub indoors before the frosts begin. A light cool environment, where the humidity does not drop excessively, constitutes an ideal winter position for this plant. As soon as the temperature rises above freezing, even in winter, the plant should be moved out of doors again. The leaves of *Laurus azorica* are not fragrant, and cannot be used for culinary purposes. The species is only for sale at highly specialized nurseries.

☼ 2°C (36°F)

Laurus azorica

Laurus canariensis

See: *Laurus azorica*

Laurus nobilis

Laurus nobilis

BAY LAUREL, SWEET BAY

The common laurel has been a favourite for centuries because of its fragrant leaves. In Roman times, victors in battle were honoured with a laurel wreath. Flavouring food with bay leaves is also an ancient custom.

The evergreen shrub originally grew in Mediterranean regions. In the late Middle Ages, the laurel was one of the first plants to be cultivated as a container plant in more northerly countries. *Laurus nobilis* is simple to clip into all kinds of shapes, and, nowadays, the front door of a stylish house is often flanked by two bay trees trimmed into pyramids, cones, spheres, or standards.

The shrubs make few demands as far as soil and position are concerned. Use a spacious container to prevent the plant being blown over easily, and ensure perfect drainage to prevent root rot.

In open ground, bay trees will tolerate temperatures as low as -10°C (14°F). Containerized specimens should be moved indoors during prolonged periods of light frost or short periods of more severe frost. Stand the shrub in a light (dark in emergencies), airy, and cool position and scarcely water. The bay tree should be taken out of doors again as soon as weather conditions permit.

Clusters of creamy yellow flowers are produced in spring. They are dioecious, and you

157

will therefore need a male as well as a female shrub to be able to admire the black berries in late summer.

○ or ● –5°C (23°F)

Lavandula angustifolia

LAVENDER

The common lavender comes from the regions bordering the western Mediterranean but, in spite of that, it is well able to withstand winters in more northerly countries. Even in a container, it may remain out of doors if the winter is not too severe. At temperatures below -10°C (14°F), the roots will need some protection, for instance by putting the pot in a hole in the garden and covering it with branches of evergreens or straw (dig the hole before the ground freezes).

Lavandula angustifolia

In summer, the greyish shrub prefers full sun. Ideally, the soil should be light, sandy, and mixed with some limy clay, but plants cultivated in standard potting compost also do well. Ensure good drainage and do not water until the soil has dried out almost entirely, as lavender definitely dislikes waterlogged roots. Cultivating lavender causes no further problems, and you will be able to enjoy the spikes of fragrant blue flowers in late summer. Cut off a bunch on a hot day, and hang it up to dry. Later on, you will be able to put the lavender among your clothes or household linen to give them a delightful fragrance.

❊

Lavandula officinalis

See: *Lavandula angustifolia*

Lavatera acerifolia

See: *Lavatera maritima*

Lavatera arborea

TREE MALLOW

The tree mallow's stems ripen to form a knobbly trunk with thick branches. Abundant clusters of lilac flowers with aubergine-coloured streaks in the centre are borne on the plant's numerous stems during the first summer after it was sown. They are followed by the typical 'cheese-shaped' fruits. The plant is a biennial and is easily propagated from seed.

Lavatera arborea

Put the tree mallow in a large tub or pot filled with light, sandy soil. Water moderately and do not feed. Stand the pot in a very sunny position, where the leaves will remain a lovely shade of greyish green. The plant prefers a light, dry location indoors in winter.

○ 0°C (32°F)

Lavatera bicolor

See: *Lavatera maritima*

Lavatera maritima

BUSH MALLOW

At garden centres and specialist nurseries, you will also find *Lavatera maritima* labelled *Lavatera acerifolia* or *Lavatera bicolor*. The latter name obviously refers to the flower's two colours. Because this species is more fragile than other lavateras, it is highly suitable for growing in containers. Light soil, average moisture, and a sunny position are all it requires in summer. In winter, it prefers a well-lit location and almost dry potting compost. If you cut back the plant in early spring, you will encourage the development of a fine, compact shape.

☼ 0°C (32°F)

Lavatera olbia

See: *Lavatera thuringiaca*

Lavatera thuringiaca 'Rosea'

Lavatera thuringiaca

BUSH MALLOW

This bush mallow, officially called *Lavatera olbia* nowadays, will easily grow to 2m (6ft) in height, and requires a large pot or tub. In

Lavatera maritima

regions with a mild climate, the species is fully hardy in open ground (minimum temperature about -10°C/14°F).

Use light potting compost, water moderately, and do not feed. If this method is adopted, the plant will produce an abundance of flowers rather than excessive foliage. The flowers of the popular cultivar *Lavatera* 'Rosea' are deep pink. The plant should be kept fairly dry in a cool and, above all, light environment in winter.

☼ 0°C (32°F)

Leonotis leonurus

LION'S EAR

This South African herbaceous perennial can grow to 2m (6ft) in height, and produces whorls of orange flowers in late summer and autumn. In spring, when the frosts have ceased, the plant may be placed in a sunny, sheltered spot out of doors. As it prefers moist, nutritive soil, it should be given water

Leonotis leonurus

and fertilizer regularly. From about August, new whorls of flowers are borne successively in tiers starting from the bottom, and the plant is likely to be in full flower when it needs to be moved indoors after the first night frost. *Leonotis leonurus* var. *alba* and the cultivar 'Harrismith White' have white flowers.

Let the plant overwinter in a cool location, and keep the soil almost dry during that period. As the leaves will fall anyway, a well-lit winter storage space is not absolutely necessary. Cut the plant back hard in spring and and renew the potting compost.

☼ or ● 0°C (32°F)

Leonotis ocymifolia

See: *Leonotis leonurus*

Leptospermum citratum

See: *Leptospermum petersonii*

Leptospermum petersonii

In addition to the well-known *Leptospermum scoparium*, which is for sale at every garden centre, there are countless other beautiful species of *Leptospermum* which, unfortunately, are only available from specialized container plant nurseries. They include: *Leptospermum polygalifolium* (better known as *L. flavescens*), *Leptospermum laevigatum*, *Leptospermum lanigerum* (the least frost-tender species), *Leptospermum rupestre*, and *Leptospermum petersonii* (better known as *L. citratum*). All these make magnificent container plants.

Leptospermum petersonii, from eastern Australia, has a loose habit, white flowers in summer, and lemon-scented foliage. The shrub is frost-tender, but may otherwise be managed just like *Leptospermum scoparium*.

☼ 2°C (36°F)

Leptospermum petersonii

160

Leptospermum scoparium

In mainland Australia, New Zealand, and Tasmania, *Leptospermum scoparium* develops into a spreading shrub or low-growing tree. In northern countries, the species is often sold as a houseplant. That, however, is not the right environment for the shrub, which likes fresh air and will only flower again after overwintering in a cool environment.

Put the plant out of doors, on a windy balcony if need be, but at least in the fresh air and in full sun or partial shade. In English coastal regions, the species is used as a windbreak, as *Leptospermum* can easily withstand salty winds. In a pot, the plant prefers light, acid soil - moorland soil is ideal. Do not water too freely, but do not let the roots dry out either. Although the plant will tolerate temperatures as low as -10°C (14°F), a containerized specimen needs to be taken indoors to a light, cool place after the first frost. A conservatory or unheated greenhouse is ideal, because the plant needs a cool period (maximum temperature 10°C/50°F) to develop buds. The plant needs very little water in winter until it can go out of doors again in early spring, where it will produce a profusion of pink-tinged white flowers later on.

A great many cultivars have been developed from this species, with flowers in every shade from white to pale pink to carmine. Some are single, with five petals, others are fully double, which immediately detracts from their graceful appearance.

☼ 0°C (32°F)

Leptospermum scoparium (fully double cultivar)

Ligularia tussilaginea

See: *Farfugium japonicum*

Leptospermum scoparium

Ligustrum coriaceum

See: *Ligustrum japonicum* 'Rotundifolium'

Ligustrum japonicum

JAPANESE PRIVET

In addition to the native *Ligustrum vulgare* and the Japanese privet *Ligustrum ovalifolium*, which is generally used for hedging purposes nowadays, there are also some fully evergreen species of privet which do very well in tubs or large pots. *Ligustrum japonicum* is the best-known example. It grows naturally in

Ligustrum japonicum 'Rotundifolium'

Ligustrum japonicum 'Texanum'

Japan and Korea, but in colder countries it is sometimes cultivated out of doors in summer and winter, although some protection is needed during severe winters.

Containerized specimens should be moved indoors when there is a slight frost, and put in a cool, light place. They should be taken back out of doors again as soon as the weather permits, because the plant likes fresh air. An unheated greenhouse is an ideal place for it to overwinter.

The cultivar most frequently available is *Ligustrum japonicum* 'Rotundifolium', as this small-leafed form grows into an attractive compact shape (rarely taller than 1m/3ft). Another one, *Ligustrum japonicum* 'Texanum', grows much taller, with strong, leathery leaves, and large panicles of fragrant white flowers in late summer.

Stand these privets in full sun or partial shade and give them average amounts of water.

☼ –5°C (23°F)

Ligustrum lucidum

CHINESE PRIVET

In China, Japan, and Korea, *Ligustrum lucidum* grows into a tree-shaped shrub, about 10m (33ft) in height. It grows rapidly, even in a container. The shrub tolerates slightly less cold than *Ligustrum japonicum*, and should therefore be taken indoors immediately after the first night frost. Only those with plenty of space will be able to accommodate this handsome, large-leafed, evergreen shrub. The leaf size varies considerably. A great many cultivars have been developed from this highly variable species, including the handsome *Ligustrum lucidum* 'Excelsum Superbum', a variegated form with deep-yellow, white-flecked leaves. For management, see: *Ligustrum japonicum*.

☼ 0°C (32°F)

Ligustrum lucidum

Ligustrum magnoliifolium

See: *Ligustrum lucidum*

Linaria

See: *Cymbalaria*

Lithodora diffusa

Lithodoras have tiny flowers in delicate shades similar to those of borage, to which the plant is in fact related. They emerge from hairy buds at the tips of prostrate shoots from May until August.

This small creeping shrub, native to the western part of southern Europe, is highly suitable for edging purposes in troughs or tubs, but it also looks extremely well by itself in a handsome pot. Even though the stems will trail over the rim, they are so transparent that they will not hide the pot itself. If you prefer a bushier growth, tip-prune the shoots in late summer after they have flowered.

In open ground, lithodoras will withstand temperatures as low as -15°C (°5F), provided

Lithodora diffusa 'Heavenly Blue'

the soil is dry. A well-drained soil mixture is also the key to success when growing container plants. Always let the sandy mixture (which must be lime-free) dry up before

watering. There is no need to feed the plant. An unheated greenhouse or cold frame is ideal for the plant in winter, but other light, cool locations are also suitable.

Keep the soil almost dry during this season.

Lithodoras are usually listed under perennials in plant catalogues.

They also include the lovely cultivars currently on the market: the light blue *Lithodora diffusa* 'Cambridge Blue', which is slightly more frost-tender than the species, whereas the azure *Lithodora diffusa* 'Heavenly Blue' tolerates rather more frost. The latter may be planted, in its pot, in a dry spot in the garden in its pot.

○ –5°C (23°F) or ❄

Lithospermum diffusum

See: *Lithodora diffusa*

Lobelia erinus

TRAILING LOBELIA

Quite a number of lovely cultivars of *Lobelia erinus*, usually labelled trailing lobelia, are on sale in spring. Their stems trail like curtains over the rims of pots and flower for months provided you do not forget to water and feed them regularly. If that is neglected, the stems

Lobelia erinus

become woody and the South African plant will begin a period of dormancy. In that case, cut back the stems drastically and give the plant adequate amounts of water and food. Its speed of recovery will surprise you.

Lobelia erinus may be cultivated in pots on a patio, and is highly suitable for hanging baskets and as underplanting in flower troughs. It is possible to keep the plants through the winter, but sowing them in spring is simpler.

(1)

Lobelia 'Richardii'

The cultivar *Lobelia* 'Richardii' closely resembles *Lobelia erinus*, but is grown from cuttings. This trailing plant is slightly more robust and flowers considerably longer, until well into autumn. You will, however, need to pay for such advantages, as these plants are considerably more expensive than the type grown from seed.

For cultivation, applications, and management, see *Lobelia erinus*.

(1)

Lobelia 'Richardii'

Lobelia tupa

Lobelia tupa is one of the very latest container plants, and is currently available only from specialist growers. This situation is likely to change fairly soon, as the plant is quite striking, and always causes a great deal of discussion among visitors to my garden. Its appearance is very special, with deep-red flowers contrasting magnificently with the greyish-green foliage.

Lobelia tupa

The plant originally came from Chile, and prefers the sunniest and warmest spot in the garden. Fill its pot or tub with ordinary soil and water moderately. It will tolerate a little frost in autumn. Ultimately, however, even this treasure needs to be taken indoors to a place that is cool, light, and as airy as possible. A greenhouse or conservatory would be ideal. Water sufficiently to prevent the root ball from drying out entirely.

☼ 0°C (32°F)

Lobelia valida

Lobelia valida's small flowers superficially resemble those of *Lobelia erinus*. The difference between the two plants is that *L. valida* is not immediately pendulous, but first grows upright for about 50cm (20in), after which the stems eventually begin to trail

Lobelia valida

untidily over the edge of the container. Starting at the lower end of the stems, the flowers begin to appear by the end of May, and will continue to be produced for several months. Propagate this perennial from seed, and let it overwinter in a light, cool, and frost-free location. The plant will retain most of its leaves in winter. Water very sparingly at that time.

☼ 2°C (36°F)

Lobularia maritima

SWEET ALYSSUM

Sweet alyssum is one of the best-known and most rewarding plants for edging purposes and flower troughs. These very low-growing, herb-like shrubs flower continuously from May until far into autumn. The brown seeds fall in a small membrane, and germinate in spring or autumn, particularly between stones and in sandy soil. Seeds may be sown out of doors from April onwards, or a little earlier in a pot indoors. Just a few plants will be enough to let you enjoy a pot full of white, fragrant flowers throughout the summer. Do not sow the seeds too close together.

Sweet alyssum is particularly suitable for growing in containers. Its roots like warmth, and poor, well-drained soil. Do not water too freely and do not feed. If flowering declines, cut back the plant halfway, after which it will produce fresh foliage and flower again.

Numerous dwarf cultivars, with flowers in very diverse colours, have been developed from the white-flowered species, which originally came from southern Europe. They include: *Lobularia maritima* 'Avalanche' (profusely and early-flowering, off-white);

'Creamery' (low-growing, warm shade of ivory); 'Navy Blue' (purple flowers); 'New Apricot' (cream with an apricot bloom); 'Rosario' (early-flowering, deep pink); 'Rosie O'Day' (spreading, fragrant, lavender-pink flowers); 'Royal Carpet' (fragrant, deep purple flowers); and 'Sneeuwkleed' (spreading, white).

(1)

Lobularia maritima 'New Apricot'

Lotus berthelotii

PARROT'S BEAK, CORAL GEM

This creeping shrub, related to the common bird's-foot, grows on sun-drenched hillsides in the Canary and Cape Verde Islands. In more temperate countries, it adds an exotic touch to a greenhouse, conservatory, or warm and sunny spot out of doors.

It has straggly branches with small greyish-green leaves resembling pine needles. Short shoots with strangely formed flowers - usually two, but sometimes more - sprout between them. The flowers resemble raised beaks, hence their English name parrot's beak. Their colour varies from blood red to orange yellow.

Lotus berthelotii will only flower in a sunny position, and the potting compost must not be left to dry out while it is in full growth. Feed the plant regularly with liquid fertilizer, or use a granular slow-acting plant food. If you keep to these rules, new flowers will be formed continually at the tips of the shoots - which grow to about 1m (3ft) long - from late spring until the end of summer.

Cut back the plant hard after flowering, to give it a good, bushy shape. The parrot's beak should be taken indoors in autumn for overwintering in a cool, dry location. The root

Lotus berthelotii

Like the underside of the light to bronze-green leaves, the stems are deep pink with light brown hairs. Compact racemes of bright yellow flowers with red centres are borne at the tips of pendulous shoots in spring and, after an interval, late summer. They arch elegantly over the edges of pots, baskets, and balcony troughs. Unfortunately, the plant does not flower right through the summer.

Lysimachia congestiflora

ball should be kept almost dry at a winter temperature between 5 and 15°C (41 and 59°F). If the plant is kept in too warm an environment in winter, it will not flower well the following season.

Propagate in late summer by pulling short, heeled side-shoots off the main stem. Put the cuttings in moist, sandy soil and stand in a warm and light, but not excessively sunny, position. It is also possible to sow *Lotus* indoors in spring.

☼ 5°C (41°F)

Lycianthes rantonnetii

See: *Solanum rantonnetii*

Lysimachia congestiflora

LOOSESTRIFE

Most species of loosestrife are difficult to keep in check and, because of their preference for constantly moist soil, they are also difficult to cultivate in containers.

Lysimachia congestiflora, originally Chinese in origin, is exceptional in both respects. This species has only been on the market since 1992, but has already become very popular.

Loosestrife is satisfied with standard potting compost, a sunny or half-shady position, and average amounts of water.

Although this evergreen plant will tolerate a few degrees of frost, it is better to take it indoors to a cool, light, and well-ventilated location in winter.

Propagation by layering is extremely simple. The stems produce aerial roots, which easily take root when in contact with the soil, without any further action being required.

There are currently also a few cultivars on the market: *Lysimachia congestiflora* 'Lissy', which does not differ much from the species, and the brand new *Lysimachia congestiflora* 'Outback Sunset', which does not flower very readily, but has beautiful variegated foliage. Its leaves are yellowish green with a pattern of green spots along their midribs.

☼ 0°C (32°F)

M

m

Mackaya bella

Mackaya's large, magnificent flowers would undoubtedly make it one of the most desirable of all container plants, were it not that this shrub also has some drawbacks: a short flowering season and no simple way of accommodating it in winter.

The white to pale violet flowers appear in early summer, and last for about two to three weeks.

Because the shrub is evergreen, it needs a light, airy, frost-free location in winter. If it continues to grow, the lax shoots should be cut back hard in spring.

The plant likes a warm and sunny position in summer, but it should also be airy, preferably in a conservatory or well-ventilated greenhouse, or else out of doors in a sheltered spot.

Fill the pot with nutritive and very well-drained potting compost, water freely, and feed it regularly when in full growth.

☼ 5°C (41°F)

Malphigia coccigera

The glossy green leaves of *Malphigia coccigera* have a few spines, and this shrub, which grows to a maximum of 1m (3ft) in height, is therefore also called mini-holly. The branches grow into a compact shape, and are easy to prune. Pale pink flowers with fimbriate petals are borne repeatedly throughout the summer.

The shrub is a native of the Caribbean region, but it is also grown as a hedging plant in the southern states of the US. The plant likes humid heat, and therefore prefers to be out of doors in a sunny or semi-shady position during the hottest months. Water moderately and make sure that the roots do not become waterlogged.

In winter, the *Malphigia* prefers a place that is light but not too cool (about 15°C/59°F). It will therefore need watering from time to time to prevent the evergreen foliage from drying out.

☼ 10°C (50°F)

Mackaya bella

Malphigia coccigera

Malus 'Flamenco'

Malus 'Flamenco'

Even the smallest garden or balcony has room for an apple tree such as this *Malus* 'Flamenco', which is highly suitable for cultivating in a container. It has a vertical trunk and produces short side-shoots. Even without pruning, they remain so short that the small tree never becomes top-heavy. Wind has little effect on it.

The pinkish-white flowers appear in mid-May, and are followed in autumn by firm, dark red apples. 'Flamenco' apples, which belong to the Cox group, are ready to pick in October, and may be stored for a long time afterwards.

Cultivate the apple in clayey, nutritive, and definitely well-drained soil. Keep the soil slightly moist at all times, and add some fertilizer in the period between flowering and harvesting.

The tree may remain out of doors in winter, but stand it against the house, and wrap it in straw or bubble plastic in the event of severe frost.

Do not water if the tree is overwintering out of doors, but it will require a little water from time to time if moved indoors.

Malus 'Flamenco' is one of the six cultivars marketed under the brand name Ballerina. Five other cultivars are sold as containerized apple trees under the same brand name: 'Bolero, 'Charlotte', 'Maypole' (an ornamental apple), 'Polka', and 'Waltz'.

❊

Malva capensis

See: *Anisodontea capensis*

Malva sylvestris

MALLOW

The grey, downy stems of this species of mallow from the Mediterranean regions and Asia Minor can grow to 1m (3ft) in height. Its mauve flowers appear between the greyish-green leaves from midsummer. *Malva sylvestris* is a perennial often cultivated as a biennial. If you propagate the plant from cuttings in early spring, it may flower during the summer of the same year. The plant will withstand temperatures as low as -15°C (5°F) in dry open ground. Containerized specimens, however, need to be taken indoors to overwinter in a cool and light location, where they will scarcely need watering. Several handsome cultivars have been developed from the species, including *Malva sylvestris* 'Brave Heart', with mauve veins in the centre of the light purple flowers merging to form a dark stain, and the low-growing *Malva sylvestris* 'Primley Blue', which only grows about 20-30cm (8-12in) tall, and bears violet flowers with mauve stripes in summer.

○ –5°C (23°F)

Malva sylvestris 'Primley Blue'

Malvastrum capense

See: *Anisodontea capensis*

Mandevilla 'Aphrodite'

The best-known examples of the over 100 species of *Mandevilla* are often for sale labelled *Dipladenia*. The plants concerned are usually pink-flowered hybrids which include *Mandevilla splendens* among their ancestors. Their large flowers superficially resemble those of oleanders, but the mandevillas' blooms appear among coiling stems, which will only develop satisfactorily when they can climb to at least 1m (3ft). The flowers are borne on new wood. In summer, you should find a sunny, sheltered spot for these climbers from tropical America.

If you water the plants freely and feed them regularly, they will continue to flower well into autumn. In winter, they prefer a cool, light location, where the minimum temperature is 10°C (50°F). Cut off lax shoots in early spring, but be careful: the latex is poisonous. Repot *Mandevilla* 'Aphrodite' as little as possible. To propagate the plant, take cuttings in spring from sturdy sections of stems that are still green. Several other hybrids may be treated in the same way, including the popular *Mandevilla* 'Alice du Pont', which is clas-

sified under *Mandevilla* x *amoena*. That hybrid is a cross between *Mandevilla splendens* and the cultivated hybrid *Mandevilla* x *amabilis*. The last-named hybrid is therefore also descended from *Mandevilla splendens*.

☼ 10°C (50°F)

Mandevilla boliviensis

The large white flowers of *Mandevilla boliviensis* have a fairytale quality but, even so, this climber from Bolivia and Ecuador is rarely for sale. In their native environment, the stems grow to 4m (13ft) tall, whereas their maximum height is about 2m (3ft) in more

Mandevilla boliviensis

Mandevilla 'Aphrodite'

northerly European countries. New clusters of flowers are formed continually from late spring until well into autumn. They have a delightful fragrance and are easily distinguished from the totally white calyces of *Mandevilla laxa* by the yellow eyes in the centres. For their management, see *Mandevilla* 'Aphrodite'.

☼ 10°C (50°F)

Mandevilla laxa

CHILEAN JASMINE

This *Mandevilla laxa* from Argentina is something of an oddity. Its white flowers have a sweet, heavy fragrance, and the inside of the flower tube is covered in white down. In summer, the flowers are formed in clusters on the climbing stems. The plant will easily withstand a few degrees of frost, but will then shed its leaves. After a severe frost, the roots are often all that survives. In spite of all this, the pot should be taken indoors in winter unless you live in an area with a very mild climate. The plant will hold its leaves at temperatures above 5°C (41°F). It will then need a light location to prevent lax growth.

For further management, see *Mandevilla* 'Aphrodite'. Voor verdere verzorging zie bij *Mandevilla* 'Aphrodite'.

☼ 5°C (41°F) or ● 0°C (32°F)

Mandevilla laxa

Mandevilla suaveolens

See: *Mandevilla laxa*

Manettia bicolor

See: *Manettia luteo-rubra*

Manettia luteo-rubra

BRAZILIAN FIRECRACKER

The tubular flowers of this South American climber resemble squibs, hence its English name. In greenhouses, the plant's coiling stems climb up a support to a height of about 2m (6ft). If you use a low trellis, the plant will remain shorter and the stems will intertwine at the top. Orange-red flowers with yellow tips are produced continually from spring until the end of summer. Although this manettia is now sold as a container plant, its leaves cannot tolerate cool, wet summers, and the climber therefore only keeps its good looks if the summer is hot. When out of doors, the plant should in any event be placed in a sheltered position in partial shade, as it cannot withstand much wind either. In a greenhouse or a room, however, you will be able to enjoy the plant all through the summer. *Manettia* is evergreen, and can therefore overwinter in a cool, light place. By its second year, however, the plant's appearance deteriorates, and it is therefore sensible to take cuttings in spring and let them take root in warm, moist soil.

☼ 7°C (45°F)

Manettia luteo-rubra

Melampodium paludosum

Melampodium paludosum is still relatively unknown, and has only been cultivated in Europe for some ten years. The plant comes from Sri Lanka, where it is accustomed to a hot and relatively humid climate. The species itself grows somewhat erratically and is not much inclined to flower. Currently, however, there are some compact cultivars on the market, which have abundant foliage and produce yellow flowers over a lengthy period. Well-known cultivars include 'Showstar' (flowers profusely), 'Derby' (more compact with smaller leaves and relatively larger flowers), and 'Discovery'.

The plants are grown as annuals. Professional growers sow at a temperature of about 20°C (68°F) during the first months of the year. Flowering plants are on sale about three months later. They will only flower profusely in a warm and sunny position. Plant in a large pot and keep it out of doors for as long as possible, as fresh air is good for the plant, and cool, thoroughly moist soil keeps it healthy. (1)

Melampodium paludosum 'Discovery'

Melia azedarach

See: *Melia azederach*

Melia azederach

BEAD TREE, PERSIAN LILAC

The bead tree sheds its leaves in winter, but not the yellow, poisonous (!) fruits which remain suspended in clusters from the bare branches. Each berry contains a rock-hard seed used at one time to make bead necklaces and rosaries.

One of the plant's Dutch names, Chinese berry, refers to its oriental origins.

In subtropical countries, *Melia azederach* is a popular ornamental tree because of its graceful, doubly pinnate leaves, fragrant, pale lilac flowers with aubergine-coloured tubes and yellow stone-fruits.

The tree will withstand a few degrees of frost in open ground, but needs to be cultivated as a conservatory plant in northern countries, preferably in a large container with nutritive soil. Water freely and feed regularly while the tree is in full growth.

Put the container in a warm and sunny position.

After the leaves have fallen, you should move the container indoors to as cool as possible a frost-free place, which need not be light.

The tree, however, will need light as soon as it begins to sprout in late winter.

Gradually begin to water more freely at this stage.

● 0°C (32°F)

Melia azederach

Metrosideros citrina

See: *Callistemon citrinus*

Metrosideros excelsa

NEW ZEALAND CHRISTMAS TREE, POHUTUKAWA

In subtropical regions, the pohutukawa adorns avenues and parks with its heavy crown of evergreen foliage and red bristles. Those bristles are the flowers, which appear to consist entirely of red stamens. The best-known species, *Metrosideros excelsa*, is native to New Zealand, where it grows into a spreading tree, some 20m (65ft) tall. Because of its evergreen foliage and flowers that appear in the New Zealand winter, it is also called Christmas tree there. In the northern hemisphere, the flowers appear in midsum-

Metrosideros excelsa

mer. Containerized pohutukawas grow slowly, and it will be several years before they are more than 1m (3ft) tall. Fortunately, even young plants produce flowers, particularly when they have been grown from cuttings. Stand the pohutukawa in a warm and sunny position in summer, and water the well-drained, slightly acid soil moderately. If you wish to prune the tree, it is best to do so after it has flowered.

It is advisable to take the container plant indoors in late autumn, as it will tolerate a few degrees of frost. Stand it in a light, airy, and, above all, cool (2-10°C/36-50°F) place for the winter, so that new buds can form; water occasionally to prevent the root ball from drying out. Sprinkle the tree with lime-free water which must not be colder than the root ball. In spring, the new leaves will not tolerate any frost at all. *Metrosideros excelsa* 'Varie-

gata' has variegated leaves - they are dark green or greyish green with butter-yellow margins.

☼ 0°C (32°F)

Metrosideros excelsa 'Variegata'

Metrosideros tomentosa

See: *Metrosideros excelsa*

Mimulus aurantiacus

MONKEY MUSK

The ultimate length of this mimulus' sticky branches is about 1m (3ft). In the western regions of the United States, the plant grows as a shrub, but its stems are more herbaceous, and arch over horizontally unless supported. This makes the mimulus eminently suitable for a relatively large pot which is hidden by its graceful stems. In late spring and summer, the

Mimulus aurantiacus

Mimulus aurantiacus, flower

stems are adorned with salmon to deep orange flowers, about 4cm (1 3/4in) across.
Find a warm and sunny position for the plant in summer, water moderately, and feed from time to time.
Keep it relatively dry in winter and stand it in a cool, frost-free, and light place so that it will hold its leaves. Pruning will make the small shrub bushier.

☼ 0°C (32°F)

Mimulus aurantiacus var. *puniceus*

MONKEY MUSK

This mimulus variety is also callled *Mimulus puniceus*, but the sole difference appears to be the colour of the flowers.
The variety has lovely deep-red flowers with

Mimulus aurantiacus var. *puniceus*

orange throats.   For its management, see *Mimulus aurantiacus*.

☼ 2°C (36°F)

Mimulus glutinosus

See: *Mimulus aurantiacus*

Mimulus puniceus

See: *Mimulus aurantiacus*

Mina lobata

See: *Ipomoea lobata*

Musa

BANANA

A great diversity of plants referred to as bananas is available, but the names of the species are seldom mentioned, as their origins are rarely known. It is important, however, to know what kind of plant you are buying, since that determines how it should be managed and how big it will grow.

Musa acuminata

Firstly, there is a difference between bananas grown from seed and bananas propagated by suckers. Edible bananas do not usually contain seeds. The plant's main shoot dies down after flowering, after which the banana growers cut through the false stem with a single blow of a machete. The stem appears to consist of no more than a collection of leaf sheaths. At banana plantations, it is possible to see new shoots growing out of the rootstock alongside the base of the dying false stem. The strongest shoots are retained and will bear fruit after about six months. This type of banana is never grown from seed.

Another group of bananas does not produce suckers. These plants are grown from seed and die after flowering, when fresh seeds need to be sown. The best-known of these 'seed-bananas' is the ornamental banana, *Musa ensete*, which nowadays should really be called *Ensete ventricosum*. This is the kind of plant usually labelled as a banana at non-specialized garden centres. It is recognizable by its thick, often reddish, stem, usually with a tuberous swelling at its base. Winter temperatures for bananas vary depending on the species and cultivar. There is great confusion regarding names. What is referred to as a species by one author, is merely a cultivar to another. This entry therefore ends with a summary of commonly used names, recommended minimum temperatures, and the average size of containerized specimens.

In summer, all bananas may be moved out of doors in large containers filled with fertile soil. Choose a sheltered position in full sun or half-shade. In a windy spot, the leaves will tear along the ribs set at right angles to the midrib. It is possible for a banana to adapt to an extent that it will withstand harsh winds without its leaves breaking off, but that will certainly spoil the decorative appearance of the foliage. Give the plant plenty of water and food throughout the summer, and fill the pot with humus-rich, well-drained soil. Even in winter, the soil should never dry out entirely. The plant needs a light position and a relatively humid atmosphere. At high temperatures, it will continue to flower, which, of course, looks magnificent in a greenhouse. The atmosphere in a heated living-room is too dry for a banana, and its leaves will turn brown at the edges as a result. The plant should therefore have a cool position when it is indoors. Popular species and forms include the following: - *Musa acuminata*, the dwarf banana. Several of its cultivars grow to about 1.5m (5ft) in height; minimum temperature 10°C (50°F). - *Musa basjoo*, Japanese banana. This species can withstand a considerable amount of cold. In countries like the Netherlands, it will survive a mild winter under a winter covering. The leaves will die down, but will sprout again in spring. In a light position, and at temperatures above 5°C (41°F), the Japanese banana will hold its long leaves and subsequently become a spreading plant, nearly 3m (10ft) tall.

Musa

- *Musa ensete* (syn. *Ensete ventricosum*) grows in East Africa at altitudes over 2,000m (6,000ft), for instance in the mountains of Ethiopia. Abyssinian banana is another popular name for the species. This seed banana grows about 3m (10ft) tall in a container, and will tolerate 5°C (41°F) in winter. - *Musa nana*, see *Musa acuminata*

- *Musa* x *paradisiaca*, banana. A collective name for the numerous species that have developed from crosses between *Musa acuminata* and *Musa balbisiana*. Both the sweet edible bananas and the cooking bananas belong to this group. The forms cultivated in South America grow tall and do not tolerate temperatures below 10°C (50°F). That also applies to the cultivar 'Dwarf Chyla', which grows to a maximum height of 2m (6ft) when containerized. Other forms stay relatively shorter and also tolerate lower temperatures. The bananas grown in the Canary Islands, including *Musa* x *paradisiaca* 'Dwarf Cavendish' and 'Lacetan' (which is sometimes classified as belonging to the species *Musa acuminata*), do not grow more than about 2m (6ft) tall, and can survive the winter at a minimum temperature of 5°C (41°F). - *Musa velutina*, Assam banana. This seed-banana may grow to 1.5m (5ft) in height, and does not tolerate temperatures below 5°C (41°F). - *Musa violacea*, red banana. This seed-banana has red-flecked foliage and can grow up to 1.5m (5ft) in height. It does not tolerate temperatures below 5°C.

☼ 5°C (41°F) or 10°C (50°F)

Muscari azureum

GRAPE HYACINTH

When the annual pot plants have died in autumn, the empty frost-resistant pots may be filled with hardy bulbs. Grape hyacinths are eminently suitable for the purpose. *Muscari azureum* produces azure flowers in early spring. For the bulb's management, see *Muscari botryoides* 'Album'.

❋

Muscari botryoides 'Album'

WHITE GRAPE HYACINTH

The white form of the grape hyacinth (*Muscari botryoides*) has been known since 1596. The cultivar 'Album' is currently much easier to obtain than the blue-flowered species

Muscari botryoides 'Album'

itself. The spikes of white flowers grow to a maximum height of 20cm (8in) but, in spite of that, are very popular as cut flowers because of their light, sweet fragrance. That scent also makes them very suitable for cultivating in pots, so that they can be placed close to you, on a patio table for instance, when they flower in April-May.

Plant the small bulbs in pots, baskets or bowls in the course of September, October or No-

Muscari azureum

vember. Any kind of soil is suitable, provided it is kept permanently moist, even in winter. Stand the grape hyacinths in a cool place, for instance in an unheated shed, or simply out of doors. Heat will cause the bulbs to sprout prematurely, in which case they will fail to flower. The plants need light as soon as the leaves appear. The bulbs are fully hardy in open ground, but may freeze in an unprotected pot in the event of a severe frost. In that case, put the pot close to the house or wrap it in straw or some other insulating material. Pots of grape hyacinths dug into the garden will survive the frost without any problems.

❄

Muscari latifolium

BROAD-LEAFED GRAPE HYACINTH

The name of this plant indicates how it differs from other grape hyacinths. Each bulb usually produces a single leaf. It is as broad as those of some wild tulips and encloses the slender stem on which the navy-blue flowers are borne. Strongly contrasting, light blue, sterile flowers are borne at the top. For their management, see *Muscari botryoides* 'Album'.

❄

Muscari latifolium

Myosotis sylvatica

FORGET-ME-NOT

In spring, forget-me-nots produce flowers in delicate shades of blue, or sometimes pink, with small yellow eyes. The flowers stems

Myosotis sylvatica

continue to grow during the summer and self-seed. The plants are fully hardy.

Forget-me-nots are easy to cultivate in a pot. Use standard potting compost and water normally. To prevent the soil from drying out too quickly, they should not be placed in too sunny a position. The plant is otherwise undemanding.

✳

Myrtus communis

MYRTLE

The bruised leaves of myrtle have a characteristic aroma, familiar ever since antiquity. Oil is still pressed from leaves and seeds. Even the flowers, which consist mainly of 3cm (1 1/4in) stamens, are delightfully fragrant.

Some brides still wear small myrtle wreathes, a custom going back to the distant past, when myrtle was regarded as a symbol of purety and virginity.

The best-known species, *Myrtus communis*,

Myrtus communis

grows in arid scrub, the maquis, in countries around the Mediterranean. The evergreen shrub will withstand temperatures of -15°C (5°F) in open ground, but, if grown as a container plant, should be taken indoors as soon as the first frost occurs. The plant is often on sale as a houseplant, although it is not really suitable for our warm living-rooms. A cool and light position (2-12°C/36-53°F) is far better for it.

Out of doors, the plant requires a position in full sun or semi-shade. The roots should never become waterlogged, but letting them dry out is equally disastrous. Even in winter, the root ball should never dry out entirely. Keep the soil uniformly moist in summer, using lime-free rainwater or boiled water. Propagation is by by seed or cuttings.

Cut through a leaf bud to take greenwood cuttings in spring, or semi-ripe cuttings in late summer; plant in warm soil (20-25°C/68-77°F), and cover with glass or plastic. Afterwards, a warm spot in full sun is best.

Myrtle may eventually grow to over 2m (6ft) in a container, but the plant is suitable for pruning and can therefore be cultivated in whatever size or shape is required. *Myrtus communis* is consequently often used for topiary.

☼ –5°C (23°F)

Myrtus communis 'Variegata'

MYRTLE

This is only one out of many variegated forms of myrtle.

The leathery, pointed leaves are adorned with butter-yellow flecks and stripes, particularly at the margins.

Take the variegated forms indoors before the frosts begin, and stand the shrubs in a lighter position than the common myrtle, both in summer and in winter.

For further management, see *Myrtus communis*.

☼ 0°C (32°F)

Myrtus communis 'Variegata'

N _____ *n*

Nandina domestica

HEAVENLY BAMBOO, SACRED BAMBOO

As the nights grow colder, *Nandina*'s green leaves change to wonderful autumn colours. A surprise follows: instead of falling, they turn green again in the course of the winter. Panicles of white flowers appear among the leaves in spring, and are followed by white berries which eventually turn red. The long thin stems, which may grow to about 1.5m (5ft) in height, look like bamboo.

Nandina domestica

In regions where temperatures never fall below -10°C (14°F), *Nandina* can be grown in open ground. Elsewhere, it makes an ideal container plant. If you stand the tub or pot in a sheltered position in full sun or semi-shade, the flowers will be followed by an abundance of fruit. Even though the plant is self-pollinating, it will bear more fruit if there is another flowering *Nandina* in its vicinity. The plant does best in standard, well-drained potting compost. Water quite freely in summer, but keep it dry and frost-free in a well-lit location in winter.
There are numerous cultivars of *Nandina domestica*, including:
- 'Alba' -matt white berries;
- 'Compacta' - low-growing, about 70cm (28in) tall;

preceding page: Nerium oleander

- 'Flava' - yellow berries;
- *forma heterophylla*, see 'Nana Purpurea';
- 'Nana Purpurea' - low-growing, with leaves tinged with purplish red changing to a magnificent bright red in autumn;
- 'Purpurea', see 'Nana Purpurea';
- 'Richmond' - scarlet berries in winter;
- var. *leucocarpa*, see 'Alba';
- 'Variegata' - leaves with white, creamy white, or pink marbling;
- 'Woods Dwarf' - golden-yellow foliage which turns red in winter.

☼ 0°C (32°F)

Nandina domestica

Nemesia versicolor 'Blue Bird'

The word *versicolor* refers to a major characteristic of this South African annual: the flowers vary in colour. There are blue to mauvish blue, white, or yellow specimens, but they nearly always have contrasting lips. 'Blue Bird' has blue and white, or blue and yellow flowers. They grow about 30cm (12in) tall, and because of their slender growth are good for combining with bushier annuals such as *Silene coeli-rosa*.
Sow the small seeds indoors in March-April, or out of doors in April-May. The seedlings will flower from late June until well into September. Remove flowers after they have

faded to encourage a second flush. Keep the plants growing vigorously in a sunny or semi-shady position throughout the summer. Ensure that excess water can drain away satisfactorily, as the roots of this *Nemesia* are very prone to rot.

(1)

Nemesia versicolor 'Blue Bird'

Nemophila insignis

See: *Nemophila menziesii*

Nemophila menziesii

BABY BLUE-EYES

The watery stems of this plant grow in all directions. They grow about 10cm (4in) tall in a border, and are broadly pendulous in a hanging basket. The small flowers, over 2cm (3/4in) across, appear among the succulent foliage from April onwards. The colour of the flowers varies: they are often clearly bi-coloured, white and deep mauve, or blue and white, and, at times, shades of purple or yellow are also discernible. Sow the nemophilas in autumn or early spring. The seedlings are fully hardy and may be put out of doors as early as March, If you sow in

autumn, they will flower from April onwards, otherwise a little later. The flowers continue to appear until well into September. Stand the pot of nemophilas in a sheltered, semi-shady spot, and water freely. They will even flower in a light position on the north-facing side of the house.

(1)

Nemophila menziesii

Nemophila 'Snow Storm'

BABY BLUE-EYES

This cultivar is a nemophila with tiny white flowers (1cm/1/4in across). If you look carefully, you will see that they have delicate blackish-purple dots. *Nemophila menziesii* var. *atromaria*, which is also sold labelled *Nemophila* 'Atomaria', has exactly the same kind of small flowers. For the plant's management, see *Nemophila menziesii*.

(1)

Nemophila 'Snow Storm'

Nerium oleander

OLEANDER

Oleanders grow naturally in a long narrow strip of land around the Mediterranean, in eastern Asia Minor, and along the southern edge of the Himalayas into western China. The Mediterranean species is stronger than the one in the east, where the shrubs are more fragile and bear fragrant flowers. These varieties were formerly described as separate species and included the Indian oleander (*Nerium indicum*), but now they are all regarded as part of a single, variable, species: *Nerium oleander*.

These huge variations have made it possible for hundreds of different cultivars to be developed. The original flower has five petals, but now there are also cultivars with double or fully double flowers. The original flowers were pink, but that palette has been extended to include white, cream, yellow, apricot, salmon, flesh-coloured, orange, red, carmine, and mauve shades.

In their natural environment, the shrubs grow mainly along rivers and in wadis (river beds that are dry most of the year and only contain water in the rainy season). There, even in dry seasons, with the sun beating down on the plants, they are rooted in moist soil.

The best oleanders are therefore cultivated in soil that is always kept moist, and in as much sun as possible. In countries like the Netherlands, however, oleanders really do not have enough warmth and sunshine, and that is the main reason why they flower so poorly. A greenhouse or conservatory provides a good solution to the problem, as the plants will flower better in that kind of environment.

There are also some other reasons for poor flowering. First, some cultivars simply flower better than others, and are clearly more inclined to flower. Winter temperatures may also be significant: overwintering in too hot a atmosphere has an adverse effect on flowering. Strong species will tolerate temperatures as low as -5°C (23°F) after a warm summer. The ideal winter temperature for strong cultivars is between 2 and 12°C (36 and 53°F). If temperatures rise above 12°C (53°F), oleanders will end their dormant phase and begin to grow. It is better for tender cultivars to be kept a little warmer, between 8 and 12°C (46-53°F). Oleanders are evergreen, and their winter position should therefore be as light as possible. In spite of that, however, they will shed some of their leaves during the dark months, and because the new foliage will not be produced in the same places, the branches will eventually become bare. You can avoid the consequences of this natural process by pruning, as oleanders can tolerate that very well. Even the stumps of old shrubs will bring forth fresh new shoots after rigorous pruning, but they will usually not flower the same year.

Oleanders gradually begin to grow again in late winter. A very light position then becomes essential to prevent lax growth. Sprinkle the plants regularly in winter (and certainly in spring), as that will suppress red spider mite. You should also try to keep the plants' position as well-ventilated as possible in winter and spring. Frequent airing helps to prevent fungal diseases. Check the plants regularly for scale insects, which are recognizable by the smooth, raised, light brown spots on the underside of the leaves. Scrape off the scales and spray the leaves with a solution of soap and methylated (mineral) spirits, or a good biologically degradable pesticide.

Oleanders may be repotted in spring. Larger plants in large pots or tubs eventually need no further repotting, and then renewing the top layer is all that is required. Oleanders naturally prefer nutritive soil, but do not feed them excessively. Large amounts of fertilizer combined with insufficient sunshine will lead to abundant foliage but few flowers.

Nerium oleander, pappus

It is really a matter of watering freely and waiting for the magnificent flowers which, depending on the cultivar, will appear between April and late summer. The cultivars with fully double or fragrant flowers, and those with yellow or flesh-coloured blooms, will require most warmth to come into full flower, and it is therefore better to cultivate them under glass.

Oleanders may be propagated by cutting off tips just below one of several whorls of leaves, and putting them in moist soil at a soil temperature a little over 20°C (68°F).
Oleanders are pollinated by moths, in the Netherlands often by Y-moths, which also visit flowers in daytime. Fruits are sometimes formed in warm summers, or if the plant is cultivated in a greenhouse.
As the fruit bursts open, brown seeds attached to pappus become visible. The seeds may be sown in spring, but plants grown from them rarely resemble the parent plant. Identical cultivars can only be produced by cuttings.
The oleander is a highly poisonous plant - every part of it, from the wood to the flowers, is poisonous.
There have even been cases of people who ate the flowers and died. Burning the wood or using oleander twigs as skewers for barbecuing meat is extremely dangerous. Do not use the blooms for cut-flower arrangements, and do not put flowering plants in living rooms or bedrooms, as the flowers have a stupefying

effect. Make sure that clippings do not end up in places where cattle may eat them.

◌ 0°C (32°F) or 5°C (41°F)

Nerium oleander 'Angiolo Pucci'

This strong cultivar has pale yellow single flowers. Their egg-yolk yellow throats are adorned with honey guides consisting of orange-red lines. The plant itself grows to a maximum height of 2m (6ft), and was first described in 1952.
For management, see *Nerium oleander*.

◌ 0°C (32°F)

Nerium oleander 'Angiolo Pucci'

Nerium oleander

Nerium oleander 'Bianco Rosato Semplice'

The precise data relating to this cultivar cannot be traced, but it resembles *Nerium oleander* 'Roseum' in almost every respect. The sole difference is the colour of the flowers. 'Bianco Rosato Semplice' has creamy white flowers with a pale pink bloom.
For management, see *Nerium oleander*.

☼ 0°C (32°F)

Nerium oleander 'Bianco Rosato Semplice'

Nerium oleander 'Emile Sahut'

The influence of the Indian oleander is very noticeable in this cultivar: its large, single flowers are borne in profusion and have a delightful fragrance.
They are deep red with carmine-striped throats.
The well-known specialist Claude Sahut developed the robust cultivar at his nursery in Montpellier in 1872, where he cultivated as many as 170 different forms. He thus became more or less the 'father' of most of the cultivars currently available.
For management, see *Nerium oleander*.

☼ 0°C (32°F)

Nerium oleander 'Papa Gambetta'

This is one of the more recent cultivars, a fragile form developed by the Italian expert Gambetta in the early 1970s. The large single flowers are pinkish red with orange centres.
For management, see *Nerium oleander*.

☼ 5°C (41°F)

Nerium oleander 'Papa Gambetta'

Nerium oleander 'Roseum'

This vigorously spreading shrub has single pink flowers which are borne in full clusters at the tips of stems.
A honey guide in a deeper shade of pink can be seen in the centre of each flower. The first information on this strong cultivar was published in 1872.
For management, see *Nerium oleander*.

☼ 0°C (32°F)

Nerium oleander 'Emile Sahut'

Nerium oleander 'Roseum'

Nerium oleander 'Soeur Agnès'

This cultivar has pure white flowers. They are large, single and fragrant, with creamy throats, but there is no honey guide. This profusely flowering, sturdy shrub, which can tolerate some adverse conditions, was developed by Claude Sahut in 1868. It is often sold incorrectly labelled 'Mont Blanc'.
The latter plant is a cultivar with fully double flowers.
For management, see *Nerium oleander*.

☼ 0°C (32°F)

Nerium oleander 'Soeur Agnès'

Nerium oleander 'Splendens Foliis Variegatis'

This variegated cultivar was developed in 1854; its fully double, pink flowers sometimes have white stripes. The dark green leaves have irregular deep yellow streaks and patches, particularly clear at the margins. Only the green parts of the leaves are capable of converting sunlight into energy, and the fragile plant therefore grows slowly to a maximum height of 1.5m (5ft).
For management, see *Nerium oleander*.

☼ 5°C (41°F)

Nicotiana alata

TOBACCO PLANT

Nicotiana alata becomes fragrant towards evening, and thus attracts moths which take care of pollination. The flowers are white, which makes them show up most clearly at

Nicotiana alata 'White Bedder'

night. Anyone wishing to have a delightfully fragrant tobacco plant near the patio would be well advised to choose a white-flowered species or cultivar such as *Nicotiana alata* 'White Bedder'. Other suitable examples include white-flowered cultivars of *Nicotiana* x *sanderae* (about 50cm/20in tall), or the robust *Nicotiana sylvestris*, which can only be cultivated in large pots or tubs.
For management, see *Nicotiana* 'Havana Apple Blossom'

(1)

Nerium oleander 'Splendens Foliis Variegatis'

Nicotiana 'Havana Apple Blossom'

TOBACCO PLANT

Buying tobacco plants is often a matter of making choices. If you want the wonderful fragrance, which is released mainly in the evening and at night, you will automatically need to think in terms of the white-flowered species (see *Nicotiana alata*). Anyone wishing to add colour to a patio is likely to choose cultivars with coloured flowers, such as *Nicotiana* 'Havana Apple Blossom', one of the many forms of *Nicotiana* x *sanderae*. This tobacco plant, also known as *Nicotiana* 'Apple Blossom', is sold as a bedding plant, but does extremely well in a container. It grows 40cm (16in) tall and is scarcely scented. Vast quantities of flowering tobacco plants are on sale in spring, but it is also possible to grow them from seed. Sow early, because the seedlings need at least three months to come into flower. Sow in moist soil at room temperature, and do not cover the seed. The young plants may be put out of doors after the final night frost. Find a position for them in full sun or semi-shade. They can withstand rain, are reasonably tolerant of wind (they are therefore suitable for balcony troughs), and have no special requirements.

(1)

Nicotiana 'Havana Apple Blossom'

Nierembergia caerulea var. *violacea* 'Mont Blanc'

Nierembergia caerulea

In the year when they are sown, Nierembergias form small shrubs bearing a profusion of blue to violet-blue flowers from midsummer until far into autumn. They may be planted in the garden in summer, but only in sheltered positions, as strong winds are likely to spoil their appearance. This decorative member of the potato family is best cultivated in a pot. Sow the small seeds at room temperature in March-April, and plant them out in light, well-drained soil. The small shrubs will begin to flower by the end of June. Water moderately throughout the summer and autumn and put them in a sunny position.

The subspecies *Nierembergia caerulea* var. *violacea* 'Purple Robe' is more robust and its flowers are rather more violet in colour.

Nierembergia caerulea var. *violacea* 'Mont Blanc' has snowy white flowers with yellow centres.

(1)

Nierembergia caerulea var. *violacea* 'Purple Robe'

Nierembergia hippomanica

See: *Nierembergia caerulea*

Olea europaea

OLIVE

The Old Testament narrator could not have chosen a worse example than the olive. In the tale about the Flood, he describes how Noah released a dove which soon returned because the whole world was still under water. A week later, Noah tried again, and the dove returned with an olive branch in its beak as a sign that some land had re-emerged.

Whatever the dove found, it could never have been an olive branch. Olive trees grow very slowly, and definitely cannot tolerate being waterlogged, which will definitely kill them.
They prefer to grow on dry slopes in a Mediterranean climate. The atmosphere should not be too humid, and fresh cool air is required in winter to enable the trees to develop buds. Olive-growing is therefore restricted to the countries around the Mediterranean and regions with a similar climate (Australia and South Africa).
In countries like the Netherlands, olives like

Olea europaea

Olea europaea

to be in the sunniest part of the garden, but you should choose a spot where the air is fresh. They are very tolerant of wind. In autumn, containerized olives should be taken indoors at the time of the first night frost, though in open ground the tree will tolerate brief spells of frost, with temperatures as low as -10°C (14°F). A well-lit winter location is essential, or the leaves will fall. Although new leaves will be formed in spring in that case, the growth of this very slow-growing plant will be further retarded. The olive tolerates a dry atmosphere, and can therefore overwinter in a heated living-room if necessary, although buds will not be formed in that case. The development of buds requires a period of several months during which the temperature should fall to below 10°C (50°F) at night.
Plant the olive in very well-drained, sandy clay, preferably containing some lime. As noted above, "wet feet" are positively fatal to olives. Water moderately in summer, and sparingly in winter at the ideal winter temperature of 2-10°C (36-50°F). Be careful, though, because the soil should never dry out entirely either in summer or in winter.
Light pruning may help to correct the loose untidy growth of a young olive tree to some extent, but this will usually be at the expense

of the flowers, which are formed on the previous year's growth. The flowers have a pleasantly sweet, spicy fragrance, and if you have a hermaphrodite plant (or two different cultivars), fruits may develop in hot summers, though they will not, unfortunately, acquire much flavour.

☼ 0°C (32°F)

Omphalodes linifolia

VENUS' NAVELWORT

Omphalodes linifolia's white flowers will confound the worst cynics - there are few plants that flower as sweetly. In a pot, unfortunately, it is a short-lived joy. Over a period of three to five weeks, the small flowers will work their way up the 40cm (16in) stems, close up, and develop seed. The flowering period may be extended a little if you sow the seeds in several different pots at intervals of about a month between March and June.

After they have flowered, you can plant the root balls in the garden and, with luck, the plants will self-seed there. The seedlings, which will appear in September and October, are fully hardy.

(1)

Omphalodes linifolia

Origanum rotundifolium

DITTANY

If you see a small shrub and what appear to be hop flowers trailing over the edge of a pot, you will be looking at *Origanum rotundifolium*. Its flowers are pink or white, and appear unobtrusively between the bracts.

Dittany grows on rocks and walls around the Black Sea.

Despite the fact that there are frequent severe frosts in those regions, the plant is not fully hardy in countries like the Netherlands, particularly in moist soil. It is, however, highly suitable for growing as a rock plant. In winter, you should put it, in its pot, in an unheated greenhouse or cold frame, or else in a shed, a dark one if need be. The plant will sprout again in spring.

In contrast with the related marjoram, *Origanum rotundifolium* dislikes lime. Do not water in summer until the soil feels dry to the touch, and keep it dry in winter.

❋

Origanum rotundifolium

Osmanthus delavayi

The sweet scent of *Osmanthus* tells us that spring has arrived. Small clusters of white flowers disperse the delightful fragrance. Flowering begins at the end of March and

Osmanthus delavayi

Osteospermum 'Congo'

continues into May. The robust evergreen shrub has dark green leaves with slightly pointed tips.

In open ground, Osmanthus delavayi's hardiness is debatable. When containerized, the shrub should be moved indoors to a cool and, above all, very light location in winter, but, if there is no frost, it would rather be out of doors. Its preferred summer position is in partial shade.

In its natural environment in the Chinese province of Yunnan, this osmanthus grows on rocky limestone slopes. In countries like the Netherlands, the plant makes do with any kind of well-drained soil. Water moderately in summer and very sparingly in winter.

Other species suitable for growing in containers include *Osmanthus fragrans* (including the orange-flowered form *aurantiacus*), *Osmanthus* x *burkwoodii*, and the rather more vigorous *Osmanthus heterophyllus* which, however, may quite well be kept smaller by pruning.

☼ 0°C (32°F)

Osteospermum

Countless osteospermum cultivars in full flower appear on the market from quite early in spring. They are grown from seed sown early in the year to prevent nurserymen from missing out on spring buying sprees. By the end of May, most pots and balcony troughs are full of annuals. Although osteospermums are usually sold as annuals, it is quite possible to keep them through the winter. In that case, you should take stem cuttings in summer, which can survive in a frost-free place even in moderate light, provided they are kept almost entirely dry.

Put the plants in very well-drained, sandy soil. Do not add fertilizer, as this would be at the expense of the flowers. The soil should drain very freely, and it is best not to water until the potting compost has almost dried out. African osteospermums like a sunny position where they will flower for months on end.

The best-known cultivar is *Osteospermum* 'Whirligig', which grows about 50cm (20in) tall and bears flowers with very characteristically shaped petals throughout the summer. White ribbon-like petals surround a blueish centre and are folded halfway along, causing the open tips to resemble small spatulas.

The most popular forms of the numerous other osteospermums are currently those named after African countries or regions,

Osteospermum 'Swazi'

189

including *Osteospermum* 'Congo', with old-rose flowers, and *Osteospermum* 'Swazi', which has white ribbon-like flowers round a blueish centre.

Many osteospermums will tolerate temperatures as low as about -10°C (14°F) in open ground. It is therefore worthwhile to dig the plants in after they have flowered, and to hope for a mild winter.

☼ 0°C (32°F)

Oxalis deppei

See: *Oxalis tetraphylla*

Oxalis tetraphylla

This oxalis may serve all kinds of purposes. Depending on when it is planted, it will flower in winter, spring, or summer. Growers plant the small tubers in autumn or winter so that they will be able to sell flowering houseplants two months later. In that case, they need to be cultivated at room temperature.

If you wish to grow this oxalis on a patio, it is best to wait until March. If you put the pot of planted tubers in a warm, light place, you will be able to take the flowering plants out of doors by mid-May. The flowers do not appear in large numbers at a time, but are borne over a long period, well into summer.

Grow them in very well-drained soil and do not water until the soil has largely dried out. Remember that the tubers are sensitive to stagnant water. It is unnecessary to add fertilizer.

Put the pot in a warm position that is not too sunny, as fierce sunlight will make the flowers close up.

If you have a few tubers left over, you may like to plant them in the garden.

If you plant them in light, well-drained, warm soil in spring, they will surprise you with their foliage and flowers in late summer. The leaves wither in autumn, after which you should take the tubers indoors to overwinter in a frost-free place.

Besides the common oxalis, which has an irregular zigzagging line across its leaves, the cultivar *Oxalis tetraphylla* 'Iron Cross' is very popular. It has a purple patch at the point where the four leaflets meet.

● 0°C (32°F)

Oxypetalum

See: *Tweedia*

Oxalis tetraphylla 'Iron Cross'

P

p

Pachystachys lutea

LOLLIPOP PLANT

In summer, *Pachystachys lutea*'s spikes of yellowish-white flowers stand out proudly above the foliage of this evergreen Peruvian shrub. It is treated with growth inhibitors and marketed as a houseplant, but it usually does not survive for long in the dry atmosphere of a centrally heated home. It does far better in a greenhouse or a conservatory, where it will eventually grow to about 1m (3ft) in height.

Nowadays, *Pachystachys* is often found as a container plant on a sunny patio, where it flowers exuberantly in summer. It then needs a lot of water and very well-drained soil. Do not water until the soil is almost dry. Feed the plant occasionally in summer if you like, but stop in late summer so that it can harden off. This is essential, because the situation becomes critical in winter. The evergreen shrub will need a lot of light, even in winter, and also likes a warm position, though not too dry an atmosphere - 12-16°C (53-60°F) is ideal. Water sparingly during that period. The plant

will ultimately become rather straggling and you should then renew it by taking cuttings in summer and inserting them in warm, moist, sandy soil to root.

◯ 10°C (50°F)

Pandanus utilis

SCREW PINE

Pandanus utilis originally came from Madagascar and grows 20m (65ft) tall. In spite of its appearance, the screw pine is not a palm, although it is related to palm trees. The leaves develop like a spiral staircase on the trunk, which continues to grow. Older leaves at the base become rather unsightly and may be removed. The tree therefore gradually 'spirals' upwards.

Because the leaves may grow to 1.5m (5ft) in length, the plant takes up a lot of space and can therefore only overwinter in a large greenhouse or conservatory. The temperature should not drop below 12°C (53°F). The

Pachystachys lutea

Pandanus utilis

atmosphere in a living-room is too dry for it. The plant may be put out of doors in summer. Make sure the soil is very well-drained, and move the plant indoors in the event of prolonged rain, or it will rot from the leaf axils.

○ 12°C (53°F)

Pandorea jasminoides

BOWER VINE

Pandorea jasminoides can climb to 2m (6ft) in a single season. To do so, it will need warmth, a lot of water and food, and obviously a support of some kind. White to pink flowers with cherry-pink throats, and 4cm (1 3/4in) across, are borne on the tips of stems in summer. Move this Australian container plant indoors well before the first night frost, and cut it back as much as you like. Stand it in a very light place at a temperature of 10-20°C (50-68°F). Low humidity is tolerated reasonably well, but remember that, depending on the amount of foliage, the plant will need more light and water in a warm position. Never water excessively, or the stems will rot away. Propagation is by seed (the *Pandorea* develops germinative seed even in the north), or by taking semi-ripe stem cuttings in summer; under glass or plastic they will root after several weeks.

○ 5°C (41°F)

Pandorea jasminoides

Pandorea ricasoliana

See: *Podranea ricasoliana*

Parkinsonia aculeata

JERUSALEM THORN, MEXICAN PALO VERDE

The Jerusalem thorn is very popular in tropical and subtropical countries because of its graceful appearance and racemes of yellow flowers. The plant in the photograph is growing in the wild in the Galapagos Islands. The species is found in similarly dry places throughout tropical America.

The branches spread vigorously and have strong spines and pendent leaves, about 40cm (16in) long. Tiny leaflets are attached to the strong midribs. Racemes of yellow flowers with striking orange stamens are produced in summer. The Jerusalem thorn is highly suitable for growing as a container plant. Stand it in the warmest and sunniest spot available in summer, and use very well-drained potting compost, as it is essential for excess water to drain away immediately. In these conditions, you can water and feed the plant normally in summer.

As soon as the outdoor temperature drops below 5°C (41°F), the bushy tree should be moved (after pruning, if required) to a very light place indoors. The temperature may, if need be, drop to 5°C (41°F), but the evergreen shrub prefers higher temperatures (up to 15°C/59°F). Water very sparingly at this time.

○ 5°C (41°F)

Parkinsonia aculeata

Passiflora

PASSION FLOWER

Passion flowers normally have five sepals and
five petals (which are scarcely distinguishable
from one another), five stamens, and three
stigmas. Their common style has a crown, or
corona, consisting of a circle of filaments, a
kind of 'crown of thorns'. The species
described here have all come from America.
Some of them will survive the winter in
countries like the Netherlands, but most of
them should overwinter in a greenhouse or
cool room. All species may be cultivated in
large pots, either in a sunny to semi-shady
spot out of doors, or else in a greenhouse or
conservatory. The tendril climbers are fast-
growing and therefore need space. If they
become excessively rampant, the shoots
should be trained and pruned. Water moderately during the growing season and hardly at
all when the plant is dormant. A lot of
fertilizer will stimulate leaf growth, but only at
the expense of flowers.

Passiflora x alato-caerulea

The flowers of this cross between *Passiflora
alato* and *Passiflora caerulea* are white and
mauve and about 10cm (4in) wide. The hybrid
is sterile and can only be propagated by
cuttings.

☼ 5°C (41°F)

Passiflora x *alato-caerulea*

Passiflora alba

See: *Passiflora subpeltata*

Passiflora 'Amethyst'

The precise origins of this passion flower are
unknown. It is often sold as *Passiflora* 'Star
of Mikan' and, to add to the confusion, there
is also a species called *Passiflora
amethystina*, which was described by Mikan.
Fortunately, none of this detracts from the
plant's beauty. Three-lobed leaves and
mauvish flowers with a purple corona are
produced on slender stems.

☼ 5°C (41°F)

Passiflora 'Amethyst'

Passiflora antioquiensis

See: *Passiflora* x *exoniensis*

Passiflora x belotii

This is the only correct name for the plant which is also marketed *as Passiflora* 'Impératrice Eugénie' (or 'Kaiserin Eugénie'), named after the wife of Napoleon III. The flowers closely resemble those of *Passiflora* x *alato-caerulea*, and 'Impératrice Eugénie' is sometimes classified as such.

☼ 5°C (41°F)

Passiflora x *belotii*

Passiflora caerulea

**BLUE PASSION FLOWER,
COMMON PASSION FLOWER**

This best-known passion flower may also be grown as a garden plant against a sheltered

Passiflora x *exoniensis*

wall. It is frost-tender as a young plant, but, when older, will certainly survive temperatures as low as -15°C (5°F) in open ground, although it will then shed most of its leaves. Containerized specimens should overwinter in a frost-free environment. Beautiful cultivars have been developed from the blue passion flower; they should be managed in the same way as the species. One of the loveliest cultivars is the equally hardy *Passiflora caerulea* 'Constance Eliott', which has white flowers. It was developed by Constance Eliott in 1879.

☼ 0°C (32°F)

Passiflora edulis

The name of this passion flower refers to its edible fruits which are mainly cultivated in warm climates and can be made into a refreshing drink, full of vitamins. In Spanish-speaking countries, these fruits are called *maracuja*. As the plant flowers early, it is also possible to cultivate edible fruits out of doors in countries like the Netherlands. As the fruits need to ripen for four months, they cannot be harvested until autumn. In the case of some cultivars, they are produced by self-fertilization, the others are self-sterile, so that you will need two different plants from different clones (which therefore must not be cuttings taken from each other) to be able to enjoy the fruits. The flowers superficially resemble those of *Passiflora caerulea*, but the filaments are mainly white (with a purple to blue band round the centre of the flower), longer, and distinctly curly at the tips.

☼ 7°C (45°F)

Passiflora edulis

Passiflora x exoniensis

Most plants sold as *Passiflora antioquiensis* are really specimens of this hybrid - a cross between the species and *Passiflora mollissima*. All these forms belong to the Tacsonia subgroup, the banana passion fruit, so named because of the banana-like appearance of the fruits. They grow in the higher regions of South America and require low temperatures and a great deal of moisture throughout the year.

The pinkish-red flower is more than 10cm (4in) across, and is remarkable because of its very small violet corona.

This clearly distinguishes the hybrid from *Passiflora antioquiensis*, as the species has no corona at all. It will be several years before either the species or the hybrid begin to flower.

○ 0°C (32°F)

Passiflora mollisima

Passiflora foetida

The scientific name of this variable species means stinking passion flower and refers to the unpleasant odour emitted by the plant if people brush past it. This action breaks off hairs on stems and leaves, and a malodorous liquid is released. The flowers, 3cm (1 1/4in) across, are white with old-rose centres, and are followed by edible fruits wrapped in antler-like protruberances. They are fairly small (2-3cm/3/4-1 1/4in long) and are only edible when ripe.

○ 10°C (50°F)

Passiflora foetida

Passiflora 'Imperatrice Eugénie'

See: *Passiflora x belotii*

Passiflora 'Incense'

'Incense's magnificently curled corona appeals to the imagination. Dr Knight developed the form from *Passiflora incarnata* and *Passiflora cincinnata* in Florida in 1973.

The parent plant (*P. incarnata*) grows in the eastern states of the US, where frosts can be severe. The climber sheds its leaves and stems in those regions, and is often covered in snow. Under a winter cover in open ground, it will tolerate temperates as low as about -15°C (5°F). The consequence, however, is that growth will be so retarded in spring that the plant will hardly come into flower before the next winter.

The species can only be cultivated satisfactorily in a large container, which should be moved indoors before the first night frost. If the species overwinters in the cold, it loses its foliage and needs to be forced in a conservatory or greenhouse in spring if it is to flower in time.

If you do not have a greenhouse or a conservatory, you should take the plant indoors earlier on in autumn, and put it in a light place where the temperature should be at least 12°C (53°F). In that case, the plant will hold its leaves and simply continue to grow in spring, after which flowering will begin on time.

Passiflora 'Incense' is striking because of its large corona of curled filaments extending beyond the actual petals. The corona is lilac mauve with darker bands, interspersed with circles of white dots - all of which makes the form a favourite treasure.

○ 12°C (53°F) or ● 0°C (32°F)

Passiflora mollissima

BANANA PASSION FLOWER

The magnificent, pendent, pale pink flowers of this species from the Andes regions will also develop fully in European climates similar to that of the Netherlands. The plant grows very well in large containers, particularly if the summer is damp and not excessively hot. It will, however, be several seasons before plants grown from seed come into flower. Because the plant does not flower until late summer in countries like the Netherlands, the banana-like fruits cannot develop properly there. This is a pity, as they appear to be so delicious that they were proclaimed the national fruit of Colombia.

○ 5°C (41°F)

Passiflora 'Incense'

Passiflora 'Star of Mikan'

See: *Passiflora* 'Amethyst'

Passiflora subpeltata

The pure white flowers of this passion flower from tropical America measure 5cm (2in) across and are produced from spring until autumn. The flowers are followed by greenish yellow fruits. The plant is self-pollinating and

Passiflora caerulea 'Constance Eliott'

produces good germinative seed. It is best to grow the species as an annual, particularly as it is not easy to keep the plants through the winter. They will then need a cool, light location.

(1) or ○ 10°C (50°F)

Passiflora subpeltata

Passiflora 'Sunburst'

The flowers of this cross between *Passiflora gilbertiana* and *Passiflora jorullensis* are relatively small. The petals are fairly inconspicuous, and it is the corona of the young hybrid (grown by Patrick Worley in 1983) that steals the show with a circle of 'filaments' changing from orange red to orange yellow. 'Sunburst' is easy to grow and flowers all through the summer. Characteristic features of the foliage include the two projecting outer lobes, light green stripes along the ribs, and small specks scattered over the leaves.

Passiflora 'Sunburst'

Unfortunately, the flowers are somewhat malodorous, so that it is advisable not to stand the plant in a conservatory or too near the patio.

○ 5°C (41°F)

Passiflora vitifolia

These red-flowered passion flowers are some of the most beautiful, but also among the most difficult to cultivate. *Passiflora vitifolia* grows naturally in the warm, damp forests of Nicaragua and the northern countries of South America. As it is never very cold in those regions, the species should overwinter at a minimum temperature of 12°C (53°F), or the leaves will fall, and the plant will not necessarily revive in spring. The name refers to the close resemblance between the leaves of this passion flower and those of the vine. The flowers are a dazzling shade of bright red, and begin to appear in spring. You can also enjoy the plant in winter if you keep it in a place that is light and warm enough, for instance a heated conservatory or winter garden.

○ 12°C (53°F)

Passiflora vitifolia

Pelargonium

GERANIUM

The plants sold as geraniums are officially called *Pelargonium*. They are distantly related to wild geraniums such as *Geranium pratense* (Meadow cranesbill), but require totally different management. Pelargoniums are mostly indigenous to South African coastal regions, and the species from which most of the cultivated pelargoniums available elsewhere were developed, come from an area with summer rains.

Besides these undemanding plants, there are also species which have adapted to extremely inclement climates. Some survive largely on mists or very brief rainy seasons. They tide over the long dry spells by storing moisture in roots or thickened stems.

Hybridization of species and selection of the results have led to the development of thousands of cultivars from the less succulent species.

The balcony 'geraniums' are among the very strongest container plants. They survive in windy places and look attractive for long periods, even if you occasionally forget to water them. Their long flowering season, from spring until far into autumn, has made them immensely popular.

In addition to the popular 'garden geranium', there are 250 natural species and thousands of cultivars. The most important of the many groups into which they are divided are described in the following entries.

Pelargonium acetosum

Pelargonium acetosum is the model for the approximately 250 species of botanical pelargonium. *Pelargonium acetosum* is a wild

species growing in several places on the East Cape, on clayey soil deposited by rivers in the vicinity. It has thin, smooth, and fragile stems, grows about 40cm (16in) tall, and produces small, succulent, greyish-green leaves. In summer, the plant develops thin stems bearing pale salmon-pink flowers. The narrow petals

Pelargonium acetosum

Pelargonium

have cherry-red veins. For the plant's management, see *Pelargonium* x *hortorum*, but make sure that the soil is particularly well-drained.

Many of the botanical pelargoniums are genuine collectors' plants.

Depending on their natural environment, they have special requirements relating to their management.

☼ 2°C (36°F)

Pelargonium 'Bildeston'

DWARF BIRD'S EGG

The cultivar 'Bildeston' belongs to a Hortorum subgroup (see *Pelargonium* x *hortorum*), a group with characteristic spotted and speckled flowers.

They are referred to as 'Bird's Eggs' because those, too, are often speckled. As 'Bildeston' is small (under 25cm/10in), it is a dwarf. Plants less than 15cm (6in) tall are sometimes called miniatures.

'Bildeston' is single-flowered, and its salmon-pink petals have irregular, bright red markings.

Some petals have small spots or stripes, and others are entirely covered in vibrant colours.

For management, see *Pelargonium* x *hortorum*.

☼ 2°C (36°F)

Pelargonium 'Bildeston'

Pelargonium 'Cathay'

STELLAR

Pelargonium 'Cathay' belongs to the Stellars, a Hortorum subgroup (see *Pelargonium* x

hortorum). The plants, about 30cm (12in) in height, have star-shaped leaves, often with a dark band.

The flower stems rise well above them and bear flowers with frayed tips to the petals. *Pelargonium* 'Cathay' has salmon-pink flowers, as do 'Bird's Dancer' (a little lighter), and 'Hannaford Star' (a slightly deeper shade). There are countless white Stellars: 'Arctic Star', 'Pixie Prince', and 'Snowflake'. Other cultivars include: 'Grenadier' (double, scarlet), 'Orange Pixie' (double, orange red), 'Pixie Fire' (red and white double flowers), and 'Scarlet Gem' (single, red).

For management see *Pelargonium* x *hortorum*.

☼ 5°C (41°F)

Pelargonium 'Cathay'

Pelargonium x *domesticum*

FRENCH GERANIUM

The countles forms of *Pelargonium* x *domesticum* (*Pelargonium* Domesticum group or *Pelargonium* Regal group) are called French geraniums. They are usually on sale as flowering houseplants (*domesticum* means 'of the house'), but grow and flower better out in the fresh air, where they are scarcely susceptible to whitefly. In living-rooms and greenhouses, however, they are highly subject to such infestation.

The plant's thread-like roots grow well in

ordinary, humus-rich potting compost, which should be left to dry out before further watering. Even though the plants may continue to flower in the shade, it is best to find a semi-shady position, where they will bear large, colourful flowers from May until late summer and beyond. If you leave Regal geraniums out of doors for as long as possible in autumn, they flower all the more profusely the following year.

☼ 2°C (36°F)

Pelargonium x domesticum

Pelargonium x *hortorum*

ZONAL GERANIUM

This is the collective name for the most popular pelargoniums. Because they have a compact, bushy shape, they are also called upright geraniums. You may also find them referred to as the Zonal group or Zonal hybrids, because of the resemblance of their leaves to *Pelargonium zonale* (one of the likely parent plants), which produces leaves marked with a darker zone. These dark zones do not occur in all forms. In professional circles, these pelargoniums are referred to as Hortorums (of gardens). The Hortorums develop a branching framework of round stems containing a lot of sap, a supply drawn on in times of drought. The plants do best if you let the soil dry out entirely after watering. Then water freely again. Be careful, however, not to let the roots become waterlogged, or they will soon rot. Stand the plants in a sunny to half-shady position which should, above all, be airy. Preferably use potting compost to which a considerable amount of clay and a little sand have been added. During the growing season, these pelargoniums like to be given some

fertilizer containing relatively little nitrogen (N). Take the plants indoors before the frosts begin, and let them overwinter in a cool, light place. The potting compost may be left to dry out almost entirely. Propagation and renewal are effected by tip cuttings taken in summer. Cut them off below the fourth leaf bud. Plant the cutting individually in sandy soil in small pots (5cm/2in diameter). Water the cuttings immediately and put them in a warm and light position, but not in the sun, and never under a plastic cover. Do not water again until the soil has dried out completely. It will take about 2 to 4 weeks for the cuttings to grow roots.

☼ 2°C (36°F)

Pelargonium x *hortorum*

Pelargonium 'L'Elégante'

TRAILING IVY-LEAFED GERANIUM

This magnificent variegated form is one of the trailing pelargoniums (trailing geraniums), referred to as *Pelargonium peltatum* or Peltatum group. Its stems are smooth and thin, and become pendulous as they grow longer. They are adorned with fleshy, glossy, more or less pointed leaves, reminiscent of ivy. In a sunny position, the plant will flower long and profusely. The Peltatums are often planted in a row in a balcony trough, with the foliage and flowers cascading over the edge like a waterfall.

Pelargonium 'L'Elégante', however, is often grown by itself. Its variegated leaves, which have a greyish-green sheen and creamy-white margins, look magnificent in a classical pot.

If you let the soil dry out in between watering sessions, the colour of the margins will change to purple at the end of the season.

Apart from requiring a slightly higher minimum temperature, management is the same as for *Pelargonium* x *hortorum*.

☼ 3°C (37°F)

Pelargonium 'L'Elégante'

Pelargonium 'Mme Layal'

ANGEL

The compact *Pelargonium* 'Mme Layal' belongs to one of the smaller groups, the Angel group. These small shrubs have branching woody stems, often with wavy leaves.

From spring until late summer, flowers with lovely markings appear above the foliage. They are sometimes classified as French geraniums, and their flowers bear a close resemblance to those of that group.

Angels tolerate more water than other pelargoniums, and are therefore eminently suitable for patios.

If the pot or tub is well-drained, you need have no fear of root rot, even in wet summers.

For further management, see *Pelargonium* x *hortorum*.

☼ 2°C (36°F)

Pelargonium Regale-groep

See: *Pelargonium* x *domesticum*

Pelargonium 'Rober's Lemon Rose'

SCENTED-LEAFED GERANIUM

The fragrance rather than the decorative appearance of foliage and flowers, is the important feature of scented-leafed pelargoniums such as 'Rober's Lemon Rose'. The flowers are nearly always rather small and the leaves are often green and felt-like. The leaves are covered in very fine hairs, and when they are broken off, for instance by someone stroking the leaf, an essential oil is released with a fragrance characteristic of the species.

The names of the plants refer to the nature of the fragrance, and the well-known lemon-scented pelargonium therefore smells of lemon; 'Old Spice' smells of cloves; 'Prince of Orange' smells of oranges, at least... in theory. The human sense of smell appears to be highly individual, and the scent of a single plant is therefore interpreted quite differently by various people. The nomenclature of scented-leafed geraniums, furthermore, is chaotic, and it is rare to find a plant with an appropriate name. If you are buying a plant, it is therefore best to rely on your nose - literally. Put the scented-leafed pelargoniums in a sunny position and give them moderate quantities of

Pelargonium 'Mme Layal'

water and food; otherwise they will lose their compact appearance and delightful fragrance. Protect the plants against prolonged spells of wet weather in summer. For further management, see *Pelargonium* x *hortorum*.

☼ 2°C (36°F)

Pelargonium 'Rober's Lemon Rose'

Pelargonium 'Shottesham Pet'

Pelargonium 'Shottesham Pet'

UNIQUE

The sturdy stems of *Pelargonium* 'Shottesham Pet' are covered in close-set curled leaves which release a spicy fragrance when touched. This spreading plant is a typical example of the Unique group with its characteristic broad and rugged growth, and often very brightly coloured flowers.

The plants like fresh air, and, because of their robust growth, are very suitable for cultivating by themselves in large pots. The ripening shoots will eventually trail over the rims.

For management, see *Pelargonium* x *hortorum*.

☼ 2°C (36°F)

Pelargonium Zonal groep

See: *Pelargonium* x *hortorum*

Penstemon 'Evelyn'

In arid regions in Central America and the southwest of the US, penstemons will survive severe frosts. In countries like the Netherlands, however, damp conditions make it

impossible for them to live through even a mild winter out of doors. Wet roots are very sensitive to cold in winter, and will therefore rot.

It is possible, however, for penstemons to overwinter in pots. Fill the pot intended for *Penstemon* 'Evelyn' with free-draining, sandy soil. Water in summer whenever the surface of the soil feels dry, and never add fertilizer. 'Evelyn' was presumably developed from *Penstemon campanulatus* and has the bushy appearance of that Mexican species. It bears pink flowers with beautiful markings from June until well into autumn.

As soon as the frosts begin, it is best to move the pot to an unheated greenhouse or cold frame, where temperatures may fall to about -10°C (14°F).

If the frosts become even more severe, the plant will require a light and cool location indoors but should not be watered.

Even if the penstemons survive the winter, they are short-lived plants. You should take cuttings as soon as they begin to show signs of deterioration in late summer. Take tip cuttings from non-flowering shoots and insert them in slightly moist, sandy soil under glass or plastic.

☼ –10°C (14°F)

Penstemon 'Evelyn'

Penstemon 'Mother of Pearl'

The white flowers of this magnificent plant are coated with a gleaming purplish-pink bloom like mother-of-pearl.

They are borne on stems about 70cm (28in) in height from midsummer.

For management and propagation, see *Penstemon* 'Evelyn'.

☼ –10°C (14°F)

Penstemon 'Mother of Pearl'

Pentas carnea

See: *Pentas lanceolata*

Pentas lanceolata

EGYPTIAN STAR, STAR-CLUSTER

The flowers are the main attraction of this small shrub from Yemen and East Africa. They first appear on young plants and are borne in convex umbels between 5 and 10cm (2 and 4in) across. They vary in colour from white to soft pink to flesh, or from pink to magenta and light mauve. All kinds of colours and mixed colours may germinate from the seed of, for example, a white-flowered plant, so it does not make much sense to give the various colours individual names. It is therefore best to buy the plants when they are in flower. You will find *Egyptian stars displayed among the*

Pentas lanceolata

houseplants or annual bedding plants, the idea being that they will be thrown away after flowering. As a container plant, Pentas can grow old. Plant it in a large pot and put it in a warm and sunny spot out of doors in late spring. Given a reasonable amount of care, the plant will grow fast and flower profusely. After the effect of the chemical growth inhibitors used by nurseries has worn off, it will eventually grow to almost 1m (3ft). The plant's shape may be kept compact and attractive by pruning after it has flowered. In winter, the plant prefers a light, airy, and cool location, where the minimum temperature is 10°C (50°F). Overwintering in a living-room is possible but, because the plant will then continue to grow, it will need to be watered regularly, whereas that is hardly necessary if it is kept in a cool place during the winter. If *Pentas* eventually becomes too woody, take cuttings from fresh stems and let them root in a sandy mixture in a frame with soil heating.

☼ 10°C (50°F)

Pentas lanceolata

Persea americana

AVOCADO

The fruit of the avocado tree contains a seed as large as a pigeon's egg. It is wonderful to watch it germinate, and if you partly fill a glass or vase with water, you may observe the entire process. Make sure the seed is suspended just above the surface of the water. The seed appears to 'smell' the water, and will germinate after several weeks or months. A sturdy stem with strong cotyledons will emerge from the stone, while the root grows down into the water. It will then be time to pot up the seedling.

Keep the glass in a warm place (20-25°C/68-77°F). You can speed up germination by increasing the humidity round the seed (by enclosing the glass), or by filing or scraping off a small part of the testa.

Over a number of years, the young avocado may grow into a magnificent foliage plant, and will look attractive on a patio or balcony. Put it in a warm position, sheltered from the sun. Although the plant will tolerate a few degrees of frost, the cold will make it shed its leaves, thus retarding its growth.

At temperatures over 5°C (41°F), the plant will hold its leaves in winter. It will then need just enough water to make up for transpiration from the leaves. You should give it plenty of water and fertilizer in summer to enable the large shiny green leaves to develop well. It will be many years before the plant flowers, and

Persea americana

204

fruits are unlikely to develop in cool European climates, since most forms of avocado need to be pollinated with pollen from a another plant. Any fruits that do develop are unlikely to have much flavour in this type of climate.

In Central America, where the avocado was cultivated 8,000 years ago, the plant will grow into a tree about 15m (50ft) tall. In countries like Great Britain, it will long remain a handsome foliage shrub, which can be kept compact by pruning.

◯ 5°C (41°F) or ● 0°C (21°F)

Petunia

Petunias have long been known as annual border plants, but it is really better to grow them in pots, where they are less likely to be spattered with muddy water. Most of the cultivars on sale are crosses between *Petunia axillaris* and *Petunia integrifolia*. Both species are short-lived, so that it is best to grow them from seed every year. Many petunias grown from cuttings are currently also on the market. They flower early, at a time when customers are looking for plants to put in their containers. The Cascade group provides petunias suitable for balcony troughs, with trailing stems cascading over the rims of containers like waterfalls. Some of the petunias grown from cuttings now have proprietary names which are used as generic names: Surfinia and Fortunia are the best-known examples. The growers registered the names to prevent others from propagating the plants. Strictly speaking, you are not even allowed to take cuttings from these plants. There are twelve Surfinia cultivars, varying from white to pink to violet, often with darker venation in the petals. They have good resistance to rain, are reasonably windproof, content with very little sun (although they do not object to a lot), and require a great deal of water and regular feeding. Unfortunately, and just like other petunias grown from cuttings, Surfinias have proved highly susceptible to viruses. An affected plant may infect other similar plants by leaf, stem, or root contact, by way of contaminated soil, or when cuttings are taken. An infected knife may cause the disease to spread rapidly. This kind of infection has occurred most frequently among the following Surfinias: Hot Pink, Pastel Pink, Violet Blue, and White. When buying plants, make sure that the leaves are unblemished and uniformly green. Infected plants develop light green spots on the leaves, which eventually become puckered and deformed. Flowers no longer

Petunia

Petunia 'Kesupite'

Petunia 'Sunsolos'

open, and the entire plant may die down eventually. If this disease can be brought under control, petunias grown from cuttings will undoubtedly remain popular. If not, plants grown from seed will probably regain lost ground, because they are not susceptible to the disease. Petunias sown in early spring will not flower until summer. To bring them on to the market early in the year, growers often sow them in autumn and winter, and therefore need to provide extra light and heat. It is better for amateur gardeners to sow them indoors between late January and the end of March. Scatter the seed very thinly in a light, poor mixture of sand and peat. Cover with glass and keep the soil temperature at about 20°C (68°F). Remove the glass after germination to prevent scorching. Grow the seedlings on in a slightly cooler and lighter position, but not in excessive sunlight; do not move them out of doors until after the final frost. Put them in a spot sheltered from the wind, in full sun or semi-shade, and make sure that the soil does not dry out or become waterlogged.

Petunias grown from seed do not need fertilizer, and will flower all the more profusely as a result. Popular cultivars include the following:
Petunia 'Kessupas' (Pastel Pink Surfinia)
Petunia 'Kessupite' (White Surfinia)
Petunia 'Kesuble' (Violet Surfinia)
Petunia 'Marrose' (Hot Pink Surfinia)
Petunia 'Pink Rising Sun'
(Fortunia Pink Rising Sun)
Petunia 'Pink Wave' (Fortunia Pink Wave)
Petunia 'Purple Wave'
(Fortunia Purple Wave)
Petunia 'Red Rising Sun'
(Fortunia Red Rising Sun)
Petunia 'Revolution' (Purple Mini Surfinia)
Petunia 'Shihi Brilliant' (Brilliant Surfinia)
Petunia 'Shihi Purple' (Purple Surfinia)
Petunia 'Summer Sun' (Multiflora F1-hybrid)
Petunia 'Sunsolos' (Blue Vein Surfinia)
Petunia 'Suntosol' (Pink Vein Surfinia)
Petunia 'Suntovan' (Pink Mini Surfinia)
Petunia 'White Rising Sun' (Fortunia White Rising Sun)
(1)

Petunia 'Revolution'

Petunia 'Suntovan'

206

Phaedranthus buccinatorius

See: *Distictis buccinatoria*

Phlox drummondii

ANNUAL PHLOX

Annual phloxes like a warm position, preferably in full sun, otherwise in partial shade. Sow indoors in early spring, or out of doors from mid April. If planted in light, nutritive soil, the seedlings will flower in the second half of the summer.

Choose low-growing cultivars for containers, so that the plants remain compact and do not become straggly. The cultivars in the Beauty series are particularly suitable. The plants' maximum height is 20cm (8in):
Phlox drummondii 'Blue Beauty' has mauvish-blue flowers fading to lighter shades;
Phlox drummondii 'Pink Beauty' bears large, bright pink to salmon-pink flowers;
Phlox drummondii 'Yellow Beauty' has soft yellow flowers.

(1)

Phlox drummondii 'Blue Beauty'

Phoenix canariensis

CANARY ISLAND DATE PALM

In the Canary Islands, where *Phoenix canariensis* originally came from, the palm ultimately grows to over 10m (33ft) in height. On winter nights, the temperature falls to about 5°C (41°F), but this palm can tolerate far more severe cold.

In places along the Côte d'Azur, the Riviera, and in southwest England, there are often several degrees of frost.

It is one of the least demanding palms for growing in a container, although even young plants require a lot of room. The feather-shaped arching leaves spread considerably from the very first, so that a space measuring at least 3m (10ft) in diameter is essential. Later on, the length of the leaves will increase to over 5m (16ft).

Stand the palm in a warm and sunny spot in summer, which may also be windy. The palm may therefore even be grown on a large balcony or on a roof.

Ensure a steady supply of softened water which must not be colder than the potting compost.

In winter, the palm should be in a light and frost-free location. A cool (5-15°C/41-59°F) and almost dry space would be best, but a heated living-room will do in an emergency. In that case, you should water regularly.

☼ 5°C (41°F)

Phoenix canariensis

Phormium colensoi

MOUNTAIN FLAX

The European discoverers of New Zealand saw how the Maoris span threads from the leaves of a plant. The vascular bundles in this so-called *Phormium* (derived from the Greek word for woven mat) are among the strongest of all natural fibres. They are woven by the Maoris.

The leaves are sword-shaped and as long as those of irises. Mature plants produce long stems bearing orange to reddish-brown flowers which are pollinated by birds.

The leaves of *Phormium colensoi* grow to over 1m (3ft) in length, which is much shorter than those of the only other species: *Phormium tenax*.

Magnificent varieties and cultivars have been developed from both species, partly in nature, and partly by targeted hybridization and selection. There are variegated forms with leaves differing in size. Cultivars are often attributed inconsistently to the species. Furthermore, both species have a cultivar called 'Tricolor' and one called 'Variegatum', which are in fact different forms.

For management, see *Phormium tenax*.

Well-known cultivars include:

Phormium colensoi 'Apricot Queen' (dark green with apricot stripes and bronze-coloured margins);

Phormium colensoi 'Dark Delight' (deep reddish brown);

Phormium colensoi 'Duet' (short, light green leaves with creamy white stripes);

Phormium colensoi 'Jack Sprat' (short, pale bronze-coloured leaves);

Phormium colensoi 'Tricolor' (lax green leaves with red margins and creamy yellow stripes);

Phormium colensoi 'Variegatum' (creamy to lemon-yellow stripes along the leaf margins).

○ of ● 0°C (32°F)

Phormium colensoi 'Variegatum'

Phormium coockianum

See: *Phormium colensoi*

Phormium hookeri

See: *Phormium colensoi*

Phormium tenax

NEW ZEALAND FLAX

In English coastal regions, New Zealand flax grows in open ground with winter protection. In that way, the plant will tolerate -10°C (14°F). When growing it in a container, you must keep the creeping rhizomes frost-free. In winter, you should find a location which is as cool as possible (not over 12°C/53°F), almost dry, and preferably well-lit. A place that is not unduly light is also tolerated if there is no

Phormium tenax

alternative. Stand Phormium in full sun in summer, which will make the leaves take on their finest colours. Water freely (*Phormium colensoi* should be watered moderately), but it must also be possible for the water to drain away freely. Do not repot until the roots have filled the entire pot, because only then can New Zealand flax be divided properly (if need be, by halving the clump with a sharp spade). Sowing is also possible, but the seedlings will only resemble their parent plants in the case of the original species and the forms that developed spontaneously in New Zealand ('Purpureum' and 'Variegatum'). In the case of hybrids developed elsewhere in the world, the seedlings are extremely variable. Numerous variegated forms have been developed from *Phormium tenax* and the only other species,

the smaller *Phormium colensoi* (see entry). Many of them are now on the market, including: *Phormium tenax* 'Aurora' (long, narrow leaves with green, red, pink to yellow and chestnut-brown stripes);
Phormium tenax 'Bronze Baby' (short, deep-red to bronze-green leaves);
Phormium tenax 'Dazzler' (bright red leaves with orange-yellow and olive-greyish-green bands);
Phormium tenax 'Purpureum' (greyish-green leaves with reddish-brown midribs and margins);
Phormium tenax 'Sundowner' (greyish-green leaves, 1.5m/5ft) long, with purple ribs, and pink to creamy yellow margins);
Phormium tenax 'Variegatum' (green with yellow, cream, and white bands);
Phormium tenax 'Yellow Wave' (broad green leaves with yellow to greenish-yellow bands).

○ or ● 0°C (32°F)

Phormium tenax 'Sundowner'

Phygelius aequalis

Phygelius species come from South Africa, and prefer a moist location in spite of their warm native environment.
They grow beside brooks and against damp rocks in the wild, preferably in a sunny spot. Stand them in a warm and sunny position, and water freely in summer.

The orange-flowered *Phygelius aequalis* has a light-yellow cultivar 'Yellow Trumpet', which is often on sale at container plant nurseries. It is sometimes called the yellow fuchsia.
In summer, pendent flowers facing in a single direction, are borne on stems approximately 1m (3ft) long. The species and yellow cultivars are less tolerant of cold than *Phygelius capensis*, and definitely need to overwinter in a frost-free place. Put them, almost dry, in a light location.

○ 2°C (36°F)

Phygelius aequalis 'Yellow Trumpet'

Phygelius capensis

Unfortunately, the best-known *Phygelius* is rarely on sale. Even so, the name is often seen at nurseries, but usually refers to one of the modern crosses between *Phygelius capensis* and *Phygelius aequalis*: see *Phygelius* x *rectus*.
The true Cape fuchsia (not illustrated) bears curved orange flowers on stems over 1.5m (5ft) tall. In areas with a maritime climate, the plant may overwinter in open ground with some form of protection. Stems and leaves will be cut by frost.
Containerized specimens should be taken indoors if they are to hold their leaves. The plant prefers a light indoor location, but will not need much water.

○ 0°C (32°F)

Phygelius x rectus

Most plants on sale labelled *Phygelius capensis* are in fact crosses between that species and *Phygelius aequalis*. In the 1980s in particular, many of these x *rectus* hybrids were created at the Hillier nursery in England. They are just as hardy as *Phygelius capensis*, and can therefore remain out of doors in open ground in areas with mild winters.

For further management, see *Phygelius capensis*.

Phygelius x *rectus* 'African Queen' was created in 1969 by crossing *Phygelius aequalis* and *Phygelius capensis* 'Coccineus'. As the pale red buds open, they arch over towards the stem.

Each one has a yellow throat and is surrounded by orange-red petals.

Phygelius x *rectus* 'Trewidden Pink' is a slimmer form with narrower orange flowers.

☼ 0°C (32°F)

Phygelius x *rectus* 'African Queen'

Pinus canariensis

CANARY ISLAND PINE

There are whole forests of these pines in the Canary Islands. Thick layers of fallen pine needles carpet the forest floor beneath these trees, which grow to 20m (65ft) tall. Hardly anything can grow there. Although the islands often experience forest fires, Canary Islands pines survive as a result of a special adaptation: only the outer layer of bark will burn.

The needles, 20cm (8in) long, give the Canary Island pine a particularly attractive appearance, but, in spite of that, it is rarely on sale. If, however, you have an opportunity to gather some seed on one of the islands, you will find it quite easy to cultivate the pine. The cone-shaped tree may remain in a pot for years. Give it a sunny position in summer and water freely. It requires a well-lit, cool location indoors in winter, when the soil should be kept just moist.

☼ 0°C (32°F)

Pinus canariensis

Pinus 'Pierrick Bregeon'

PINE

Containerized pines are almost exclusively known in the form of bonsai, trees that are kept diminutive by the continual pruning of branches and roots. *Pinus* 'Pierrick Bregeon' is naturally slow-growing, which makes this pine very suitable for cultivating as a container plant. The flattened spherical shrub is supplied in a large pot when it has grown to about 30cm (12in) in height. Its growth is so slow that it will be several years before it needs a larger container.

It is essential to ensure good drainage when repotting the plant, as pine roots cannot endure boggy soil for any length of time. Mix ordinary potting compost with at least one third sharp sand, so that the soil keeps an open structure. Water with some restraint: twice weekly is quite enough in normal circumstances. It is best to use rain water, or else boiled water, as pines dislike lime.

Pinus 'Pierrick Bregeon' is very suitable for a balcony or a roof garden. The pine is impervious to wind, tolerates full sun, and is

Phygelius x *rectus*

Pinus 'Pierrick Bregeon'

fully hardy. If, however, severe frost is accompanied by a dry wind, it is better to stand the plant as close to a wall as possible. If your balcony is covered, do not forget to water

occasionally in winter, as evaporation from the surface of the leaves continues even then.

✳

Pittosporum tobira

JAPANESE PITTOSPORUM, MOCK ORANGE

The hedges of mock orange in Mediterranean countries have a sweet fragrance. It is reminiscent of orange blossom, and is exuded by the waxy, creamy-white flowers. *Pittosporum tobira*, an evergreen shrub, originally came from China or Japan.

In countries like the Netherlands, mock orange is highly popular as a container plant. It will grow into a well-branched, leafy shrub. The shiny green leaves are remarkable for their light midribs. The variegated form, *Pittosporum tobira* 'Variegatum' is often available from nurseries. The leaf margins are white to creamy yellow, a shade which changes to dull, light green in an untidy transitional zone.

In open ground, mock orange will tolerate temperatures as low as -10°C (14°F), but, when containerized, the shrub should be moved indoors for overwintering in a light location, where the potting compost should

Pittosporum tobira 'Variegatum'

Pittosporum tobira 'Variegatum'; flower

Pittosporum tobira 'Variegatum'

213

not be left to dry out entirely. Try to keep the winter temperature below 12°C (53°F), as growth during the winter season makes the shrub highly attractive to red spider mite and other pests.

In summer, the plant may be placed in full sun, although it does better in semi-shade. Avoid soaking-wet soil, but do not let it dry out entirely either.

☼ 0°C (32°F)

Plectostachys serphyllifolia

Plectostachys resembles the ever-popular *Helichrysum petiolare*, and is closely related to it. It is even better known by its synonym *Helichrysum microphyllum*. *Micro* means small, and *phyllum* means leaf, and the plant is most easily recognizable by these characteristics. The small leaves are no more than 1cm (1/2in) long and grow on spreading stems. The felty white hairs protect them from the fierce South African sunlight.

The species is highly suitable for use as basic planting for hanging baskets. Insert flowering plants such as trailing verbena, which will then show up all the better. *Plectostachys* will remain compact in a sunny position, especially if you water sparingly and do not add fertilizer. Growers take cuttings in summer; these are left to overwinter in a cool and light location. Amateur gardeners usually buy new plants each spring. The old plants will withstand several degrees of frost and continue to look well until far into autumn.

In addition to the white-woolly species with greyish-green leaves, there are several magnificent cultivars, including 'Aurea', which has creamy-white to yellowish leaf margins; 'Silver', which is slightly greyer than the species; and 'Yellow', which has uniformly pale yellow leaves.

(1) of ☼ 0°C (32°F)

Plectranthus coleoides

See: *Plectranthus forsteri*

Plectranthus forsteri 'Marginatus'

If these magnificent decorative foliage plants are labelled at all, they are usually given the wrong name: *Plectranthus coleoides* 'Marginatus' is what they are called in the trade, after an Asian species. *Plectranthus forsteri*, however, is the correct name. The species comes from islands in the Pacific. The trailing stems make the plant very suitable for growing as ground cover in a frost-free conservatory or greenhouse, but they may also cascade gracefully down the sides of hanging baskets or balcony troughs. The variegated form 'Marginatus' (also called 'Variegatus') is often grown up chicken wire or mesh, which the leaves will cover completely.

As a container plant *Plectranthus* will grow in full sun or partial shade. Water moderately. Feeding is scarcely required, particularly if you propagate the plant by cuttings.

Plectranthus forsteri 'Marginatus'

Plectostachys serphyllifolia

The trailing shoots root easily where they touch the soil, but you may also cut them off and use for cuttings. These should overwinter in a cool and slightly damp location, after which you pot them up in fresh soil in spring.

☼ 0°C (32°F)

Plectranthus fruticosus

This plant was at one time thought to relieve rheumatic pains, and was therefore often kept in living rooms. In fact, it grows better in a pot or container out of doors, where it will produce slender stems full of small light-blue to pink, mauve-flecked flowers.

Even so, the plants are grown mainly for the decorative appearance of their large, fragrant, downy leaves. Put them in a sheltered position to prevent the leaves from being damaged by wind. If the potting compost is kept moist enough, they may be placed in full sun, although they will grow better in partial shade. This South African plant will rapidly become a large bush in a spacious pot, but if you keep it in a smaller one, growth will remain within bounds. It is also possible to prune the plant, although this will initially affect its appearance. Clippings can be put in water and treated like cuttings at any time of the year. The plant should be moved indoors as soon as night temperatures fall below 5°C (41°F) in autumn.

In winter, it is best to treat the plectranthus like a houseplant.

☼ 5°C (41°F)

Plectranthus saccatus

Plectranthus saccatus looks as though it is a sturdy shrub, but its succulent, purple to slate-grey stems break off easily.

The leaves, too, are succulent, delicately toothed, and slightly sticky; their colour is variable. The plant presents a magnificent appearance, especially by itself in a large pot on a patio.

The blueish-mauve flowers are relatively large, but they rarely appear, and even then sparsely, so that the foliage is its main decorative feature.

Water freely in summer, as that is what the plant would expect in its natural environment (southern East Africa). Move it indoors in good time in autumn, and water sparingly in winter. The plant should have enough light, as it holds its leaves.

☼ 5°C (41°F)

Plectranthus fruticosus

Plectranthus saccatus

Plumbago auriculata

CAPE LEADWORT

Cape leadwort is well known as a houseplant, but is really more suitable for growing in a container. The stems, often tied round a hoop in a shop, rapidly grow in all directions. They may be cut back hard, but that also means cutting off the buds developing at the tips of the stems. It is therefore better to grow the plant in a large pot or container, and provide a strong support for the stems, as they do not attach themselves.

Water freely in summer, but do not feed excessively. If you stand the pot in a warm position in full sun or partial shade, the plant will bear abundant trusses of sky-blue to lavender-blue flowers. *Plumbago auriculata* 'Alba' has pure white flowers. The calyx has small sticky hairs which easily attach themselves to clothing. The name leadwort refers to the plant's use as a remedy for lead poisoning. *Plumbago* is derived from the Latin words *plumbum*, which means lead.

Plumbago will survive a mild winter in open ground, but containerized plants should be moved indoors before the frosts begin. There is a ten to one chance that the plant will still be in full flower at the time. In a conservatory, or a moderately heated greenhouse, it will continue to flower all through the winter.

In a cooler location, the plant will become dormant. Some of the leaves will dry up but remain on the plant. Water sparingly at this time, but let *Plumbago* have as much fresh air as possible. The stems may be cut back hard in early autumn or late winter.

☼ 0°C (32°F)

Plumbago capensis

See: *Plumbago auriculata*

Plumbago indica

This red-flowered *Plumbago* likes tropical heat and will therefore thrive in a greenhouse. The plant is rarely on sale in northwest Europe, perhaps because it can only grow well out of doors if it is in a warm position.

Red flowers appear on the stems from late summer.

Move the semi-climber indoors before the temperature falls to below 10°C (50°F) at night.

Stand it in a moderately warm location (minimum temperature 12°C/53°F), but not in a centrally heated living room, where the atmosphere would be too dry. A well-lit place in a cool room in a centrally heated house would be best.

☼ 12°C (53°F)

Plumbago indica

Plumbago auriculata

Plumeria rubra

FRANGIPANI

The large flowers of this small tropical tree from Central America exude a delightful fragrance. Small wonder that it has been planted in the most diverse tropical and subtropical regions. The leaves are shed in dry periods, leaving a bare candelabrum of round branches.

In more northerly climates, frangipani can only be grown as a container plant in a warm, sheltered position. You can achieve a good, compact shape by occasional tip pruning, but be careful, the latex in the plant is poisonous. In summer, large leaves are produced at the tips of stems, along with flowers measuring about 7cm (2 3/4in) across. The species has pinkish red blooms. *Plumeria rubra forma acutifolia* has white flowers; those of *forma lutea* are yellow; and *forma tricolor* has flowers in three colours: pink on the outside, white on the inside, with yellow centres. All forms, in fact, have yellow centres.

Do not water the plant in summer until the potting compost has almost dried out. Use free-draining, fertile soil. As soon as the temperature falls below 10°C (50°F) in late summer, the plant should be moved indoors. Cease watering. The plant will shed its leaves and may be put in a dark location for the winter.

● 10°C (50°F)

Podranea ricasoliana

In southern Europe, North Africa, the Canary Islands and Madeira, the stems of this South African climber meander across buildings and pergolas to a height of about 4m (13ft). Clusters of very large pink flowers (up to 5cm/2in across) hang from the tips of the stems.Although this climber will remain smaller in a pot, it still needs space. A position in the ground in an unheated greenhouse of conservatory is ideal, but *Podreana* may also be cultivated satisfactorily in a large pot if adequate support is provided. Stand the container in a warm and sunny position, and water the nutritive humus-rich soil freely in summer. Move *Podreana* indoors before the first frosts and stand it in a place which should be as cool as possible. The plant will shed its leaves at a temperature below 12°C

Plumeria rubra forma acutifolia

(53°F), after which it can overwinter in a dark and dry location. At higher temperatures, the leaves will remain on the plant, which means that it will need light and moisture.

● 0°C (32°F)

Podranea ricasoliana

Polemonium caeruleum 'Brise d'Anjou'

JACOB'S LADDER

The common Jacob's ladder, one of the least demanding of all garden plants, likes to grow in partial shade and moist soil. Sky-blue flowers appear above the doubly pinnate leaves in summer.

Polemonium caeruleum 'Brise d'Anjou'

A variegated Jacob's ladder was known in the eighteenth century, but it went out of fashion and was only recently rediscovered at a nursery in France. It has proved a real treasure for cultivating in a pot, not only because of the butter-yellow margins to its leaflets, but also because the plant stays more compact that way. Slower growth is often a characteristic of plants with variegated leaves, as there is less chlorophyll. 'Brise d'Anjou' should therefore be given a light location and plenty of water and food.

The leaves die down in autumn. The polemonium's rootstocks are fully hardy, although it would be better to protect the plant from severest frosts by putting it, in its pot, in a hole in the garden.

✳

Polygala myrtifolia

This South African plant bears purplish-red flowers at the tips of waxy-leafed shoots. The flowers have a remarkable shape and appear throughout the summer. Even so, this rewarding and profusely flowering plant is not very popular yet. This may have something to do with its requirements for overwintering. Because it is evergreen, it will need a lot of light. The plant is also rather exacting in respect of temperature, which should on no acount fall below 5°C (41°F) in winter. Nor

Polygala myrtifolia var. *grandiflora*

should it exceed 12°C (53°F), or the polygala will stop growing. Make sure that it has as much fresh air as possible.

Managing the plant is much easier in summer. The shrub grows about 1m (3ft) tall, and does well in partial shade. Water freely and ensure that the water can drain away satisfactorily, or the entire plant will be lost. Shield the slightly acid soil from prolonged periods of wet conditions in summer. The plant may be cut back hard in early spring.

The variety usually on sale at nurseries is *Polyganum myrtifolia* var. *grandiflora*. It has purple and white flowers over 2cm (over 3/4in) across.

☼ 5°C (41°F)

Polygala virgata

The thin stems of this South African species first grow vertically, and then arch over under the weight of the flowers adorning the plant from April until well into late summer.

They closely resemble those of *Polygala myrtifolia*. The difference between the two plants is most apparent in the foliage which, in the case of *Polygala virgata*, is clearly oblong and green (without a blueish-green waxy layer).

Unless the plant's winter location is well lit, it is likely to shed its leaves.

In that event, the *polygala* should be cut back hard in spring if it is to sprout satisfactorily again.

Fortunately, that is not much of a problem, since this vigorous *Polygala* grows 1.5m (5ft) tall, even in a container.

Polygala virgata

For further management, see *Polygala myrtifolia*.

☼ 5°C (41°F)

Polygonum capitatum

KNOTWEED

A containerized standard plant looks rather exposed if its tall stem emerges from the bare soil. This problem may be overcome by planting low-growing, shallow-rooted plants at its base. *Polygonum capitatum* is an excellent choice for this purpose. It is a spreading perennial from the Himalayas. Its foliage is normally green, with a darker V-shaped mark on each leaf. The leaves will turn red in the event of drought or in fierce sunlight. The creeping shoots root at each node, thus creating a broad carpet which, because of its shallow roots, scarcely competes with the standard plant. In dry locations, *Polygonum capitatum* sometimes survives the winter in northwest Europe. When containerized, however, the plants will be moved indoors with the standard plant, where a little light, a little warmth, and a few drops of moisture will satisfy their needs.

☼ or ● 0°C (32°F)

Polygonum capitatum

Portulaca grandiflora

SUN PLANT

The horizontal stems of the sun plant grow slowly and arch over in places where there is no soil to support them. The leaves are succulent and bright green. Portulacas are ideal plants for hanging baskets and balcony troughs and, because the species originally came from the border regions between Brazil, Uruguay, and Argentina, they like sunny positions. If you fill the troughs with sandy soil that is deficient in nutrients, and water moderately, numerous flowers, 2-3cm (3/4-1 1/4in) across, will appear. Depending on the plant, they may be crimson, pink, red, orange, yellow, or white. Very little seed is required for filling an entire trough. Sow directly in the trough - indoors in April, or out of doors from May onwards. Flowering begins around June, and continues until September. Purchased plants will flower as early as April-May.

(1)

Portulaca grandiflora

Pratia pedunculata

In Australia, *Pratia pedunculata* covers whole areas of damp valleys. This ground cover also spreads rapidly in other regions where frosts are unknown. The foliage of *Pratia pedunculata* 'County Park', the cultivar grown most frequently, is no more than about 2cm (3/4in) in height. Star-shaped blue to mauve flowers, barely 1.5cm (5/8in) across, appear between the leaves throughout the summer. Grow this plant in partial shade and water moderately. In very well-drained soil, it will tolerate temperatures as low as -10°C (14 °F). Containerized plants should be protected against damp cold in winter, when the pratias should be moved to an unheated greenhouse or a cold frame, or moved indoors in the event of frost. In a light, frost-free location, the plants will retain their leaves. Pratias need very little water in winter.

☼ –5°C (23°F)

Prostanthera cuneata

MINT BUSH

In dry soil, this small evergreen Australian shrub will tolerate temperatures as low as -15°C (5°F). It does not, however, survive winters that are cold and wet, and should therefore overwinter indoors in a cool and light location. A greenhouse or cold frame would be ideal. Watering is scarcely required in winter. Small flowers, about 1cm (1/2in) across, appear in summer, and on closer inspection appear to be beautifully speckled. Even so, the foliage is the plant's main attraction: the leaves are small and succulent, and have a sweet, minty fragrance when touched. Put the plant in a warm and sunny position in summer, and make sure that the soil is slightly acid and free-draining. Water at widely spaced intervals during this period.

☼ –5°C (23°F)

Pratia pedunculata 'County Park'

Prostanthera cuneata

Prostanthera rotundifolia

MINT BUSH

Like *Prostanthera cuneata*, this prostanthera has delightfully fragrant foliage, but the rounded shrub is cultivated mainly for the racemes of violet flowers borne in spring and early summer.

Prostanthera rotundifolia will tolerate a few degrees of frost, but should be moved indoors in winter if containerized. For further management, see *Prostanthera cuneata*.

○ 0°C (32°F)

Prostanthera rotundifolia

Prunus amygdalus

See: *Prunus dulcis*

Prunus dulcis

ALMOND

The wife of a Moorish caliph in southern Spain was homesick and pining away. She longed for the snow on the mountains around Baghdad, the city where she was born. "I promise," said the Caliph, "that I shall make it snow here as well," and he ordered that almond trees be planted all over the fields. After they had flowered in May, the petals drifted down, and covered the land with a white blanket. So the Caliph's wife had her

snow, albeit in an unusual form. Almonds are grown in regions with a Mediterranean climate such as southern Europe, North Africa, Australia, and California. The trees flower in March, even before the leaves appear on the branches. Although deciduous trees will survive more northerly winters in sheltered locations, they do not usually bear fruit there.

The cultivar 'Robijn' (Ruby) is most likely to be successful in open ground, but almond trees are prone to all kinds of disease in damp climates.

It is therefore preferable to grow the almond tree in a large pot or tub, and to move it to a greenhouse or cool winter garden in winter. The lovely pink or whitish pink flowers may then be enjoyed in early spring.

The trees may overwinter in the dark until the buds begin to form. In summer, almonds like a warm position, plenty of water, and well-drained soil.

○ or ● –10°C (14°F)

Punica granatum

POMEGRANATE

In the Middle East and Asia Minor, the pomegranate grows into a large shrub or small tree which flowers in summer and bears fruits the size of a large orange in autumn. Within a

Prunus dulcis

Punica granatum 'Nana'

Pyrostegia ignea

See: *Pyrostegia venusta*

Pyrostegia venusta

FLAME FLOWER, FLAME VINE, GOLDEN SHOWER

In central South America, *Pyrostegia venusta* will wind its way high up into the trees, attaching itself by its twining tendrils. Clusters of orange tubular flowers will then be suspended from the trees in winter. This inverted flowering rhythm, with buds developing in autumn, sometimes persists in European countries. You may, however, change the rhythm by watering occasionally during the autumn months. The plant will then have a dry period in March-April, and the flowers will subsequently appear in early summer. Although this climber does well in a sunny, sheltered spot out of doors, it is preferable to keep it in a conservatory, where it will have space to climb and bear a profusion of flowers. Water freely in summer, and use humus-rich, well-drained soil.

The plant is evergreen, and a well-lit location is therefore essential. Ensure good ventilation and relatively high humidity to prevent red spider mite, but do not let the temperature fall below 10°C (50°F).

☼ 10°C (50°F)

Pyrostegia venusta

leathery skin, small juicy vesicles contain the refreshing and slightly acid pulp often served with desserts.

The plants available for growing in containers are usually low-growing cultivars such as 'Nana', with smaller orange flowers and decorative miniature fruits. Such cultivars, sometimes grown as standards, are intended mainly for ornamental purposes; they bear flowers which do not fall, but swell up into decorative fruits.

Stand the container in a warm and sunny position in summer, and water freely. Pomegranates are undemanding as far as soil is concerned, but it should be well-drained and preferably contain some clay.

The pomegranate should be moved to a cool position (5-10°C/41-50°F) in winter, and given very little water. It may be cut back hard at this time. The flowers will appear on new wood the followiong summer.

Propagation by cuttings is difficult, but pomegranates are easy to grow from seed. Sow at room temperature in spring, and only use seed from ornamental specimens, as plants grown from the seeds of purchased fruits are extremely vigorous and eventually become difficult to manage; they will not flower until they are older.

● 2°C (36°F)

Q, R ———————— q, r

Quamoclit lobata

See: *Ipomoea lobata*

Quercus suber

CORK OAK

In southern countries, cork oaks are cultivated for the thick, springy bark that protects the trees against small fires in the layer of humus. The trunk is stripped of its bark every ten years, and the thick sections are then processed and made into such items as corks for wine bottles, floats for fishing nets, and floor covering.

The weathered appearance of cork oak appeals strongly to plant lovers. Because of its slow growth, it takes a long time for the plant to acquire a tree-like appearance. Cultivation is not difficult if you can provide the evergreen tree with a light, well-ventilated, and cool lo-cation in winter. A conservatory or green-house would be ideal. The plant will scarcely need watering during this period.

In summer, cork oaks like a warm and sunny position. Do not water until the soil has almost dried up. Use rain water or boiled water which should not be colder than the root ball.

☼ 0°C (32°F)

Rehmannia elata

The rehmannia's large flowers are borne on straggly stems in early summer. Despite its untidy growth, the plant is becoming popular for cultivating in containers. It originally came from China, where it is a perennial, but be-cause it scarcely tolerates frost, it is treated like an annual in northwest Europe. After the final night frost, the pot should be put out of

Quercus suber

Brak of *Quercus suber*

doors in a sheltered position to prevent the lax plants and large flowers being spoilt by the wind, and in partial shade to prevent sun scorch. You should preferably use free-draining, humus-rich soil, and water normally. Rehmannias may be propagated by cuttings or by seed, but because the plants flower early in the season, this should be done at room temperature in January-February at the latest. It is even better to sow the plants the previous summer. The seedlings require a cool, light position, and it is therefore simpler for most people to buy flowering plants in spring and to manage them like annuals.

(1)

Rehmannia elata

Rehmannia angulata

See: *Rehmannia elata*

Rhodochiton atrosanguineum

This Mexican climber has rapidly become popular among a small group of genuine plant lovers in recent years. They sow the perennial plant annually in order to see it flower in its container all through the summer. It is possible for the plant to overwinter, but there is no real need to do so, as rhodochitons are easy to grow from seed.
Sow indoors, in March or April, so that the climber may be moved out of doors in its pot after mid-May.
Water freely, feed regularly, and provide a support which should be at least 1m (3ft) tall. As the plant climbs, fresh aubergine-coloured bell-shaped flowers, about 3cm (1 1/4in) long, dangle continually from inverted burgundy

Rhodochiton atrosanguineum

calyces. Vesicular capsules containing numerous brown seeds enclosed in serrated membranes appear in late summer.

(1)

Rhododendron molle

AZALEA

Rhododendron molle blooms in late spring or early summer, bearing clusters of funnelshaped flowers at the tips of stems.
The wild species from Japan are rarely avail-

Rhododendron molle

able from garden centres; instead, there are numerous cultivars referred to as the *Rhododendron* (or *Azalea*) Mollis Group.

The large flowers vary in colour from deep red, pink, and orange, to yellow. The fresh green foliage appears at about the same time as the flowers, and changes to deep green or blueish green later on. The leaves turn beautiful shades in autumn and then fall.

This azalea is fully hardy and may be planted, in its pot, in the garden in autumn. The purpose of cultivation in a container is merely to enable people to enjoy the beautifully branching shape of this shrub (maximum height 1.5m/5ft) to the full. After flowering, it may be pruned slightly to improve its shape.

❄

Rhododendron x *obtusum*

JAPANESE AZALEA

Many rhododendron hybrids are on sale labelled Japanese azalea, and often represent one of the numerous cultivated varieties of *Rhododendron* x *obtusum*, which has been improved in Japan for centuries. Large numbers of cultivars with flowers in all manner of colours have been developed from the countless hybrids.

Japanese azaleas may be planted in sheltered positions in the garden. They will only shed their leaves in the event of severe frost. The shrubs are likely to be badly damaged by late frost and take a long time to recover fully.

Rhododendron

Unless you live in a mild climate, cultivation in containers is more suitable. Put the plant in a large pot or tub containing soil which should be slightly acid. Keep the soil moist

Rhododendron

and cool, and stand the Japanese azalea out of doors in a fresh, semi-shady spot. Do not let the soil dry out entirely even in winter, and find a location for the azalea which is frost-free, well-ventilated, and as light as possible.

☼ 0°C (32°F)

Rosa 'Cinderella'

MINIATURE ROSE

'Cinderella' is typical of the hundreds of roses suitable for growing in pots. Depending on

Rhododendron

the cultivar and method of cultivation, the widely branching bushes grow to between 15 and 40cm (6 and 16in) in height. Plants grown from cuttings will remain shorter than grafted specimens of the same species.

'Cinderella' was developed in 1953 from the polyantha rose 'Cécile Brünner', and the miniature rose 'Tom Thumb' ('Peon'). The bushes grow about 25cm (10in) tall, and have green leaves and few thorns. The fully double flowers are white with pink margins. Because of their erect growth, miniature roses are highly suitable for combining with other plants in containers. Miniature roses prefer to grow out of doors both in summer and in winter. Water normally and feed regularly, especially in spring. The plants will tolerate severe frost in open ground, but it is preferable to move containerized specimens indoors in such conditions. Alternatively, the pots may be sunk into holes in the garden.

❋

Rosa 'Cinderella' (with thyme)

Rosa 'Kent'

GROUND-COVER ROSE

This relatively new rose is highly suitable for growing in containers. *Rosa* 'Kent' (also called 'Poulcov' or 'White Cover') was developed in Denmark in 1987, and bears semidouble white flowers at brief intervals from spring until winter. The bush has a maximum spread of 1m (3ft); its maximum height is 50cm (20in). *Rosa* 'Kent' is classified as a ground-cover rose.

With the exception of extremely vigorous cultivars, other ground-cover roses are also suitable for growing in pots. They usually do

Rosa 'Kent'

well on their own roots, are not much troubled by disease, and even tolerate a shady position - *Rosa* 'Kent' is no exception.

Keep the containerized rose out of doors in summer and in winter. If you are concerned about severe frost, the pot may be sunk into a hole in the garden, covered in insulating material, or moved indoors temporarily.

❋

Rosa 'Poulcov'

See: *Rosa* 'Kent'

Rosa 'White Cover'

See: *Rosa* 'Kent'

Roscoea purpurea

Roscoeas are still relatively unfamiliar and are always a talking point. Plant lovers tell one another about the orchid-like flowers of this forgotten genus: it was described two centuries ago, but has only recently become popular as a garden plant. If you plant it deep and cover it well, this ginger-like plant from the Himalayas and Sikkim will tolerate temperatures as low as -15°C (5°F). Its small size (maximum height 30cm/12in) still impedes a complete breakthrough for garden cultivation. When planted in a large, deep pot, roscoeas may be enjoyed at close quarters. Use humus-rich leaf mould, which needs to be kept cool in summer and should never be left to dry out entirely during the warm months. The flowers appear from midsummer until well into autumn. Move the pot indoors in winter. The leaves will then die down, so that the tubers can overwinter in a dark and dry location. The plant may be divided in spring and then potted up again.

⬤ 0°C (32°F)

Roscoea purpurea

Rosmarinus officinalis

indoors to a cool location which should be as light as possible.

◯ –5°C (23°F)

Rosmarinus officinalis

ROSEMARY

Rosemary is relatively hardy in the coastal regions of western Europe, where the evergreen shrubs are grown as low hedges. Further inland, severe frost will kill rosemary, and it is therefore safer to cultivate it in a pot.

Move the pot to a sunny position out of doors in summer and water moderately.

The soil should preferably contain some clay. Excessive moisture is fatal to this plant from the maquis (the drought-loving scrub in southern Europe).

Trim rosemary to keep its bushy shape. Scatter its needle-shaped leaves over meat before grilling to give it a delicious herby flavour.

Move rosemary to an unheated greenhouse or conservatory in winter and scarcely water.

If you do not have either a greenhouse or a conservatory, leave the rosemary out of doors unless the temperature falls below -5°C (23°F). If it turns colder, the plant should be moved

Ruellia graecizans

Ruellia graecizans from tropical South America is one of the most slender of all container plants. Its stems grow vertically to about 1m (3ft), producing pointed oval leaves, and, at

Ruellia graecizans

their tips, scarlet flowers, 2-3cm (3/4-1 1/4in) long. In favourable conditions, ruellias will flower almost continuously throughout the year.

You can enjoy the plant only if you keep it in relatively warm conditions both in summer and in winter. Find a well-lit place for it in winter, where the minimum temperature should be 10°C (50°F). The humidity should not drop too sharply. Water very sparingly at this time, but make sure that the soil does not dry out. In summer, the plant should be watered freely and given plenty of food. It should be planted in humus-rich soil.

☼ 10°C (50°F)

Russelia equisetiformis

CORAL PLANT

The thin stems of this Mexican flowering plant resemble horsetail (*Equisetum*), an ancient cryptogam. The stems, which may grow to 1.5m (5ft) long, arch over under their own weight. Bright red tubular flowers are borne on young shoots throughout the summer.

Grow the plant in a sunny position in summer; water normally, but do not feed. Find a well-lit location in winter, where you may keep the plant almost dry at a temperature between 5 and 12°C (41 and 53°F). The russelia need not be moved indoors until quite late in the season, since it will tolerate a certain amount of frost. Rejuvenate the plant by cutting back the oldest hardwood stems down to the ground. The plant propagates itself as the pendent stems will root in places where they touch the soil.

☼ 2°C (36°F)

Ruta graveolens

COMMON RUE

Although rue is a herb for the kitchen or medicine cabinet, its effect is so powerful that it should be used with the greatest possible caution. Be careful with the sap, which may cause blisters on some skin types.

Apart from the above, this herb is a magnificent and easily cultivated plant, especially the cultivar 'Jackman's Blue', which has foliage with a blueish green bloom and creates a highly decorative effect in the garden. The plant is fully hardy in open ground, although the leaves may be damaged by severe frost. In winter, plant rue, in its pot, in the garden. In summer, this plant prefers a sunny or partially shady position in light, well-drained soil, which should really contain some lime or clay.

Russelia equisetiformis

Ruta graveolens 'Jackman's Blue'

Water moderately in summer and sparingly in winter.

✳

Ruttya fruticosa

Ruttya's slender stems grow untidily in all directions. It is best to tie them up just to give the plant a better shape. This East African plant is worth growing just for its flowers. They are borne in spring and summer, and present a very exotic appearance, with orange petals and a shiny dark brown, aubergine, or black spot in the centre of each flower.

The plant grows well in any kind of soil. Give it normal quantities of water and food, and a warm position in full sun or partial shade.

It is open to question, however, whether the species, which recently has been cultivated on an increasingly large scale, will ever become genuinely popular. It needs to be kept in a light and fairly warm place in winter. The temperature should not fall below 10°C (50°F) - a slightly higher temperature is preferable - and the humidity should not drop too much either.

○ 10°C (50°F)

Ruttya fruticosa

S

S

Salvia coccinea

SAGE

From halfway through the summer until well into October, *Salvia coccinea* bears bright red flowers. Apart from the species, there are numerous cultivars with flowers in different shades: 'Lactea', 'White Dove', and the sub-species *alba* all have white flowers; 'Rose-Salmon' is whitish pink with salmon pink; 'Coral Nymph' is soft pinkish white; 'Splendens' and 'Red Indian' have scarlet flowers; and 'Lady in Red' has blood-red flowers. The herbaceous shrubs grow between 60 and 90cm (24 and 36in) tall, except for 'Nana' and 'Nana Compacta', which are very compact. *Salvia coccinea* originally came from tropical South America and is frost-tender. Fortunately, all forms are easy to grow from seed. Sow indoors between February and April, and do not move the seedlings out of doors until after the final night frost. They are

preceding page: *Senecio viravira*

Salvia coccinea 'Rose-Salmon'

grown in ordinary potting compost in a sunny or partially shady position. Water normally to moderately and feed liberally.

(1)

Salvia grahamii

See: *Salvia microphylla*

Salvia involucrata

The rigidly upright stems of *Salvia involucrata* grow to over 1m (3ft) in height. They produce large green leaves with wine-red midribs. From midsummer until far into autumn, the flower stems are adorned with bladder-shaped, rose-red flowers. A strange berry-shaped flower often appears at the top of the racemes. This Central American plant is frost-tender when containerized, and should be moved indoors well before the first frost (in open ground it will tolerate temperatures as low as -5°C/23°F). Let the plant overwinter in a light, well-ventilated, and cool (5-12°C/41-53°F) location and kept almost dry, or in a dark and definitely cool place (0-10°C/32-50°F). If the latter alternative is chosen, the plant should be cut back to about 10cm (4in) above ground. As soon as this salvia begins to grow again in spring, it should be repotted and placed in a well-lit location. After the final

Salvia involucrata

frost it may be moved out of doors again to a sunny, warm, and sheltered position. Water freely and fill the pot with nutritive soil. If you repot *Salvia involucrata* annually, fertilizers will not be required.

○ or ● 0°C (32°F)

Salvia microphylla

If the Latin name is translated literally, this species is called small-leafed sage, and its small leaves are in fact only 2cm (3/4in) long. They grow on succulent stems which bear small rose-red or bright red to deep red flowers in late summer. Because of its dense and well-branched growth, this Mexican plant is one of the most rewarding species of salvia for cultivating in containers. *Salvia microphylla* is very easy to propagate by cuttings and, if space is in short supply, it may also overwinter as a cutting. For management, see *Salvia involucrata*.

○ of ● 0°C (32°F)

Salvia microphylla

Salvia officinalis

SAGE

The true sage has been a familiar medicinal herb for thousands of years, and its name is derived from these properties. *Salvia* comes

from the Latin *salvere*, which means 'to be healthy'. The herb may also be used for culinary purposes, but with moderation, as it has a strong flavour. Most people regard sage as an ornamental plant which evokes a Mediterranean atmosphere.

In a sunny position, the foliage will remain a handsome shade of greyish-green. Flower spikes appear at the tips of the shoots in late summer, and bear blue, purple to pink flowers for weeks on end.

Cut back the plant hard after it has flowered to retain its compact growth. Water moderately in summer, and provide sandy, clayey, preferably limy soil and good drainage.

In open ground, sage will survive temperatures as low as -10°C (14°F), but containerized specimens should be moved indoors before the frosts begin. The plant should overwinter in a very light and above all cool place, where it will stop growing altogether.

A cold frame, greenhouse, or unheated conservatory would be ideal for this purpose.

○ 0°C (32°F)

Salvia officinalis

Salvia patens

Although the Mexican *Salvia patens* is a perennial, it is best grown as an annual in northwest European countries. If you sow

Salvia patens 'Cambridge Blue'

early (in February-March), the seedlings will begin to flower in June and continue until far into October if there is a mild autumn.

The flowers are over 5cm (2in) long and are borne on stems that grow to more than 50cm (20in) in height. Their colour varies depending on the cultivar: *Salvia patens* 'Alba' and 'White Perfection' are white; 'Cambridge Blue' is light blue; 'Chilcombe' is mauve; and 'Oxford Blue' is dark blue.

All forms are easy to grow in ordinary potting compost. Normal amounts of water and a sunny to partially shady position are all they require.

It is possible to keep the tuberous roots through the winter in a cool place. The foliage will die down, which makes overwintering in the dark a possibility. Do not let the soil dry out completely.

(1) or ● 0°C (32°F)

Salvia uliginosa

BOG SAGE

This species of sage does not really reach full growth until most container plants are past their prime. In September-October, its long,

Salvia patens 'Chilcombe'

lax stems spread out from the pot with bright blue flowers at their tips, thus presenting a very cheerful appearance. Grow these salvias in large pots and water freely in summer. The pots should be moved indoors in winter, as this South American perennial is not fully hardy.

☼ 0°C (32°F)

Salvia uliginosa

Santolina chamaecyparissus

they may also overwinter indoors in a place which should be as cool and well-lit as possible. As soon as the temperature rises above -5°C (23°F), you should move the plant out of doors again.

Make sure that the soil is completely dry and remains so out of doors.

☼ –5°C (23°F)

Santolina incana

See: *Santolina chamaecyparissus*

Sanvitalia procumbens

CREEPING ZINNIA

The flowers of *Sanvitalia procumbens* measure 2cm (3/4in) across and have a striking dark centre varying from purple to black. This prostrate Central American plant flowers throughout the summer. The cultivars in particular are low-growing and trail gracefully over the rim of a pot. The plants are available in spring, but may also be sown: indoors in March-April, or out of doors from May onwards. The seedlings rapidly grow into flowering plants, and show up best in a sunny position. Water normally and make sure that excess water can drain away easily. In addition to the species, which grows to a maximum height of 15cm (6in), it is possible to buy seeds of even shorter cultivars such as

Santolina chamaecyparissus

COTTON LAVENDER, LAVENDER COTTON

In Mediterranean countries, low-growing cotton lavender bushes are to be seen on dry, sunny hillsides. The species has adapted well to dry conditions by reducing its leaves to short stumps and growing white hairs to protect them from fierce sunlight and excessive transpiration. If you bear this in mind, managing santolinas is extremely simple. Put the plant in a pot containing poor, very light, sandy, preferably limy soil, and do not water until it has dried up entirely. A warm position in full sun will keep the shoots beautifully white and compact. Straggling green growth may be cut back drastically during the growing season. In dry soil, santolinas will tolerate temperatures as low as -15°C (5°F) in winter, so that they can be moved, in their pots, to a cold frame, greenhouse, or unheated conservatory. If you do not have any one of these,

Sanvitalia procumbens 'Golden Carpet' (golden yellow), 'Mandarin Orange' (deep orange), and 'Yellow Carpet' (lemon yellow).

(1)

Sanvitalia procumbens 'Golden Carpet'

Saxifraga sarmentosa

See: *Saxifraga stolonifera*

Saxifraga stolonifera

MOTHER OF THOUSANDS

The relatively unknown mother of thousands is one of the most rewarding saxifrages. It is fully hardy and thrives in damp, shady positions. From a hanging basket or a balcony trough, the rosette sends out long, thin runners which eventually dangle over the rim and bear complete new plants. The cultivar *Saxifraga stolonifera* 'Cuscutiformis' is particularly prolific.

Saxifraga stolonifera 'Cuscutiformis'

Provide humus-rich soil which should remain permanently moist and cool - that is all you need to do. In July and August, long stems grow out of the rosette and bear very small flowers which, on closer inspection, turn out to be strikingly beautiful.

Scadoxus multiflorus

See: *Haemanthus multiflorus*

Scaevola aemula

This Australian hanging plant with fan-shaped flowers has been a lightning success.
Prior to 1989 it was still wholly unknown, but now its pendent stems bearing white to lilac-blue flowers adorn countless hanging baskets and pots in many lands throughout the summer.
Five petals grow on one side of a yellow centre, thus forming a semicircle with a diameter of about 3cm (1 1/4in).
Find a sunny to semi-shady position for the species or the popular blue cultivar *Scaevola aemula* 'Blue Fan', and give the plants plenty of water and food.
Cuttings taken in late summer may overwinter

Scaevola aemula

in a light and cool location (5-12°C/41-54°F), but most devotees prefer to buy new plants every year.

(1) or ☼ 5°C (41°F)

Scaevola aemula 'Petite'

The cultivar *Scaevola aemula* 'Petite' differs considerably from the species and is therefore also called *Scaevola humile*. Its succulent stems are closely covered in short green leaves and bear fan-shaped blueish-pink flowers, only 1.5cm (5/8in) in diameter, throughout the summer. This is a lovely cultivar, as yet all too rarely for sale.

For management, see *Scaevola aemula*.

☼ 5°C (41°F)

Scaevola aemula 'Petite'

Scaevola humile

See: *Scaevola aemula* 'Petite'

Scutellaria alpina

SKULLCAP

Containerized scutellarias grow to a maximum height of about 20cm (8in), but these perennials will eventually spread. The nodes root and form new plants where they touch the soil. The plants are fully hardy in open ground. *Scutellaria alpina*, which comes from the mountains of southern and eastern Europe, flowers from June until far into September. The flowers are purplish red with yellow lips. Numerous lovely cultivars in various colours are available: *Scutellaria alpina* 'Alba' has pure white flowers; those of

'Greencourt' are mauve with white lips; and 'Rosea' bears pink flowers. Provide cool, humus-rich soil in summer and do not let the soil dry out. The pot may be planted in a hole in the garden in autumn, or put in a cold frame or unheated greenhouse.

❋

Scutellaria alpina 'Greencourt'

Scutellaria scordiifolia

SKULLCAP

Anyone who enjoys creating subtle combinations of flowers in hanging baskets will like this magnificent plant from eastern Europe and the adjacent regions of Asia. In the photograph on page 237, the tubular violet-blue flowers are mixed with the slightly lighter, mauvish blue of *Cymbalaria pilosa* (ivy-leafed toadflax, Kenilworth ivy).

The introduction to this book includes a section on how to plant up a hanging basket. One of the problems is that the root balls of the species planted in the sides need to be pushed through the sphagnum moss. In the case of *Scutellaria scordiifolia*, this is very easy to do in spring. The countless radical tubers may be pressed into the basket a few at a time, and subsequently develop into complete trailing plants.

Skullcaps are equally undemanding when it comes to further management. All you need do is make sure that the basket does not dry up entirely, which means that it should be watered daily. *Scutellaria scordiifolia* is fully hardy, even in a hanging basket. Even so, it is preferable to plant up hanging baskets every year, in which case the skullcaps should be removed and planted in the garden for the winter.

❄

Selenicereus grandiflorus

QUEEN-OF-THE-NIGHT

Most cacti prefer to be out of doors in summer rather than indoors, since glass keeps out ultraviolet light which ensures their compact growth and fine colours. In persistently rainy weather, however, cacti should be protected against excessive moisture. The queen-of-the-night is less demanding. In a spacious pot, it will successfully withstand considerable amounts of moisture. Taller specimens will need a fair-sized support frame, as the plant may become very large and heavy. The flowers have a maximum length of 30cm (12in). They open on summer evenings and exude an intense fragrance. In the Caribbean region they are pollinated by bats. The miracle of flowering is limited to older plants.

Stand *Selenicereus* in a sunny or semi-shady position in summer and water freely. In winter, the plant prefers a light position, and the potting compost may be kept almost dry at a temperature of at least 10°C (50°F).

◌ 10°C (50°F)

Selenicereus grandiflorus

Sempervivum

HOUSELEEK

Houseleeks are highly rewarding, fully hardy succulents which may withstand quite harsh

Scutellaria scordiifolia (hanging basket with *Cymbalaria*)

Sempervivum tectorum (in strawberry pot)

conditions. On a tiled roof, they will survive the severest winters. Their roots attach themselves to their base, and need scarcely any soil to nourish the rosettes. In times of drought, the rosettes will curve slightly inwards to prevent transpiration. Their fleshy leaves are full of sap which acts as a reserve supply for hard times. In summer, the oldest rosettes grow into flower stems bearing pink, white or yellow flowers. The old rosettes die after flowering.

Cultivate houseleeks in boulders, on a roof, in a roof tile on the ground, in shallow bowls, or in any other kind of small pot or container. Houseleeks cannot endure a permanently damp, shady position, or competition from other plants.

Provide a poor, sandy soil mixture and regular periods without water, or the rosettes will lose their characteristic compact appearance.

Attractive forms include:

Sempervivum arachnoideum, the cobweb houseleek, which has small rosettes concealed in a web of white hairs. This makes the species particularly suitable for dry and very sunny places. Keep as dry as podssible in winter.

Sempervivum 'Commander Hay' is a form developed in England. It has large rosettes of slightly reddish, green-tipped leaves.

Sempervivum octopodes comes from the Balkans. The species has hairy, red-tipped green leaves.

Sempervivum tectorum, the common or roof houseleek, was planted on the roofs of farmhouses in the belief that it would prevent the house being struck by lightning. The plant

Sempervivum arachnoideum with *Cymbalaria*

has glossy, spatula-shaped, pointed leaves. They are variably green and red, which has led to the selection of deviant forms such as 'Atropurpureum' a cultivar with uniformly dark red leaves.

✳

Senecio leucostachys

See: *Senecio viravira*

Senecio viravira

RAGWORT

The grey-leafed species of ragwort are excellent for combining with flowering plants, and for creating breaks in colourful borders. The drawback is that they come from dry, sunny regions and cannot tolerate the damp, changeable winters of northwest Europe.

Senecio viravira comes from Argentina. The species is questionably hardy in open ground, but is excellent for cultivating in a pot containing light and preferably poor soil. The foliage of containerized plants stays whiter, and the plant may be moved to a cold frame, greenhouse, or unheated conservatory in the event of frost. In the absence of any of these, a cool, light location indoors will also prove satisfactory.

Give the plant hardly any water during the winter months, and water sparingly in summer. In a sunny position out of doors, the deeply divided foliage will acquire a beautiful silvery brightness.

◯ 0°C (32°F)

Senecio viravira

Sesbania tripetii

See: *Sesbania punicea*

Sesbania punicea

Within two years, *Sesbania punicea* will grow from seed into a tall shrub capable of flowering. If you have enough space, this plant will prove a real treasure, with racemes of lovely orange-red papilionaceous flowers appearing between the doubly pinnate leaves in summer. By holding a single stem and cutting it off just above head height, the plant will branch out and develop into an airy parasol with flowers at eye level.

In summer, *Sesbania* should be placed in a warm, sunny spot out of the wind. Water freely, and provide humus-rich, well-drained soil. Give the plant plenty of food in spring and early summer. Then harden it off and let the soil gradually dry up in autumn before you move the plant indoors before the first frost. In a cool, dark place, the plant will gradually shed its leaves, and will then require very little water.

Sow in spring at the tropical soil temperature of approximately 25°C (77°F).

● 0°C (32°F)

Sesbania punicea

Silene coeli-rosa

CAMPION, CATCHFLY

The fragile flowers of this annual plant from the countries round the Mediterranean are borne on erect stems. In their native environment, they are found in grassy meadows, but in northwest Europe they prefer full sun. They climb up other plants in a border, but in a pot they will remain more compact.

The cultivars 'Blue Angel' and 'Rose Angel' are very low-growing (about 25cm/10in), and therefore less inclined to arch over. They flower uninterruptedly from June until well into autumn. They will tolerate a considerable amount of frost, but eventually die down in winter. They gradually become more straggly during their long flowering period. 'Blue Angel' has mauvish blue flowers; those of 'Rose Angel' are bright pink.

Sow the seeds indoors - directly in the pot - in March and prick out as little as possible, since silenes react badly to having their roots disturbed. The plants do best in non-acid soil.

There are many available cultivars of *coeli-rosa*. Besides those already mentioned, 'Albo-rosea' (white and pink) and 'Nana' (a dwarf form) are highly suitable for containers. 'Candida' (white flowers), 'Blue Pearl', and 'Kermesina' (red flowers) are larger and looser. They are particularly suitable for sowing in pressed plastic pots, after which you can push them, soil and all, into the side of a hanging basket.

(1)

Silene coeli-rosa 'Blue Angel'

Skimmia foremanii

See: *Skimmia japonica* 'Rubella'

Skimmia japonica

Skimmia japonica grows slowly, and the evergreen shrub may therefore be kept in a container for a long time. It is tolerant of wind and therefore suitable for a balcony or a roof garden, where it can remain all the year round. Stand the container against a wall in the event of severe frost, and protect the foliage from the sun to prevent the plant drying out.

Fill the container with humus-rich soil which should be kept normally moist and as cool as possible.

The fragrant foliage looks best in shade or semi-shade, although the shrub will flower more profusely in a sunny position. The flowers, too, are fragrant, and open in late winter or early spring. Female plants will bear red berries if pollinated with the pollen from a flowering male plant.

Skimmia japonica 'Rubella' (also called *Skimmia foremanii*) is a male plant, and does not produce berries itself. 'Rubella' bears red flower buds and reddish flower stems all through the winter, when even the leaves turn red. The buds open around May.

❄

Skimmia japonica 'Rubella'

Solandra hartwegii

See: *Solandra maxima*

Solandra maxima

CAPA DE ORO, GOLDEN-CHALICE VINE

A certain amount of optimism is required if

you decide to grow a solandra. This Central American climber is extremely vigorous and may grow to 7-10m (23-33ft) or more. It does not, however, flower readily. Let it spread into a bush in a large container, with the woody stems supporting one another. This creates a cluster of shiny green leaves, each of which grows 10-15cm (4-6in) long.

Provide a warm position, for instance in a conservatory or a warm place out of doors, and give the plant a lot of water and food in spring and early summer. When the solandra has reached a height at which it can flower (approximately 2m/6ft), it should be left to dry out temporarily in midsummer. Buds will then form which may develop into spectacular, fragrant flowers (pollinated by bats in Central America) in late summer. When they have opened, the flowers are pale yellow with deep purple streaks, and about 15cm (6in) across. They turn darker as they age. It is difficult to induce the plant to flower in a European climate, and the edible fruits of this poisonous plant do not ripen in these regions.

The *Solandra maxima* is only suitable for cultivation by experienced enthusiasts. The plant should be moved indoors before the first night frost. A well-lit, cool location and very little water will help it to survive the winter.

☼ 2°C (36°F)

Solandra maxima

Solanum jasminoides

POTATO VINE

In southern countries, the thin scrambling stems of the potato vine cover entire walls and low buildings. They are concealed behind a 'mountain' of leaves and flowers. Even in the Dutch climate, the plant grows rapidly and flowers over a very long period. Provided it is growing well, flowers will continue to appear. They are pale blue or, in the case of the most popular cultivar, *Solanum jasminoides* 'Album', pure white. Move the plant out of doors to a sunny or partially shady position after the final night frost. Water freely and feed liberally, so that it continues to grow well. In winter, the plant may remain out of doors until the first frost. Let it overwinter in a light and moderately cool to warm place, and water occasionally. If kept in a cold and dark location, it will shed its leaves.

☼ 10°C (50°F) or ● 0°C (32°F)

Solanum jasminoides 'Album'

Solanum melongena

EGGPLANT, AUBERGINE

The eggplant is in fact a white aubergine. The vegetable was brought to Europe from southeast Asia as early as the thirteenth century. Since then, many cultivars suitable for growing in greenhouses in cooler climates have been developed, and the eggplant is one of them. The fruits are the same size and colour as hen's eggs; older fruits change to a bright shade of orange yellow.

The eggplant, also marketed as *Solanum ovigerum*, may be kept through the winter, but should preferably be grown as an annual. If you sow under glass in spring, the seedlings

may flower from June onwards, producing the typical *Solanum* flowers that reveal their close affinity to the potato.
More and more fruits are formed during the summer; they should be cooked in exactly the same way as aubergines.
The plant grows about 1m (3ft) tall, and prefers a sunny position, sheltered from the wind, in summer. Water and feed normally during this period.

(1)

Solanum melongena

Solanum ovigerum

See: *Solanum melongena*

Solanum rantonnetii

BLUE POTATO BUSH

This solanum should really be called *Lycianthes rantonetii*, but the outdated name is generally used. The bushy plant grows about 2m (6ft) tall in a container. It flowers from early summer until far into autumn, producing clusters of handsome violet to blue flowers. They measure over 2cm (3/4in) across, and are often followed by poisonous berries which gradually turn red.
Keep the plant in a warm and sunny position in summer, and water and feed freely. Move the plant indoors before the first night frost, and then cut back hard if required. It will shed its leaves if kept in a dark, cool place, but will hold them in a well-lit location at a temperature over 10°C (50°F).

○ 10°C (50°F) or ● 2°C (36°F)

Solanum rantonnetii

Solenopsis axillaris

See: *Laurentia axillaris*

Sollya fusciformis

See: *Sollya heterophylla*

Sollya heterophylla

BLUEBELL CREEPER

Even without flowers, *Sollya heterophylla* is a magnificent plant. Its thin, twining stems produce oblong leaves which create a light and airy impression. In summer, small nodding blue flowers dangle among them; they are not very striking when seen from a distance, but look very pretty close-up.
Although the sollya originally came from western Australia, it dislikes drought. Water regularly and provide humus-rich, well-drained soil. The plant prefers a sunny or partially shady position, and likes to climb up a support. It is best to select a light support

which does justice to the *Sollya*'s airy appearance.

In winter, the plant likes a well-lit, well-ventilated location at a minimum temperature of 2°C (36°F). The evergreen leaves are prone to infestation by red spider mite, but this can usually be prevented by frequent ventilating and spraying. In winter, the plant should not be put in too warm a place in an excessively dry atmosphere.

Propagate the plant by seed (at room temperature) in spring, or by stem cuttings in summer.

☼ 2°C (36°F)

Sollya heterophylla

will tolerate a few degrees of frost, it should be moved indoors in good time in autumn. The plant will often still produce buds, which will develop into magnificent white flowers with yellow-powdered stamens in a cool room. The buds, however, will drop off in a warm, dry atmosphere. Let the plant overwinter in a place which should be as cool as possible but frost-free; water sparingly. The tree will shed its leaves if it is kept in a dark location, but new foliage will be produced on old wood in spring. African hemp will hold its leaves in a well-lit location.

☼ or ● 2°C (36°F)

Sparmannia africana

Sparmannia africana

AFRICAN HEMP

African hemp is marketed as a houseplant, but may also be grown as a highly decorative container plant. In a sheltered, semi-shady to shady position, it will do far better than in our overheated living rooms.

Be sure and choose a sheltered position, as the leaves will be significantly smaller in a windy spot.

The plant grows very rapidly in summer and will require a lot of water; it should, however, be fed sparingly. Keep the humus-rich soil cool and permanently moist, or too many leaves will be shed. Although African hemp

Spathodea campanulata

AFRICAN TULIP TREE, FLAME-OF-THE-FOREST

The African tulip tree may grow 15m (50ft) tall in (sub)tropical regions. The species originally came from West Africa, and is very popular as a street or park tree in warm countries. The pinnate leaves cast a cooling shadow, and the tree is adorned with dense clusters of reddish-orange flowers in spring.

Rain water remains cupped in the flowers after a shower.

Containerized spathodeas are suitable only for experienced enthusiasts who are able to provide a well-lit location at a minimum tem-

243

perature of 12°C (53°F) in winter. A great deal of patience is also required, as the tree needs to grow to a considerable height before it is likely to flower.

Stand the containerized plant in the warmest and sunniest spot available in summer, and give it plenty of water and fertilizer. Propagate by seed in spring.

☼ 12°C (53°F)

Spathodea campanulata

Sphaeralcea fendleri

The slender, spreading stems of *Sphaeralcea fendleri* cover sunny, rocky slopes in the southern states of the US. Its leaves are small and covered in silvery grey felt-like hairs. During the growing season, new flowers, about 1cm (1/4in) across, are produced continually at the tips of stems. The shape of the plant reveals its affinity to Malvaceae such as *Anisodontea* and *Malva*.

Cultivate the airy shrub, which has an ultimate height and spread of about 1m (3ft), in a poor, very well-drained soil mixture, and do not water until the soil has visibly dried up. In dry soil, this plant is basically hardy, but in the damp winters of countries like the Netherlands, it is better to keep it in a cold frame or unheated greenhouse. Do not water during

this period. If neither a cold frame nor a greenhouse is available, it should also be possible for the plant to overwinter indoors in a very cool and well-lit location.

Cut back in winter or early spring to encourage bushy growth. Pruning in the growing season will temporarily stop the development of flowers.

☼ –10°C (14°F)

Sphaeralcea fendleri

Sphaeralcea miniata

See: *Sphaeralcea fendleri*

Sphaeralcea munroana

The flowers of *Sphaeralcea munroana* are a vibrant shade of pinkish red, and its leaves are less white-woolly than those of *Sphaeralcea*

Sphaeralcea munroana

fendleri. The plants are otherwise very similar in their behaviour.

For management, see *Sphaeralcea fendleri*.

☼ –10°C (14°F)

Sprekelia formosissima

AZTEC LILY, JACOBEAN LILY

In spring, a single stem, 30cm (12in) tall, grows out of this large bulb from Mexico. It is the flower of the Aztec lily, which opens in early summer and grows to 12cm (5in) in width and length. When cultivated in a pot, it looks an incredible shade of red among the leaves that are just beginning to develop.

Put the plant in a sunny spot and water freely. Stop watering as soon as the leaves die down in autumn. Store the bulb in a cool place in winter (preferably between 5 and 12°C/41 and 53°F), and plant it in fresh soil in very early spring. Propagate by bulblets which may be removed from the large bulb at the time of repotting.

● 5°C (41°F)

Sprekelia formosissima

Strelitzia reginae

BIRD-OF-PARADISE FLOWER

In South Africa, the bird-of-paradise flower is pollinated by birds. They can easily alight on the horizontal bracts from which the orange and deep blue flowers emerge. If the bird-of-paradise flower is placed in the warmest, sunniest, and most sheltered spot available, these flowers will also appear in northwest Europe. A certain amount of patience will be required, as strelitzias are slow growers, and do not flower until the plants are mature.

It is possible to sow strelizias, but the seedlings grow so slowly that it is preferable to split up the plants. When the roots eventually threaten to break out of the pot, the clump may be carefully divided. Provide fresh, highly nutritive soil and water whenever you think it is required during the warm summer months.

In winter the potting compost should be kept almost dry, and the plant should be moved to a well-lit cool location where the temperature fluctuates between 5 and 12°C (41 and 53°F).

☼ 5°C (41°F)

Strelitzia reginae

Streptocarpus saxorum

FALSE AFRICAN VIOLET

This streptocarpus is one of the loveliest species, and needs a warm and sheltered position if it is to be cultivated in a hanging basket out of doors. The East African *saxorum* has prostrate stems which arch over when there is no soil to support them. The leaves are covered in velvety hairs, and trail over the rim of the pot; thin stems bearing one or two lilac to carmine flowers with white eyes occasionally appear amidst the foliage. They hover about 20cm (8in) above the leaves - a truly beautiful sight.

To achieve all this, you should hang the plant

in a light, but not excessively sunny spot. Water at longish intervals, and hang the streptocarpus in a dry place during persistently rainy weather, as the soil should not remain soaking wet all the time. As soon as the temperature drops below 10°C (50°F), the plant should be hung up indoors, where it will adorn the living room until the following summer.

☼ 10°C (50°F)

Streptocarpus saxorum

Streptosolen jamesonii

MARMALADE BUSH

In Mediterranean countries and on the islands in the Atlantic, the marmalade bush grows into a rugged, scrambling shrub which bears a profusion of yellowish-orange flowers. If you would like to see these flowers in your own garden, you should put the plant in as light and airy a position as possible. This will imitate the natural conditions in the northern Andes, where the species originated. The light in those regions is very brilliant, and the nights are cool, but mainly frost-free. A profusion of flowers may be expected only if similar airy, light conditions can be provided. Otherwise, just an occasional flower will appear. The flowers are borne in spring if the marmalade bush is cultivated in a greenhouse; the plant will flower in summer out of doors. It should be moved indoors before any frosts occur. The slightly wrinkled leaves remain on

Streptosolen jamesonii

the plant, and a well-lit location is therefore required. Keep the temperature at moderate levels (preferably at 5-12°C/41-53°F), and ventilate as frequently as possible to prevent mildew and infestation by whitefly and red spider mite.

☼ 2°C (36°F)

Sutera cordata 'Snowflake'

The brief history of Sutera cordata 'Snowflake' is one of success. The compact hanging plant was introduced in 1993 under the name of Bacopa 'Snowflake'. Even before it was realized that this name was incorrect, the plant had become immensely popular, and had been propagated at top speed. It is now known to many keen plant lovers by the familiar name Bacopa. The rapid rise of Sutera coincided with the increasing popularity of hanging baskets, for which Sutera cordata 'Snowflake' is particularly suitable. The woody stems grow horizontally and eventually arch over. They remain a handsome shade of green, and bear small white flowers that are highly suitable for combining with other plants in hanging baskets throughout the summer. Hang the basket, or stand the pot (because the plant will also thrive in containers) in a light position out of doors in summer. It may be in full sun, provided the soil is not left to dry up. Provide a cool, airy location indoors in winter, or there will be a considerable risk of grey mould. The actual temperature is less important. In a light position in a heated room, you should continue to water freely. A cool room is therefore preferable, because then you will scarcely need to water in winter, and the plant will remain quite happy. Sutera is easy to propagate by cuttings. Cut off sections of stems, preferably in August or September, and let them root in a light mixture of moderately moist soil. There is no need to wrap the pot in plastic. Recent developments have removed the need to confine yourself to white-flowered plants. The names speak for themselves: Sutera diffusa 'Blue Form'; Sutera diffusa 'Pink Domino' (which, in fact, has magenta flowers); and Sutera diffusa 'Rosea'.

☼ 10°C (50°F)

Sutera diffusa 'Snowflake'

See: Sutera cordata 'Snowflake'

Sutera cordata 'Snowflake'

T

t

Tagetes tenuifolia 'Paprika'

Even those who are not really fond of tagetes will make an exception for this low-growing (20cm/8in) cultivar.

The colour of its flowers goes well with terracotta pots. Cultivation of this annual is very simple.

Its needle-shaped seeds are sown indoors in spring, and the seedlings may be put out of doors in full sun or partial shade after the final frost.

Pinch out the first buds to encourage bushy growth and then enjoy the display of flowers which will continue right up to the first frost.

Tagetes tenuifolia 'Lemon Gem' resembles the above cultivar in every respect except that its flowers are lemon yellow.

(1)

Tagetes 'Paprika'

Tapien

See: *Verbena* 'Sunvop' en *Verbena* 'Sunver'

Tecoma capensis

See: *Tecomaria capensis*

Preceding page: *Tropaeolum majus*

Tecoma-hybrid

See: *Campsis* x *tagliabuana*

Tecoma stans

YELLOW BELLS, YELLOW ELDER

Tecoma stans is native to Central America, where the plant grows about 5m (16ft) tall. Containerized specimens remain bushy and may be kept in shape by pruning in winter. If you stand the pot in a sheltered, warm, and sunny spot in summer, flowers, 5cm (2in) long and wide, will be produced in profusion. They flower in clusters and are followed by bean-shaped pods. If you do not wish to harvest the seeds, the beans should be removed to extend the flowering period. Water and feed freely in summer and preferably provide limy soil which should be well-drained. Move the shrub indoors well before the first night frost, and let it overwinter in a light, cool place (preferably 5-12°C/41-53°F). If kept in the dark, the shrub will shed its leaves, and should hardly be watered at all. In the latter circumstances, make quite sure that the temperature does not drop below 10°C (50°F). Seed will germinate best in heated soil in spring. This method will also encourage tip cuttings to take root in summer.

○ or ● 2°C (36°F)

Tecoma stans

Tecomaria capensis

CAPE HONEYSUCKLE

In (sub)tropical countries, this South African climber covers whole areas, not only vertically, but also horizontally, as it develops into a bushy shape. Arching, reddish-orange flowers are produced in small groups at the tips of stems, even those of very young plants.

In a warm and sunny position in a sheltered garden, cape honeysuckle will flower profusely over a long period, from June until well into winter, even in northwest Europe. Plant in nutritive soil and water freely.

In winter, the plant prefers a light location at a minimum temperature of 12°C (53°F). The glossy, pinnate leaves remain on the plant at this time, so that occasional watering is required. It is also possible to let the plant overwinter in a cool and dark place, but in that case the temperature should be kept as low as possible and the plant should not be watered. For propagation, see *Tecoma stans*.

○ 12°C (53°F) or ● 2°C (36°F)

Thevetia neriifolia

See: *Thevetia peruviana*

Thevetia peruviana

YELLOW OLEANDER

The foliage of this shrub from tropical America closely resembles that of the *Nerium oleander*, hence its former name *neriifolia*.

Thevetia peruviana

The plant is related to the oleander and all parts are equally poisonous. Oblong, fragrant flowers appear on side stems in summer, but never open fully. They are usually yellow, sometimes salmon pink. *Thevetia peruviana* 'Alba' has pure white flowers. Thevetias are container plants for experienced enthusiasts. They will flower moderately, producing just a few blooms on each plant, even in favourable circumstances. Plant in nutritive, moisture-retentive soil. Stand the container in as warm and sunny a position as possible in summer, and water freely. In winter, the plant should be kept in a place that is light and not too cold (at a temperature around 12°C/53°F); it should be watered occasionally.

☼ 10°C (50°F)

Thunbergia alata

BLACK-EYED SUSAN

Sowing *Thunbergia alata* is child's play. If you push the large brown seeds into a big pot early in March, you will be able to enjoy the first flowers about six weeks later. They are orange with deep violet centres closely resembling pupils, hence the name black-eyed Susan. Black-eyed Susan is native to South Africa, where it is a rampant climber. In northwest Europe, in open ground, the stems will coil their way up stakes, string, or mesh to a height of 2m (6ft). Containerized plants are more restrained, but even they will flower for months on end. For those disinclined to sow, flowering plants are on sale from April onwards. Stand them in a warm and sunny

Thunbergia alata 'Alba'

position, with some protection from hot mid-day sun. Because there is considerable transpiration, plentiful watering is required.
Spherical fruits develop from the flowers and burst open when they have ripened, thus scattering the seeds. Take special note of the name when buying seeds. Besides the species, with its orange flowers with dark centres, seed mixtures are also available. These are sometimes labelled *Thunbergia alata* mixed, but are also given fancy names such as Susie Mix or Florist mixture. They grow into plants with orange, yellow, or white flowers, with or without black centres. There are also fine selections of, for instance, plants with white flowers only, and almost black eyes, imcluding *Thunbergia alata* 'Alba'. The cultivar 'Fryeri' bears yellow flowers with white eyes.

(1)

Thunbergia alata

Thunbergia battiscombei

Superficially, *Thunbergia battiscombei* closely resembles *Thunbergia erecta*, but distinct differences become apparent on closer inspection: the leaves are broader, the flowers a much deeper shade of blueish-mauve, and the hairy bracts are larger and have a clear pattern of reticulation.
This species is one of the latest additions to

the range of available container plants, and is currently on sale at highly specialized nurseries only.

For management, see *Thunbergia grandiflora*.

☼ 10°C (50°F)

Thunbergia battiscombei

Thunbergia erecta

The outstandingly beautiful flowers of *Thunbergia erecta* are produced in the year after the plant was sown. It should therefore be managed as a container plant and kept

Thunbergia erecta

through the winter in a light, cool location. Water sparingly at that time and cut back in spring, but not too hard, or there will be fewer flowers. The stems should preferably be trained up stakes or mesh, as that will create a fresh green screen which may grow 1.5m (5ft) tall, a magnificent sight in itself.

Water freely while the plant is in full growth and feed from time to time. Let *Thunbergia erecta*, which originally came from tropical West Africa, harden off at the end of the season. Stop feeding and gradually water less freely.

☼ 5°C (41°F)

Thunbergia gibsonii

See: *Thunbergia gregorii*

Thunbergia grandiflora

BLUE TRUMPET VINE

The blue to mauve flowers of *Thunbergia grandiflora* can grow to 8cm (3 1/4in) in diameter. Until recently, they were only to be seen in collections of tropical plants. Now, however, this climber from India is gradually becoming available as a conservatory plant. To keep the plant in flower, it must continue

Thunbergia grandiflora

in full growth, and this is only possible in a warm position, and with frequent and plentiful watering.

This evergreen climber may overwinter in a light location, where the temperature should be kept at a minimum of 10°C (50°F). Take tip cuttings in spring and let them root in moist soil in a warm place (around 25°C/77°F).

☼ 10°C (50°F)

Thunbergia gregorii

Thunbergia gregorii is usually grown as an annual (for sowing method, see Thunbergia alata). In very mild climates, however, this rampant climber from Africa will survive the winter out of doors, albeit without leaves or stems.

If you wish to keep a containerized specimen through the winter, make sure that the stems stay alive as much as possible - this is easiest at a temperature around 12-16°C (53-61°F). The plant will of course need some water and adequate light in these conditions.

In summer, the plant produces bright orange flowers which emerge from handsomely marked bracts. Water freely while in flower and feed regularly.

☼ 10°C (50°F)

Thunbergia gregorii

Thymus x citriodorus

LEMON THYME

Lemon thyme is a cross between Thymus pulegioides and the common thyme (Thymus vulgaris). Leaves and stems exude a lemony fragrance when touched. Its aromatic oil is used for such purposes as flavouring liqueurs. The variegated forms are particularly popular as container plants.

They include: Thymus x citridorus 'Archer's Gold' (yellow-leafed); 'Aureus' (green and golden-green foliage); 'Gold King' (green leaves with gold margins); and the highly popular 'Silver Queen' (silvery green with cream margins). This final cultivar is also known as 'Argenteus', 'Silver Beauty', and 'Silver Posie'.

For management, see Thymus vulgaris.

❋

Thymus x citriodorus 'Silver Queen'

Thymus vulgaris

COMMON THYME

The countless species of thyme grow as ground cover in dry, sunny positions in Mediterranean countries and Asia Minor. Because of their preference for well-drained, warm, and limy soil, they are highly suitable for cultivating in containers.

Stand the pot in as warm and sunny a position as possible and do not water until the soil has dried out entirely.

Common thyme is a favourite culinary herb which is added to stocks, soups, and sauces along with other herbs such as parsley.

The flavour is best when the plant is in full flower.

These small, white, pink to purple flowers attract countless bees and bumblebees. Common thyme is fully hardy in a dry position, but protect the small plant from rain during the winter.

❋

Thymus vulgaris (with *Rosa* 'Cinderella')

Tibouchina semidecandra

See: *Tibouchina urvilleana*

Tibouchina urvilleana

GLORY BUSH

In South America, this shrub grows in light areas at the foot of wooded slopes in mountainous regions. The leaves are covered in downy hairs and are produced on long, square, hairy stems. A cultivated plants may flower for a large part of the year, even in winter, if it is in a light and warm location.
It will survive the winter even in a cool (5-12°C/41-53°F) and light position, but should be watered sparingly at that time to prevent continued growth. In early spring, the plant should be cut back hard and provided with fresh, nutritive soil and gradually increasing warmth. This will encourage the plant to start growing again. After the final frost, it should preferably be moved out of doors to a sheltered, warm position shaded from the very hottest summer sunlight. The mauvish-blue

Tibouchina urvilleana

flowers, approximately 10cm (4in) wide, begin to appear around midsummer. Water freely with decalcified water during this period, and feed regularly with non-calcareous plant food. If you follow these guidelines, this magnificent plant will continue to flower far into autumn. Some of the 350 species of *Tibouchina* produce white flowers. Hybrids developed from them have recently come onto the market.

◯ 2°C (36°F)

Tibouchina hybrid

Trachelospermum asiaticum

JAPANESE STAR JASMINE

Japanese star jasmine grows naturally in Korea and Japan. The pale yellow flowers resemble those of the oleander, although they are much smaller. Japanese star jasmine is known as a climber, but in fact grows into an erect bush. The thick, glossy leaves remain on the plant in winter, and turn a reddish colour in the event of drought or frost. In a sheltered position, the plant will tolerate temperatures as low as -15°C (5°F). For further management, see *Trachelospermum jasminoides*.

☼ –5°C (23°F)

Trachelospermum asiaticum

Trachelospermum jasminoides

CONFEDERATE JASMINE, STAR JASMINE

The white flowers of this evergreen Chinese plant have an intense fragrance. This scent is too powerful for many people indoors, but on a balcony or patio it is a delight. Star jasmine is by nature a climber, but, when grown in a large pot, will long remain a modest shrub with straggly stems. Cultivation is problem-free. The plant prefers full sun or partial shade, grows in normal potting compost, and tolerates a good deal of water in summer. If, however, you occasionally forget to water, that is not a problem either. The plant may remain out of doors for a long time in autumn, as it will easily tolerate temperatures as low as

-5°C (23°F), and will survive -10°C (14°F) in a sheltered position in open ground.
The thick leathery leaves will require light indoors in winter, or too many of them will be shed. You may cut back the long stems as much as you please in spring. Be careful, though: the entire plant is poisonous.

☼ –5°C (23°F)

Trachelospermum jasminoides

Trachelospermum majus

See: *Trachelospermum asiaticum*

Tropaeolum canariense

See: *Tropaeolum peregrinum*

Tropaeolum majus

GARDEN NASTURTIUM, INDIAN CRESS

Nasturtiums are annual garden plants which are highly suitable for cultivating in containers. The genuine species needs support, as it may climb to 1.5m (5ft) in height. Without a support, its long stems will creep or trail. Low-growing cultivars such as 'Tom Thumb' make bushy plants, but will also trail gracefully over the rim of a pot.

Tropaeolum majus 'Alaska'

Sow directly in the pot, tub or trough, indoors in March-April, or out of doors in April-May. Water adequately while in full growth, but never feed. The plant will flower much better in poor soil, usually producing orange or yellow flowers. Stand the tub or pot out of doors in full sun or partial shade in a spot where it is not too windy.

For a time, nasturtiums were regarded as old-fashioned plants, but since the arrival of eye-catching cultivars, they are right back in fashion again:

'Alaska' has very striking green, greyish-green and creamy white leaves;

'Cherry Rose Whirlybird' produces old-rose flowers;

'Double Golden Gleam' has deep yellow (double) flowers;

'Empress of India' has carmine flowers;

'Mahogany Jewel' is a dark red cultivar;

'Peach Melba' has peach-coloured flowers with scarlet centres;

'Primrose Jewel' has soft yellow flowers;

'Strawberries and Cream' has cream flowers with red specks.

(1)

Tropaeolum peregrinum

CANARY CREEPER

Canary creepers have more vigorous climbing tendencies than nasturtiums. Leaves resembling miniature fig leaves are produced on succulent stems. When the plant is in full growth, new buds develop continually in the axils nearer the top, and open out into highly

Tropaeolum majus

Tropaeolum peregrinum

Tulbaghia violacea

remarkable orange-yellow, fringed flowers. Sow canary creepers indoors in spring, and move them out of doors after the final night frost. Use ordinary potting compost and never let it dry out. Provide a support, as the stems easily grow over 2m (6ft) tall.

(1)

Tulbaghia violacea

Tulbaghias look like small versions of *Agapanthus*. They come from South Africa, and bear lilac flowers. Agapanthuses flower for several weeks in late summer, but tulbaghias start flowering in early summer and continue, with brief intervals, until well into autumn. The flowers are carried in umbels at

Tropaeolum majus 'Peach Melba'

the tips of stems which may grow about 50cm (20in) tall. The ribbon-shaped leaves, which smell of onions, grow to around 30cm (12in) in length. *Tulbaghia violacea* is a totally undemanding container plant which may be kept out of doors throughout the summer and far into autumn, as it will tolerate several degrees of frost. Stand the plant in a cool, well-ventilated, and well-lit location, and give it just enough water to prevent the root ball from drying out entirely.

Water and feed liberally in spring until the flower stems become visible. Keep the soil slightly drier after that, and find a warm and sunny position for the plant. Propagate by division or by seed.

○ 0°C (32°F)

Tulipa

TULIP

After the annuals have died down, the empty pots, tubs and baskets may be used for tulip bulbs. After they have flowered (between March and May), the bulbs should be removed, foliage and all, and heeled in somewhere in the garden. The pots, tubs, and

Tulipa 'Diana'

baskets are then ready for planting up with annuals again.

Plant tulip bulbs in autumn or winter. Stand the pot, tub, or basket in a cool position (not indoors!) and make sure the soil does not dry out. Protect the pot from frost by standing it close up to the house, perhaps along with other pots, and wrap straw, blankets, or bubble plastic round it. In the event of severe frost, the bulbs may be moved indoors temporarily, and stored in a cool location.

Preferably choose bulbs of cultivars suitable for containerization, for instance the the early-flowering *Tulipa* 'Diana' (white to creamy yellow), the early-flowering *Tulipa* 'Bellona' (canary yellow), and botanical tulips such as *Tulipa tarda* or *Tulipa violacea*.

❋

Tweedia caerulea

The flowers of *Tweedia caerulea* are a magnificent shade of sky blue when they open. As they age, they gradually fade to lilac. This South American climber never grows more than 1m (3ft) tall. *Tweedia caerulea* makes an excellent perennial for cultivating in a container, but it should overwinter in a light, well-ventilated and cool location (minimum temperature 5°C/41°F). It may also be grown as an annual from seed sown indoors in early spring. In that case, the plants will not flower until after midsummer. Stand the pot in a sunny, sheltered, and warm position out of doors in summer. The plant should be grown in nutritive, humus-rich, and very well-drained soil.

(1) of ○ 5°C (41°F)

Tweedia caerulea

V

v

Verbena x *hybrida*

The numerous hybrids and selections of verbena are favourite bedding and container plants.

The shoots spread and eventually arch over the rims of pots or balcony troughs. This type of growth, combined with their long, fragrant, flowering period (from late spring until well into autumn) has made these plants highly popular.

Their flowering period may be further extended by removing dead heads.

Never let the plants dry out, and occasionally give them some fertilizer (with a relatively low nitrogen content), which benefits flowering. Verbenas are sun-loving plants.

It is theoretically possible to keep the perennials through the winter, perhaps as stem cuttings taken in late summer.

Most forms may also be grown from seed during the first months of the year, although results tend to be rather disappointing. First soak the seeds in tepid water for 24 hours, then sow them in a tray with slightly moist soil at room temperature, and cover with light-proof foil.

(1) or ☼ 0°C (32°F)

Verbena x *hybrida* 'Silver Ann'

Verbena x *hybrida* 'Peaches and Cream'

This award-winning cultivar has a modern colour: peaches and cream, as the name indicates.

The shoots are covered in velvety hairs amd tend to be more erect than those of most other hybrids.

Verbena 'Peaches and Cream' is usually propagated annually by seed.

For management, see *Verbena* x *hybrida*.

(1) or ☼ 0°C (32°F)

Verbena x *hybrida* 'Peaches and Cream'

Verbena x *hybrida* 'Sissinghurst Pink'

Attractive pale pink flower heads with magenta centres are formed at the tips of shoots with deeply divided leaves.

For management, see *Verbena* x *hybrida*.

(1) or ☼ 0°C (32°F)

Verbena x *hybrida* 'Sissinghurst Pink'

Verbena x *hybrida* 'Sunver'

This is the sibling of *Verbena* x *hybrida* 'Sunvop' (Violet Tapien).
'Sunver' is marketed under its trade name Pink Tapien and produces pale pink flowers with deeper pink centres.
Propagation is by cuttings.

For management, see *Verbena* x *hybrida*.

☼ 0°C (32°F)

Verbena x *hybrida* 'Sunvop'

This plant was introduced in 1994, and was given the trade name Violet Tapien by its grower.
The name is protected by plant breeder's rights, and only the grower concerned may propagate the plants.
According to the supplier, it is a very strong plant which forms such a dense mat that weeds choke underneath it - it should also be possible to walk on it.
'Sunvop' is one of the verbenas propagated by cuttings, and seeds are therefore not available in the trade.
For management, see *Verbena* x *hybrida*.

☼ 0°C (32°F)

Viburnum carlesii

Viburnum carlesii is highly suitable for culti-vating as a standard plant and clipping into a spherical shape to plant in the garden or in a

Verbena x *hybrida* 'Sunvop' and 'Sunver' (Tapien)

container. In open ground, the deciduous shrub is fully hardy. Greyish-green leaves are produced in spring, along with pink buds that open to white flowers. Their strong fragrance is enjoyed by some people, but others find it unpleasant.

When containerized, the viburnum's roots will need some protection from frost.

The plant is otherwise undemanding and will grow in any soil and in any location. The shrub's maximum height is about 1.5-2m (5-6ft). It may be cut back after flowering.

Viburnum carlesii

Viburnum tinus

LAURESTINUS

In Mediterranean countries, the evergreen *Viburnum tinus* flowers in winter, when heads of white flowers, about 5cm (2in) across, are produced. Further north, the shrub sometimes begins to flower in autumn, or else does so in early spring. As long as there are no severe frosts, viburnums prefer to be out of doors, but if the temperature falls below -5°C (23°F), the plant should be moved indoors to as cool a location as possible. Plenty of light and fresh air will keep the plant healthy during this period. Take it out of doors again as soon as possible. In summer, this viburnum prefers prefers a warm position, sheltered from harsh sunlight, in partial shade if need be. Provide normal soil, moderate quantities of food, and water normally.

☼ –5°C (32°F)

Viola cornuta

HORNED VIOLET

The horned violet originally came from the Pyrenées, and has been hybridized to produce countless garden forms, including some of the most rewarding of all violets.

In spring, the blueish-mauve and creamy white to white forms are for sale in their thousands to provide small plants for balcony troughs and pots. They flower continuously for many months, especially if they are not placed in full sun.

Horned violets are sown in cool, moist soil in late summer. The seedlings are almost fully hardy in open ground and will flower in

Viola cornuta

Viburnum tinus 'Eve Price'

spring. Most enthusiasts, however, prefer to buy the plants in spring.

(1) and ❋

Viola cornuta 'Belmont Blue'

See: *Viola cornuta* 'Boughton Blue'

Viola cornuta 'Boughton Blue'

HORNED VIOLET

Because of its 'washed-out' mauvish-blue colour, this horned violet is very suitable for combining with other plants. *Viola* 'Boughton Blue' is named after Boughton House in the English county of Northamptonshire, but nowadays the plant is increasingly marketed as the cultivar 'Belmont Blue'.

This form is particularly suitable for hanging baskets in partial shade. The relatively small root ball is easy to insert in the side of the basket. When you empty the basket in autumn, you can easily plant the horned violet in a dry, sunny spot in the garden, where it will survive as a perennial if the winter is not too severe.

❋

Viola cornuta 'Boughton Blue' ('Belmont Blue')

Viola hederacea

AUSTRALIAN VIOLET, IVY-LEAFED VIOLET

The Australian violet is not fully hardy everywhere in northwest Europe. The evergreen leaves are produced on ground-covering, prostrate stems which trail over the rims of pots and troughs. The small flowers are mauve and white and have a characteristic convex

Viola hedereacea

shape. Growing this violet as underplanting in tubs and pots serves a dual purpose: it covers the bare area surrounding the base of certain container plants, and when the containers are moved indoors to a light and cool location in winter, the violas will certainly stay alive, even in fairly dry, or almost dry soil. Overwintering in a cold frame or unheated alpine house is another possibility. In addition to the species, there is a very rare and sought-after cultivar called *Viola hederacea* 'Blue Form', with entirely lilac-blue flowers. It may be managed in exactly the same way as *Viola hederacea*.

☼ 0°C (32°F)

Viola hederacea 'Blue Form'

Viola 'Rebecca'

This very special violet has creamy white flowers, and is enlivened at the margins of its undulate leaves by violet spots and streaks. The flowers have a strong and agreeable fragrance.

Because of its compact growth, this violet is particularly suitable for pots or tubs.
For management, see *Viola cornuta*.

(1) and ❋

Viola 'Rebecca'

Viola tricolor 'Hortensis'

HEARTSEASE, WILD PANSY

This collective name is used for all kinds of violets closely related to the wild pansy. They are often the result of hybridization with other species and forms. *Viola tricolor* is native to many European countries. It grows in partial shade in lush meadows, and self-seeds profusely in such places. This species and the numerous cultivars developed from it are sown in late summer and subsequently flower from spring until far into summer.

(1) and ❋

Viola tricolor 'Hortensis'

Viola x *wittrockiana*

PANSY

Pansies were on sale in Greek markets 2,400 years ago. There has been so much hybridization with wild species since then that it is often impossible to trace their precise ancestry. Most cultivars are considered to belong to the Wittrockiana hybrids. These developed as a result of the frequent crossing of forms including *Viola tricolor* with *Viola tricolor sudetica* and *Viola altaica*.

Choose the plants for their colour and fragrance, if desired. They are for sale in spring and also in autumn (as winter pansies). They will flower in borders, troughs, or pots over a long period if the humus-rich soil is kept permanently moist and the pots are not placed in intense sunlight.

Winter pansies will tolerate a considerable amount of frost in open ground or large troughs, but small pots should be well-insulated to extend the flowering period for as long as possible. They may also be moved indoors to overwinter in a very light and well-ventilated location.

For propagation see *Viola cornuta*.

(1) and ❋

Viola x *wittrockiana*

Viscaria oculata

See: *Silene coeli-rosa*

263

W,Y,Z _w,y,z_

Wattakaka sinensis

See: _Dregea sinensis_

Yucca gloriosa

SPANISH DAGGER

This yucca from the eastern United States will tolerate temperatures as low as -15°C (5°F), and is therefore also available as a garden plant. It is, however, preferable to cultivate it as a container plant and keep it out of doors in summer and indoors in midwinter. If it is cut by severe frost, which will be evident from the somewhat waxy appearance of the leaves, all it is good for is the compost heap. The yucca will require a cool, dry, unheated location indoors. Allow for the fact that the plant will occupy a lot of space, as it will eventually have a spread of more than 1m (3ft).

If you take good care of the yucca, huge panicles of pendent, bell-shaped white flowers, each one about 7cm (2 3/4in) long, will appear in late summer. Unlike those of the related agaves, the yucca's flowering rosettes do not die down.
Plant the yucca in very well-drained soil, stand it in full sun, and water moderately. This is the only way to preserve its handsome shape.
In addition to the illustrated species, there are numerous other rewarding yuccas suitable for growing in containers: _Yucca aloifolia_, which closely resembles _Yucca gloriosa_, and _Yucca elephantipes_, which has shorter, wider, leaves with a waxy sheen, and a well-branched structure.

○ 0°C (32°F)

Yucca recurvifolia

See: _Yucca gloriosa_

Preceding page: A _Yucca gloriosa_ in full bloom presenting a dazzling array of flowers

Zantedeschia aethiopica

ARUM LILY

In many countries, this South African arum lily is cultivated to provide flowers for cemeteries, but it is also highly effective as a container plant cultivated to enhance a stylish house. _Zantedeschia aethiopica_ is hardy in open ground, where it will tolerate temperatures as low as -10°C (14°F). If you are growing the tubers in a pot, it is advisable not to take any risks, and the plant should therefore be moved indoors when the first night frost occurs. This arum lily grows in swamps around Cape Town, and is consequently also suitable for cultivating as an aquarium or pond plant. In that case, it should be planted more than 50cm (20in) under water to prevent the tubers freezing in winter. When containerized, fairly moist soil will suffice. The plant thrives either in full sun or in semi-shade.

○ 0°C (32°F)

Zantedeschia aethiopica

265

Useful addresses

The Netherlands

Koninklijke Maatschappij Tuinbouw
en Plantkunde
(Royal Horticultural and Botanical Society)
PO Box 97910
2508 DH The Hague

Nationale Collectie Passiflora's
Veerweg 35, 4471 BJ
Wolphaartsdijk
Zeeland
*Speciality: passion flowers and container
plants (admittance by appointment only)*

United Kingdom

The Huntingdon Library, *art collections and
botanical gardens in San Marino
(California), has thirteen different gardens.
For information in the UK, contact:*

Harry Mays
Woodsleigh
Moss Lane
St Michaels on Wyre
Preston PR3 0TY
Royal Horticultural Society
Horticultural Hall
Vincent Square
London SW1P 2PE

*The foremost horticultural organization in
the country, the society has a wide range of
activities, from organizing national
exhibitions (including the Chelsea Flower
Show) and lecture programmes to providing
information to members and running its own
garden and training schemes at Wisley.*

Scotland's Garden Scheme
31 Castle Terrace
Edinburgh EH1 2EL

Winter storage of fuchsias

Fulfills the same function in Scotland as the National Garden Scheme does in England and wales.

Ulster Gardens Scheme
c/o The National Trust
Rowallane House
Saintfield
Co. Down

United States of America

American Horticultural Society
7931 East Boulevard Drive
Alexandria, VA 22308-1300

Massachusetts Horticultural Society
300 Massachusetts Avenue
Boston, MA 02115

Pacific Horticultural Foundation
Box 485
Berkeley, CA 94941

Conservatories and orangeries (to visit)

United Kingdom
Belfast Botanic Gardens, Belfast, Northern Ireland (palm house)

Bicton Park Gardens, Budleigh Salterton, Devon (palm house)
Blithfield Hall, Abbots Bromley, Staffordshire (orangery)
Carrow Abbey, Carrow, Norfolk
Castle Ashby, Castle Ashby, Northamptonshire (orangery)
Chatsworth, Bakewell, Derbyshire
Chiswick House, Burlington Lane, Chiswick, London W4 (camellia house)
East Cliff Lodge, Ramsgate, Kent
Howsham Hall, Howsham, North Yorkshire
Kensington Palace, London W8 (orangery)
Kew Gardens, Richmond, Surrey (palm house, orangery, Temperate House and Princess of Wales conservatory)
Royal Horticultural Society, Wisley Garden, Ripley, Surrey
Sezincote, Moreton-in-Marsh, Gloucestershire (orangery)
Shrubland Park, Barham, Suffolk (now a health farm, but has retained the winter garden conservatory)
Syon House, Brenford, Middlesex
Wollaton Hall National History Museum, Wollaton Park, Nottingham, Nottinghamshire (camellia house)
Wrest Park, Silsoe, Bedfordshire (orangery)

Winter storage of container plants in the Netherlands

Canada

Jardin Botanique de Montréal
(Montreal Botanic Garden)
4101 Rue Sherbrooke Est
Montréal (Québec)
H1X 2B2

Botanic Gardens
University of British Columbia
Vancouver
British Columbia

United States of America

Brooklyn Botanic garden
1000 Washington Avenue
Brooklyn, NY 11225

The Huntingdon Botanical Gardens
San Marino
California

New York Botanical Garden
Southern Boulevard & 200th Street
Bronx, NY 10438

For more information on orangeries and greenhouses, please contact your local Cooperative Extension Agent or your State University Department of Agriculture.

[KU115]

Index

Acknowledgments

The author and publishers wish to express their thanks to the following people, without whose co-operation this book could not have been produced.

Ans Advocaat of De Paardestal in Peize; the Brederoo family of the Kwekerij Brederoo, Honselersdijk; Pauline Brummelaar and Geerle Wijma of the Hoveniersbedrijf Pastel, Sebaldeburen; the Buurman family of the Kwekerij Overhagen, Velp; Koen Delaey of the Kwekerij Sollya, Hertsberghe; Henk van Engen and the staff of Intratuin Groningen; Mia Esser of the Nederlandse pelargonium- en geraniumvereniging (Dutch pelargonium and geranium association), Haulerwijk; Ans van den Hoek of the Federatie van Nederlandse Tuinbouw Studiegroepen (federation of Dutch horticultural study groups), Honselersdijk; Jan Hummel of the Nederlandse kring van fuchsiavrienden (Dutch circle of fuchsia fanciers), Zevenhuizen; Amy van Ierssel of the Kwekerij De Rhulenhof, Ottersum; Wim Kersten of the Oranjerievereniging (orangery association), Haelen; Jacques Klerx of the Kwekerij Klerx, Malden; Cor Laurens of the Nationale Collectie Passiflora's (national collection of passion flowers), Wolphaartsdijk; Truus Manders-Vanlier of the Oranjerievereniging (orangery association), Heel; the Van der Meer family of the Kwekerij Van der Meer, Hoek van Holland; Mrs M. Paulus of the Kring Oleander van de oranjerievereniging (oleander circle of the orangery association), Maasbracht; Mr Hetterscheid of the Vaste Keurings Commissie (permanent inspection committee), Aalsmeer; Hannie Wouda and Bob Foltz of De Eglantier, Paterswolde; Fleur van Sonneveld and Eric Spruit of the Kwekerij De Kleine Plantage, Eenrum.